IMAGES
of America

ELON

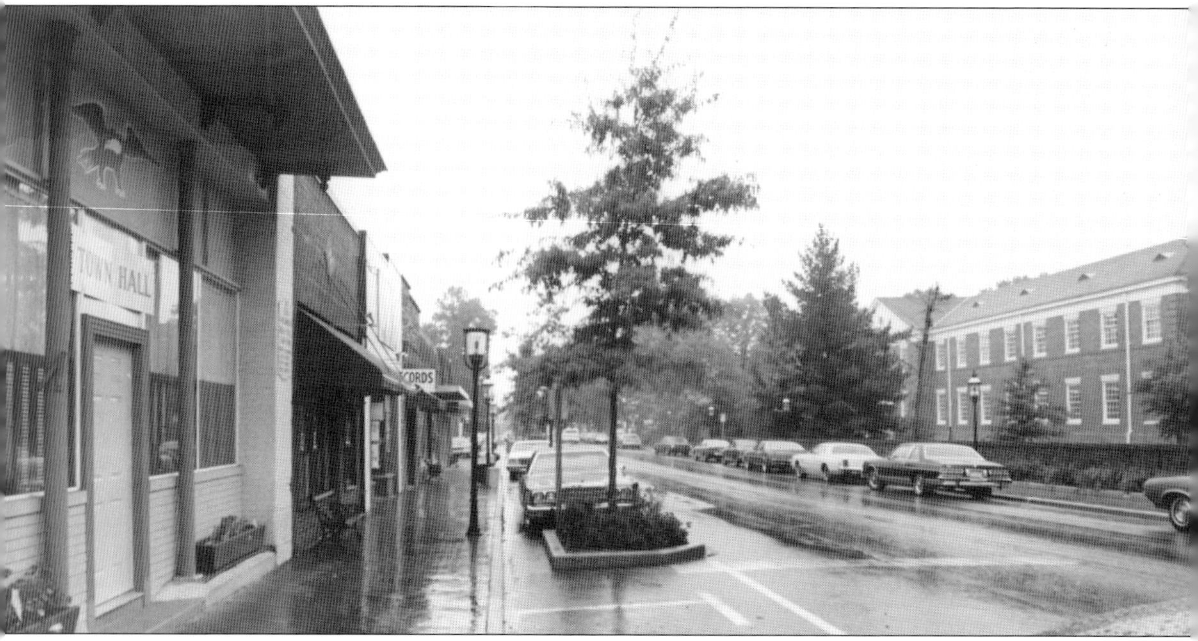

When Elon College (the town) and Elon College (the college) were born near the end of the 19th century, North Williamson Avenue was the dividing line between the two—Elon businesses to the left, the college to the right, each supporting the other—and that is how it has been for 125 years to the benefit of both as they have grown and prospered together with the passing of time. (Author's collection).

On the Cover: In the 1947–1948 school year, fourth graders at Elon Public School gathered for their class photograph. Teacher Leffy Lowe is at right. Several of these youngsters still live in the area: Dr. James Powell, back row, third from left (starting on the back cover); then his brother John, fourth from left; Wes Reynolds, fifth from left; and Jean Toms, fourth from right on the front. (Dr. James B. Powell.)

IMAGES
of America

ELON

Don Bolden

ARCADIA
PUBLISHING

ISBN 978-1-4671-2811-7

Published by Arcadia Publishing
Charleston, South Carolina

Printed in the United States of America

Library of Congress Control Number: 2017949018

For all general information, please contact Arcadia Publishing:
Telephone 843-853-2070
Fax 843-853-0044
E-mail sales@arcadiapublishing.com
For customer service and orders:
Toll-Free 1-888-313-2665

Visit us on the Internet at www.arcadiapublishing.com

To the memory of Billie Faye, an Elon College graduate and my wife for 60 years, who passed away on April 1, 2017

Contents

ACKNOWLEDGMENTS

A large number of the photographs in this book came from the archives of Elon University in Belk Library, and special thanks go to Chrystal Carpenter, archivist, and others on her staff for opening the files and assisting in making the photographs ready for publication. Without their help, this book would not have been possible.

Thanks also go to Kathleen Patterson, Downtown Development administrator for the Town of Elon, who supported the idea of the book from the beginning and provided photographs and links to others who had photographs as well.

A number of others from Elon or with links to the community also searched storage spaces and scrapbooks at home in order to share their own photographic memories of the Elon community. They are given credit at the end of the captions accompanying their respective photographs. Any photographs without credit came from the personal collection of the author.

My main resources were *Town of Elon College* by Mary L. and T.H. Mackintosh; *Elon College, Its History and Traditions* by Dr. Durward T. Stokes; and *From a Grove of Oaks—The Story of Elon University* by Dr. George Troxler.

Thanks also go to Angel Hisnanick, my title manager at Arcadia Publishing, for guiding me through the publication process and having answers for all my questions.

INTRODUCTION

The town of Elon is located in piedmont North Carolina, a couple of hours from the Blue Ridge Mountains to the west and a bit longer to the beautiful beaches to the east. It is situated in Alamance County, home to several other municipalities and communities that have become well known for various industrial operations of national and international importance.

Burlington, which abuts Elon to the east, was the founding location of Burlington Mills in 1923. This became known as Burlington Industries and was at one time the largest maker of textiles in the world. There is Glen Raven Mills next door as well. This was a textile and hosiery company (it patented panty hose) and now produces the Sunbrella line of fabrics for awnings and other products internationally. Carolina Biological Supply Company, the nation's largest supplier of biological teaching supplies, is just over the town limits, as is the major laboratory of LabCorp, a health-care diagnostics company that changed the way medical testing was done, made DNA a household term, and employs some 50,000 people around the world. Western Electric was also located in Burlington for several decades, first producing telephone products but eventually producing major defense products for the United States government, including the Nike antimissile system. Copland Fabrics continues as a nationally known textile company in the Hopedale-Carolina community.

Those are impressive names and impressive success stories. But what about Elon? What has it produced? Over the years, Elon has sent thousands of young men and women into the world armed with an Elon College degree—now an Elon University degree—that has prepared them to take their places in helping set the future of state, national, and world communities. The town has found its place as the support system for the university that has been in operation since 1889 and now graduates more than 1,400 students per year.

But education is not why the town came to be. Elon was born of the railroad and the needs of two early textile companies. In the early 1850s, the North Carolina Railroad began laying track for its line from Goldsboro to Charlotte, and trains started moving over that line in 1856. Near the center of that line, the company established facilities for the construction and maintenance of the train engines and cars. That place was known for many years as Company Shops. In 1887, the name was changed to Burlington. Burlington, however, was not incorporated until 1893, the same year as Elon.

A dirt road ran along the tracks from Company Shops to the town of Gibsonville to the west. There was another dirt road that ran from Ossipee in northwestern Alamance County south to a stagecoach inn that was at today's intersection of South Church Street and Williamson Avenue just inside Burlington's city limits. John Boon operated an inn there, just south of today's Elon. The place where those two roads crossed was known as Boon's Crossing, according to local histories. The railroad brought a lot of activity and growth to Company Shops, and Gibsonville enjoyed growth as well. But the area in between remained just a country crossroads for many years. That changed, however, in 1887.

In 1976, Mary and T.H. Mackintosh produced *Town of Elon College: A Brief History* as part of the community's participation in the nation's bicentennial celebration. In it, they note that in 1887 there were rumors that a railroad depot was to be built at Boon's Crossing. By April 1888, the depot was operating and it had been named Mill Point. By that time, textile mills had been operating several years at Ossipee and Altamahaw on Haw River a few miles north of Mill Point. The depot was needed by those mills to receive supplies and to ship their goods to market.

Col. James N. Williamson owned the Ossipee mill, and he was a major force in getting the Mill Point depot opened. In 1889, Williamson built a two-story house across the road from the depot, but he never lived there. His residence was in Graham. The Mackintosh history says the Elon house was first occupied by S.A. Holleman and his family, and it also served briefly as a women's dormitory. Holleman was a professor at Elon College and was the first to plat the town. The Williamson house stills stands at 111 East Trollinger Avenue and is now the home of Dolores Truitt. When the depot was opened in 1888, a post office was opened there. John Q. Gant, owner of the Altamahaw mill, was the first postmaster. In the application for that post office, according to the Mackintosh history, Mill Point is described as "new place—no settlement."

It was not long, however, before that changed, and in a big way. While the post office was being established, the Christian Church was trying to establish a four-year college. The church had long desired a seminary, all the way back to 1852 when Graham Institute was founded. The Civil War put a hold on plans; and in the years that followed, Graham Normal College was established just south of the Alamance County courthouse. Eventually, it was decided to form a four-year college, but at another location.

W.H. Trollinger was a prominent business figure in Haw River who had provided some of the land needed to lure the railroad to Alamance County to build its shops. He owned 50 acres of land in the Mill Point area, and he offered some of it to be used for the new college. He was also a friend of the mill owners to the north.

In the end, Trollinger gave 32 acres of land, and Capt. James Williamson of the Ossipee mill gave a donation of $2,500, according to the 2014 history of Elon University—*From a Grove of Oaks: The Story of Elon University*, by Dr. George Troxler, professor emeritus of history at the university.

A number of things were considered in selecting a location, according to Dr. Troxler's work. He writes that those making the decision wanted to ensure that students would be protected from "corrupting influences," so a rural location was best. There was discussion of amending Graham's charter to eliminate the manufacture and sale of liquor in the town to make it attractive to the college, but that did not work out. Those "corrupting influences" remained important, and Elon's original charter prohibited such sale and manufacture and also any game of chance, gambling, or houses of ill fame within one and a half miles of the college.

With the selection of the Mill Point site, work began in 1889, and Elon College was born. College trustees had chosen the name "Elon" for the word in Hebrew meaning "oak" or "grove of oak trees." The new college site was home to many large oak trees.

In May 1890, the Mill Point Post Office was renamed as the Elon College Post Office. While the name of the town changed also, the town of Elon College was not officially incorporated until April 7, 1893. In 1890, Prof. S.A. Holleman, a faculty member, platted the town with the college at its center. There were no "streets," only "avenues." Williamson Avenue was named for James N. Williamson, the textile executive; Trollinger, for land donor W.H. Trollinger; O'Kelly, for the Rev. James O'Kelly, founder of the Christian Church; and Haggard, for Rice Haggard, who first offered the name "Christian" for the denomination. Others were named for Biblical locations or other persons of importance in the Christian denomination. With the college in operation and more activity at the depot, businesses began to appear along Williamson Avenue. The first store was at 100 North Williamson, built by W.L. Smith, station agent at the depot. That building burned in 1891 and was replaced quickly by the present structure there. Other buildings appeared along that block in the 1890s as well.

The town and the college were joined by a third entity in 1907 when the Christian Church opened an orphanage south of the railroad just east of the college. Lela Mae Canada of Durham was the first child to enter the orphanage, and 22 others would follow her the first year. Orphans and half orphans were admitted, and hundreds would be served in the years to come. The orphanage continued over the years and grew in its service. Several cottages were built around the property for children of various ages, and a gymnasium and swimming pool were also added. As laws regarding child care changed over the years, the orphanage became the Elon Home for Children, and foster care programs became an important part of the home's work. Eventually, the Elon campus closed and operations were moved to Charlotte, where the organization continues to serve young people in that area of the state. When Elon Homes for Children ended its operations at Elon, the university bought the property and the facilities that were once part of the homes. Most of the buildings have now been converted to university use, and the farmland is used for student athletic activities.

There were many periods of difficulty for the college over the years. There was World War I and the 1918 flu epidemic. There was the Great Depression, when staff could not be paid. And then there was World War II. The most serious problem perhaps was the fire in 1923 that destroyed the most important structure on campus—the Main Building. It housed the college administration offices as well as classrooms and other facilities. That one incident could have closed the college had it not been for resourceful leaders and the great support of residents of the town of Elon College and Alamance County. The ashes literally were still smoldering when the faculty was called together, and in Burlington businessmen were meeting that day to raise money to help the college in rebuilding its facilities. Thus Elon rose from those ashes, and the new facility was named the Alamance Building in appreciation to those in the surrounding area who helped with its construction.

Elon's link to education goes back several decades before Elon College was formed, and there is living proof of that fact today. In the 1850s, a little school was built on property owned for many years by the Cable family. The old Cable School property adjoins the parking lot for the football field house at Rhodes Stadium, and it was restored to original condition by the university in 2014. A plaque reads, "Built in the 1850s as part of the first state supported system of education in North Carolina." It was just before 1900 that another state-supported school was opened in Elon with a six-month term and 28 pupils with one teacher. It was the Elon College Public School. In 1912, a brick building was built on East Haggard Avenue, and it served as the town's only school into the 1960s, when school consolidation came to Alamance County.

Over the years, the university grew but remained within the old brick wall that girded the campus for so many years. It was in 1949 that Alumni Gym was built outside the wall across Haggard Avenue, and in the years that followed, the little college began a period of growth that still continues at amazing speed in 2018. New dormitories were built, an arts center appeared, and the college spread quickly north.

Dr. Leon Smith was president during the very early beginnings of the growth, followed by an Alamance County graduate of Elon College, Dr. J. Earl Danieley, who took the school into new territory in both buildings and academic programs. Dr. Fred Young was president for 25 years leading up to the 21st century, and during his years, the school became established as one of the leading colleges along the heavily populated Eastern Seaboard of the United States. The college greatly expanded the area from which it drew students, no longer confining its search to North Carolina and eastern Virginia. Then, in 1999, Dr. Leo Lambert came to lead Elon College, and changes came at a more rapid clip than ever before. Elon College became Elon University, a title more appropriate to its programs, and the old Fightin' Christian athletic mascot gave way to the Phoenix. The Fightin' Christian reflected the school's beginning with the church, but the scope of the university had spread far beyond a single denomination or even a single faith. So the Phoenix was chosen to reflect the school's rising from the ashes of the 1923 fire to the soaring successes of the new century.

Today, the town of Elon has become a vibrant community of businesses, churches, and residential communities that provide support to a university with more than 6,000 students and facilities second to none, ranking as one of the nation's finest private universities.

One

The Town

At one time, there were two entities that bore the name Elon College. There was Elon College, the college, and there was Elon College, the town. It had been that way since 1890. Elon College, the college, had been formed in 1889 at the site of a railroad depot known as Mill Point. Between Burlington and Gibsonville, the depot served textile mills several miles north of the depot location. A post office had also opened at Mill Point in 1888, and in 1890, the name of that post office was changed to Elon College. The town and the college grew together over the years, both continuing to have the same name.

Toward the end of the 20th century, the college was undergoing rapid growth in student numbers, in facilities, in academic programs, and in many other areas. As a result, the college trustees voted to rename the school Elon University. That left the community as Elon College, home of Elon University. That would not work. Soon after the decision to change the name of the school, the town also agreed to take a new name—Elon. Both institutions made their name changes official on June 1, 2001.

Today, the town of Elon occupies five square miles of Alamance County between Burlington and Gibsonville, and its population is approximately 10,000 residents, including Elon students in town but off campus. It is home to a variety of businesses, and there are two large retirement and adult-care communities in the area—Twin Lakes and Blakey Hall.

The railroad now divides both the town and the campus, but the depot that started it all is no longer in existence, and the trains no longer stop in town.

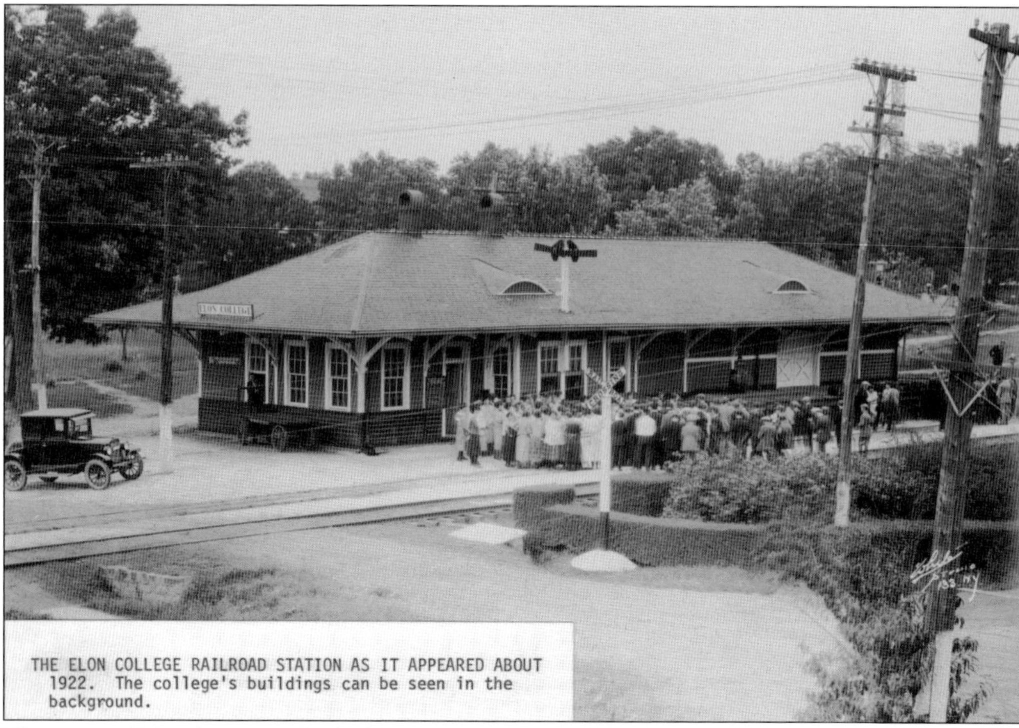

The story of Elon began with the location of a railroad depot at a crossroads in a remote area of Alamance County between the fall of 1887 and the spring of 1888. It was built to provide rail service to two textile mills a few miles to the north. The depot was known as Mill Point, and this image shows the depot as it appeared in 1922. (Elon University.)

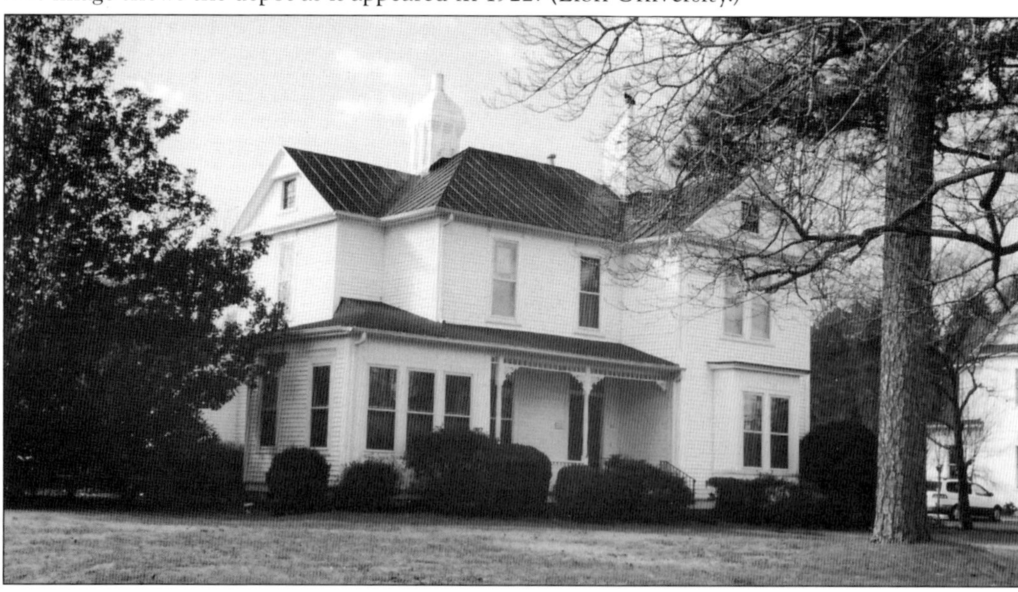

Capt. James Williamson, owner of the mill at Ossipee, north of Elon, and a resident of nearby Graham, built this house in 1889 across the road from the new depot. He never lived there, but some faculty and students lived there later. The home is at 111 East Trollinger Avenue overlooking the university campus and is the residence of Dolores Truitt in 2018.

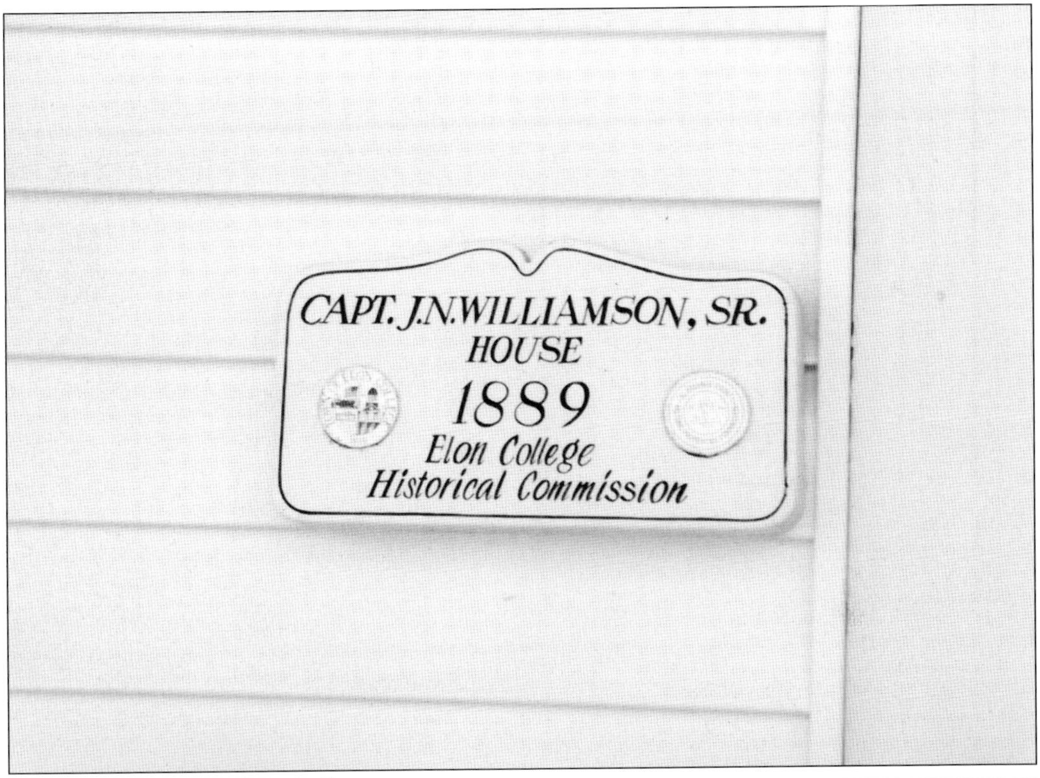

Some years ago, the Elon College Historical Commission placed plaques on the vintage houses in the community. This one is on the Captain Williamson house on Trollinger Avenue, which is one of the oldest residences in Elon today. Several of the early homes in Elon were on Trollinger Avenue, and this is one of three very similar dwellings still located together on that street.

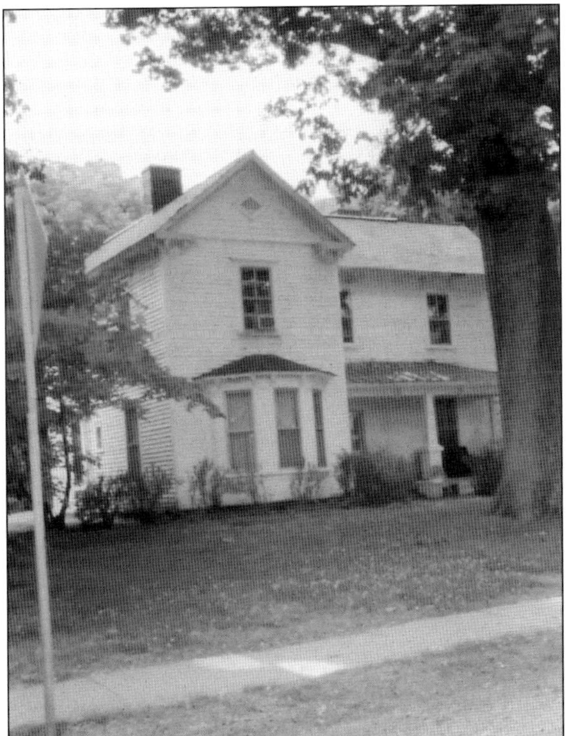

W.L. Smith, the first agent for the freight depot at Mill Point, built this house on West Trollinger Avenue a short distance from his workplace. It is one of the two earliest houses built in Elon College, and it continues in use today. Smith later built the first store in Elon at 100 North Williamson Avenue.

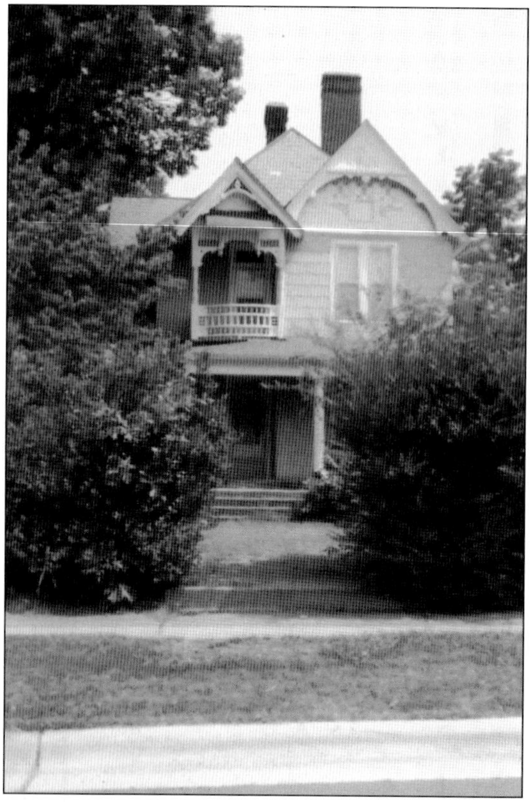

The family of the Reverend M.L. Hurley was the first to occupy this house located at 402 East Lebanon Avenue. Like all the homes along Lebanon and Trollinger Avenues, it faces the railroad tracks. This residence, like many others along those two streets, was likely built in the 1890s. This is one of but a few houses remaining on East Lebanon as the university has spread along that street.

Joseph Charles McAdams came to Elon College as the contractor for West Dormitory. He completed this house at 202 South Williamson Avenue in 1904. His daughter later lived there, and today granddaughter Jo McAdams Grimley and her husband, Dr. Eugene Grimley, reside there. They did extensive renovation but used all the original doors, frames, flooring, and windows, returning each space to its original use. (Jo and Dr. Eugene Grimley.)

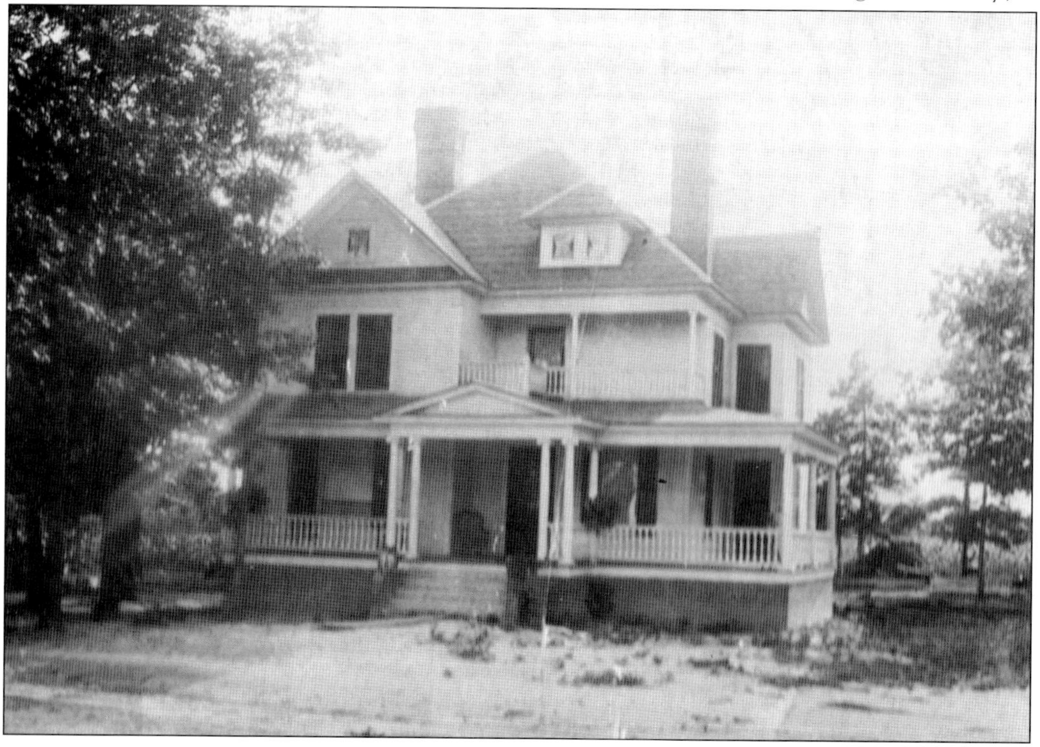

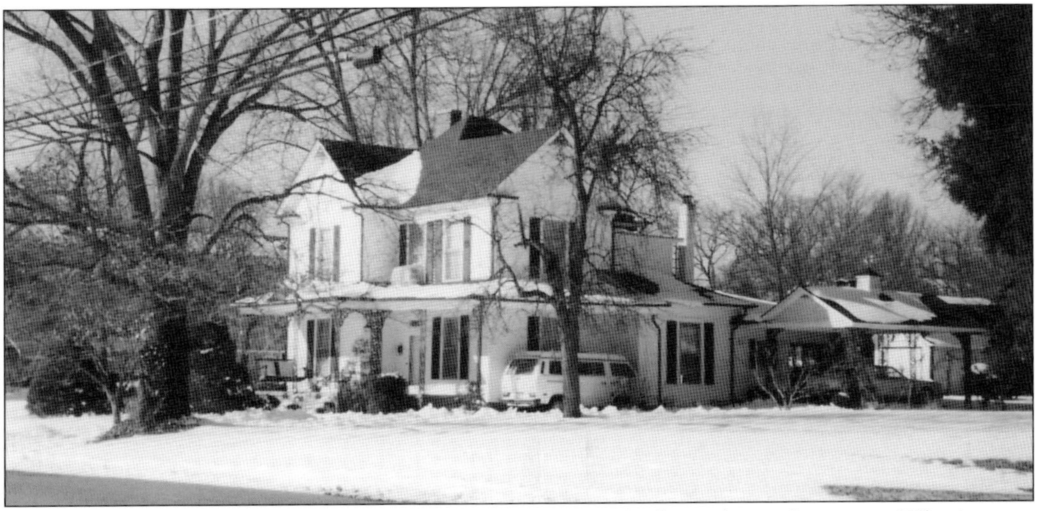

This house at 310 Lebanon Avenue is another of those built in the early years of Elon's town history. For many years, it was owned by Dee and Mona Atkinson and was surrounded by several other similar houses of that era. The dwelling is gone now, and the Martha and Carl Lindner III Hall is located there in the university's Academic Village. (Mona Atkinson.)

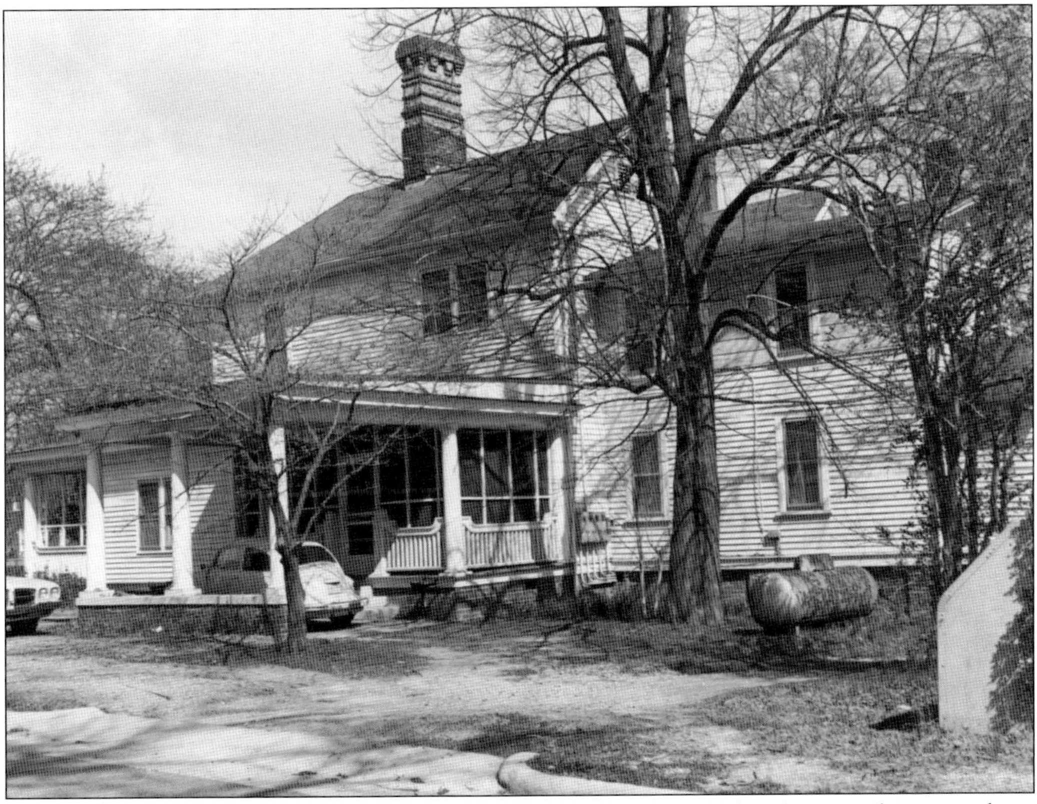

This is the side view of the house at 201 East Trollinger Avenue. The photograph was made in the 1970s. The house was built in 1892 by J.A. Long, brother of Dr. W.S. Long, president of Elon College. In later years, the structure was divided into apartments and is now owned by Richard Goodson. (Elon University.)

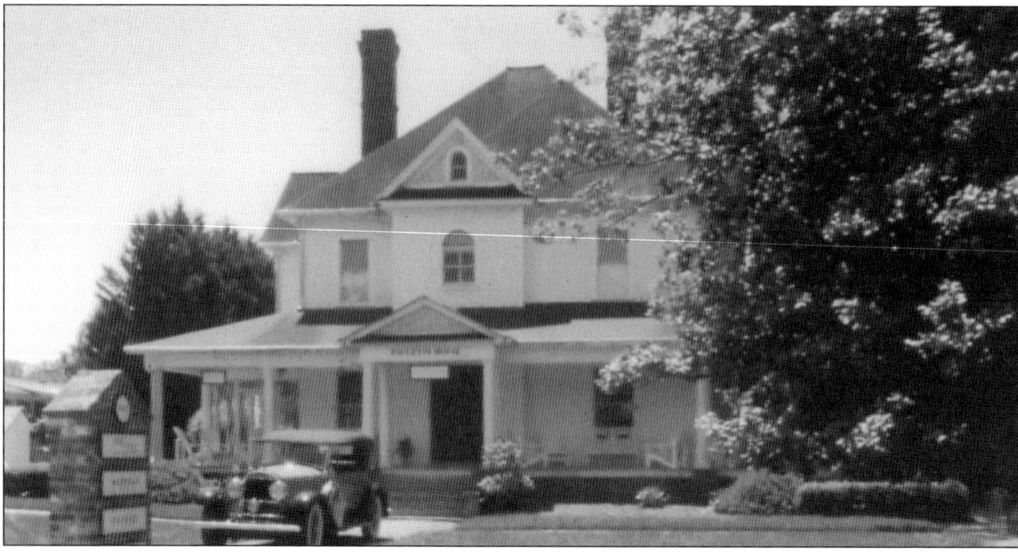

This house at 105 East Trollinger Avenue is next to the Williamson house, and is another of those built in the town's early years and still in use today. Charles D. Johnston lived there, and later, so did Dr. John G. Truitt Sr. Both were superintendents of the Elon Orphanage. It is now known as Faucette House, and Della and Lowell Faucette live there and operate a hair salon and a wine shop in it.

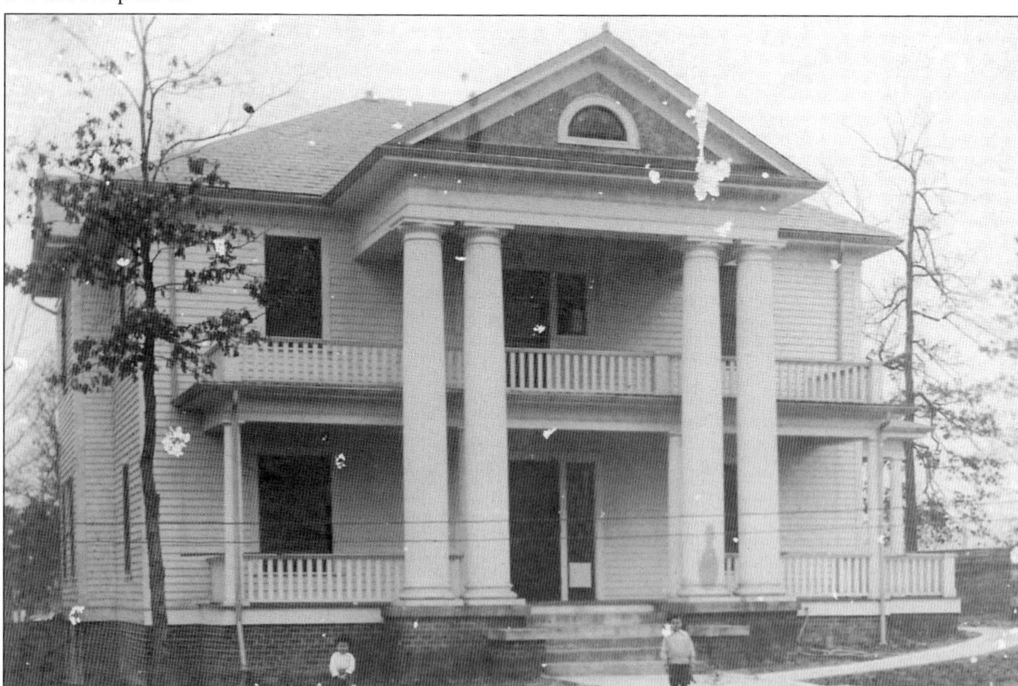

Dr. W.P. Lawrence, who filled many roles on the faculty of Elon College, built this house on Haggard Avenue at O'Kelly Avenue in 1910–1911. After his death in 1926, the house was used as a residence for female honor students and for other college uses before it was again used as a residence. Finally, it was removed for the construction of the McMichael Science Building. (Walter Boyd.)

Dr. W.P. Lawrence entered Elon College the year it opened and graduated in 1894. He joined the faculty and served in various positions for 32 years. Lawrence was dean, headed the English Department, edited a newspaper, and had a role in politics. He was mayor of the town of Elon College and served in the North Carolina General Assembly for one term beginning in 1921. (Walter Boyd.)

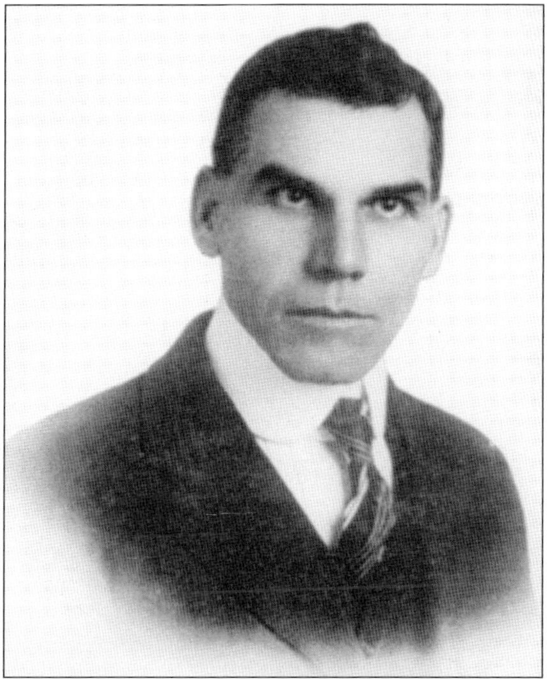

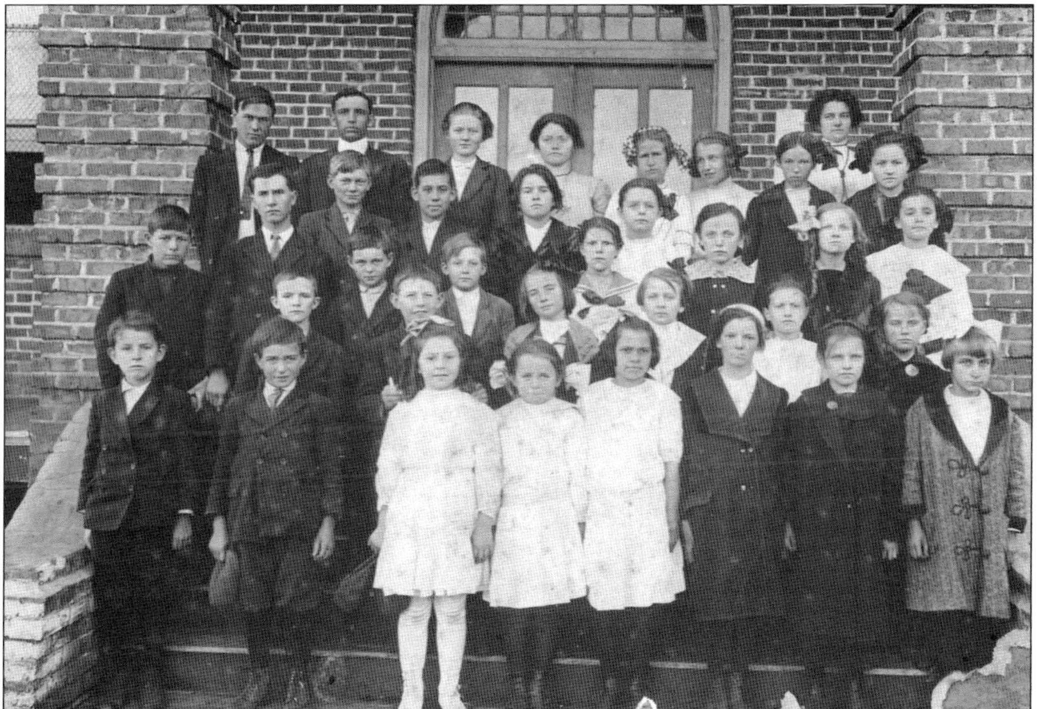

While Elon students were making their way through college work, there were some much younger students just down the street at the Elon College Public School. As with most of the early schools in Alamance County, the school included all grade levels. Students here were from various class and age levels.

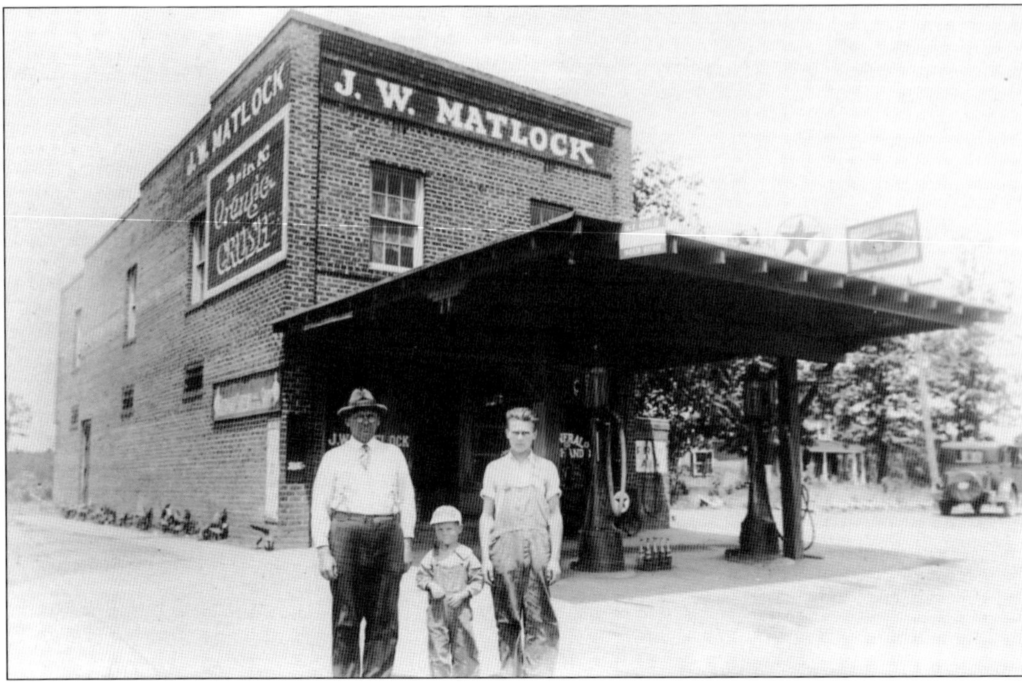

Matlock Store was a landmark in Elon College for many decades in the 20th century. Shown here in 1922, it was a general store and gasoline station. Pictured from left to right in front of the store are John William Matlock Sr., Corey Rufus Matlock, and John William Matlock Jr. The store was at the corner of Haggard and Manning Avenues, just west of the university campus. (Nina Matlock.)

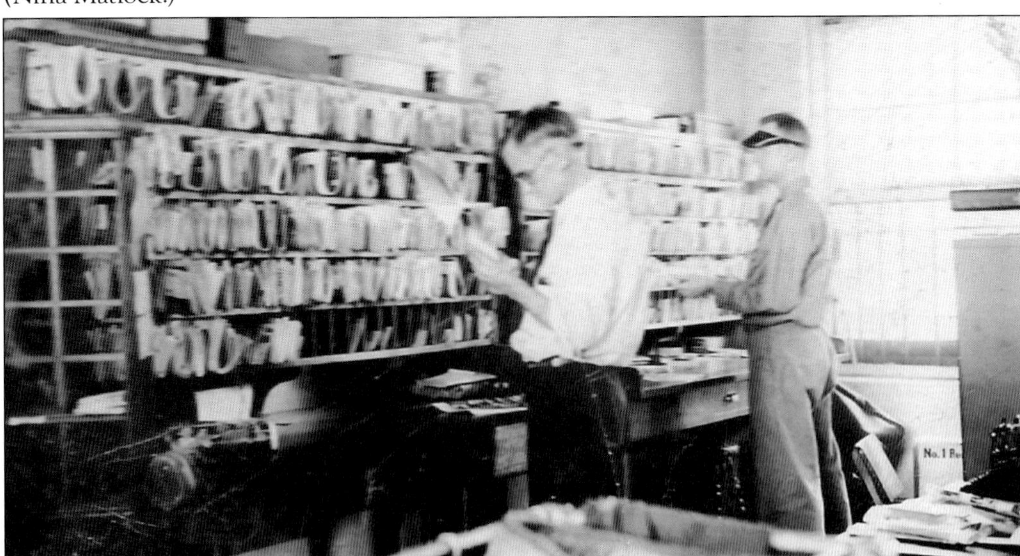

The Elon College Post Office has moved many times. There were two early locations on West Lebanon Avenue, then three sites on North Williamson Avenue, and finally the present site at South Williamson Avenue and Trollinger Avenue. Pictured is one of the early locations on North Williamson Avenue, and its size reflects the fact that Elon College was a very small town in those years. (Earl Vickers.)

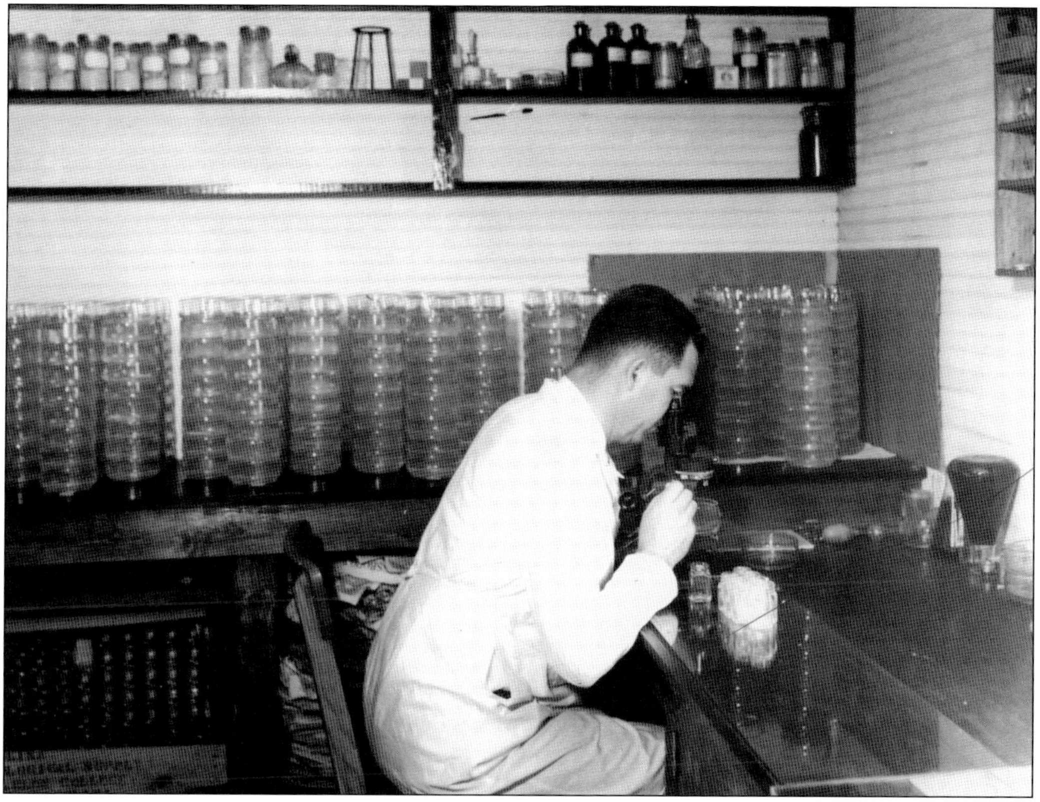

Dr. Thomas E. Powell Jr. graduated from Elon College in 1919 and immediately joined the faculty, teaching biology and geology. He found it difficult to locate supplies needed for his classes, so in 1927 he founded Carolina Biological Supply Company near campus as he continued teaching. In 1936, Powell resigned to operate his company, now the major supplier of biological supplies in the nation. (Dr. James B. Powell.)

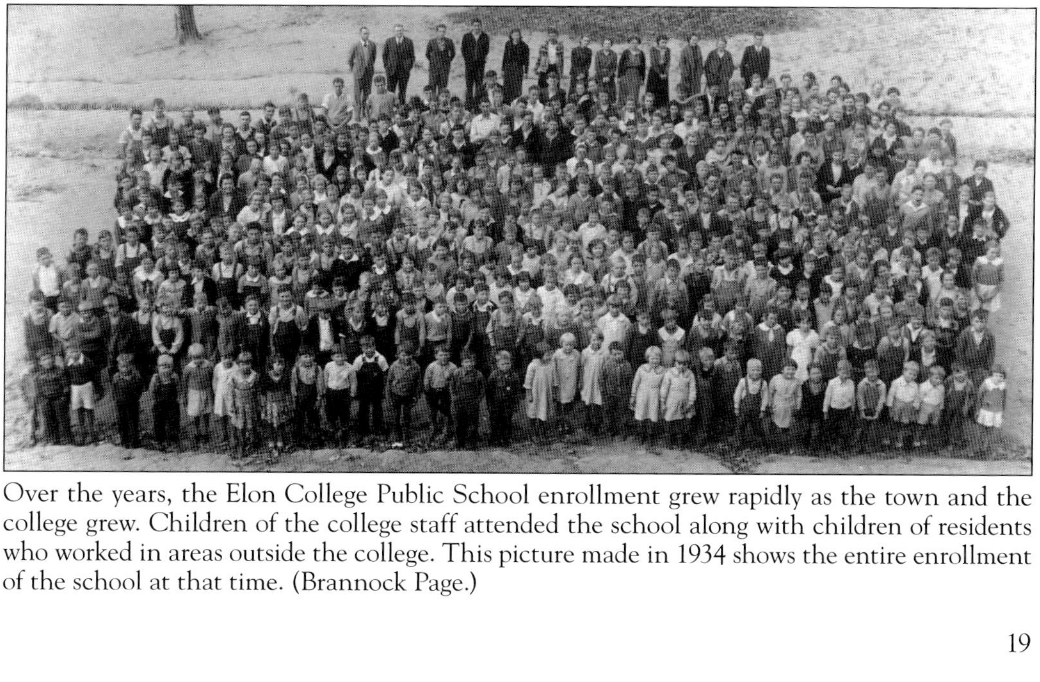

Over the years, the Elon College Public School enrollment grew rapidly as the town and the college grew. Children of the college staff attended the school along with children of residents who worked in areas outside the college. This picture made in 1934 shows the entire enrollment of the school at that time. (Brannock Page.)

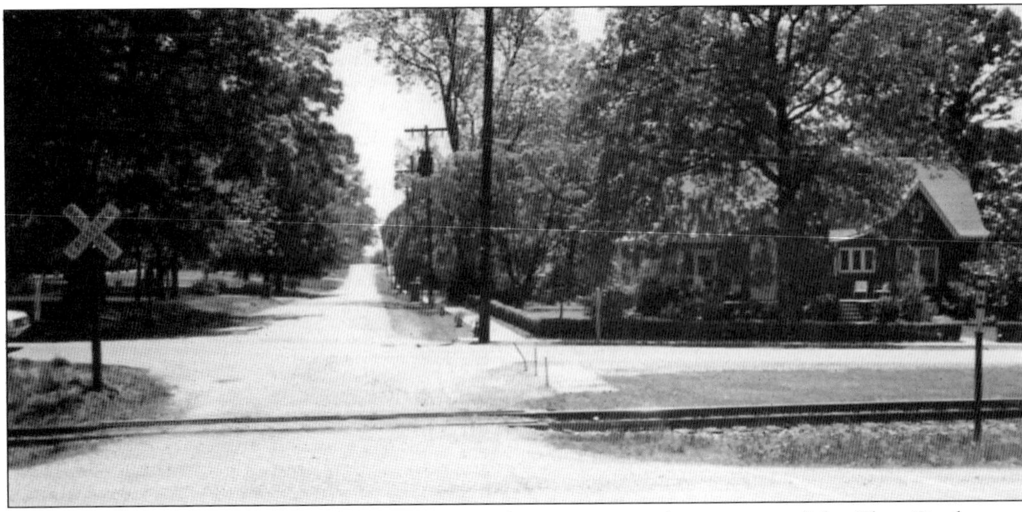

This photograph shows Antioch Avenue stretching out into the campus of the Elon Orphanage in the 1930s. East Trollinger Avenue crosses just beyond the railroad tracks. Note that there are no warning lights and no gates to stop traffic as trains approach. There is only a sign. For safety reasons, this crossing and one other in town were closed in later years. (Dr. Eugene and Jo Grimley.)

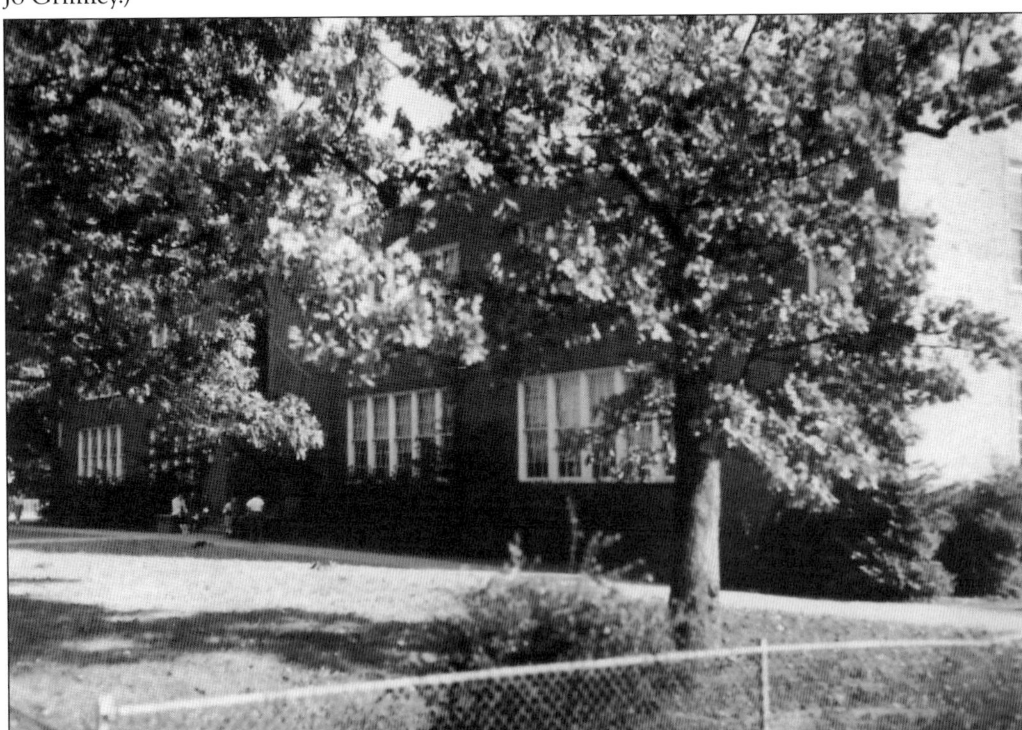

Built in the early part of the 20th century, the Elon Public School served the community until the 1960s when a major school consolidation program took place in Alamance County. High school students moved to Western Alamance High School, and the Elon school became a junior high school. It was later replaced by Western Middle School, and Elon University obtained this property. (Elon University.)

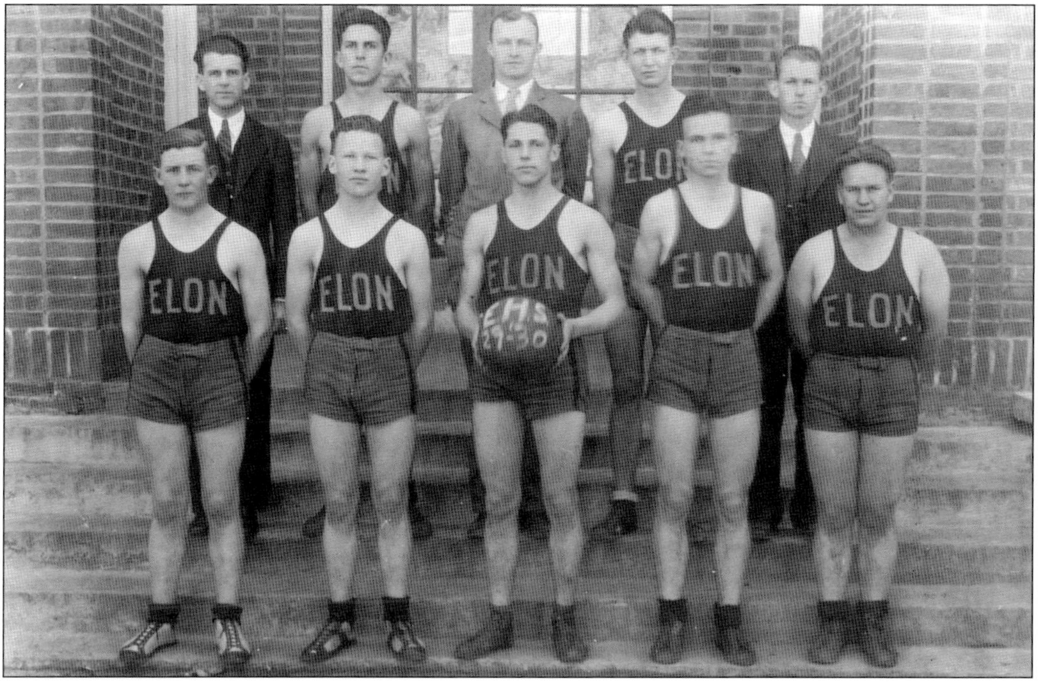

The Elon High School men's basketball team in 1929–1930 was small in both size and numbers. There are only seven players on the team in this photograph on the school steps. The Elon teams played those from other high schools in its immediate area, including Burlington High School and other Alamance County schools. (Jean Loy Toms.)

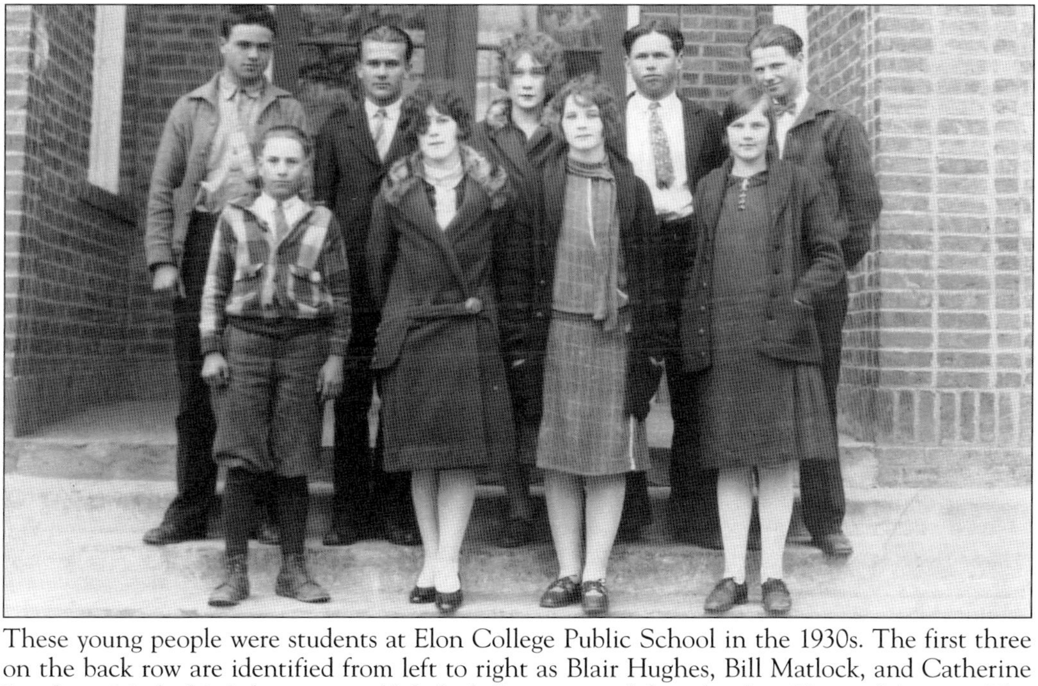

These young people were students at Elon College Public School in the 1930s. The first three on the back row are identified from left to right as Blair Hughes, Bill Matlock, and Catherine Pritchett. Matlock's father operated Matlock Store west of the school on Haggard Avenue. The group's identity (a class or a school club or other) is not listed. (Nina Matlock.)

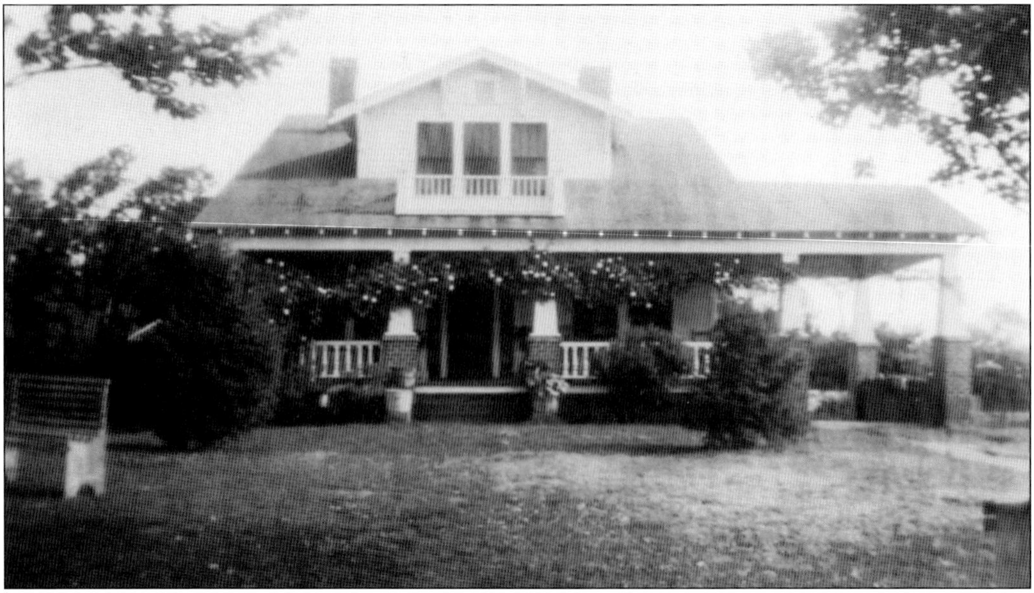

This house sat on the property now occupied by the Loy Center on the Elon University campus. It was the home of the Apple family. When Lib Apple Loy died, her husband, Bill, gave the land for the center, now home to the university sororities and fraternities. Lib Apple's family also gave land for the Loy Center Courtyard in 1987. (Brannock Page.)

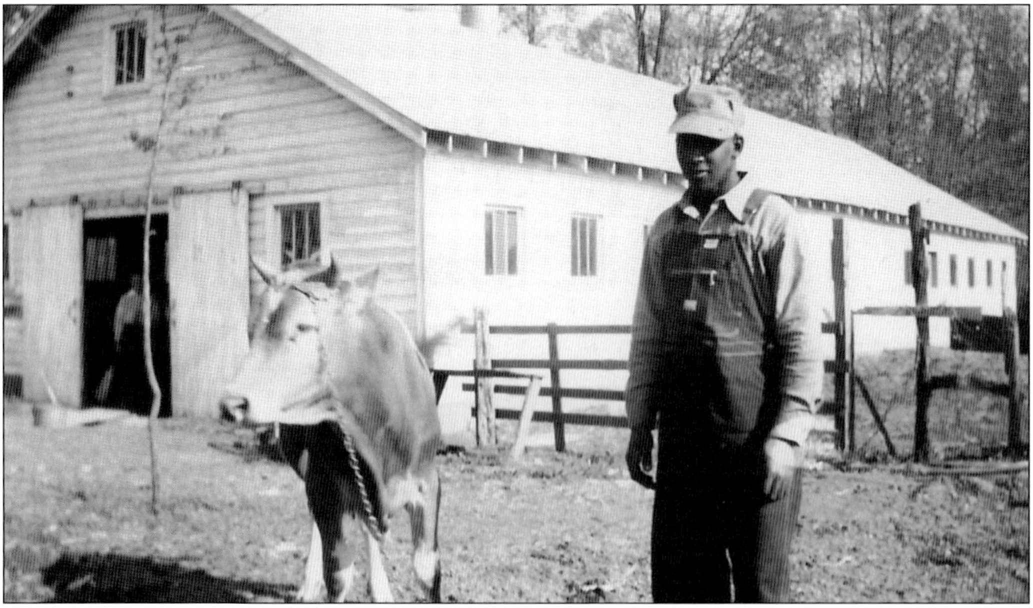

John Mack Johnston worked on the Apple farm, now the location of the Loy Center on the Elon University campus. He is shown here with one of the cows and the barn, which was a part of a large farm operation for many years. Donations from the Apple and Loy families made it possible for the university to create Loy Center as the home for sorority and fraternity houses. (Brannock Page.)

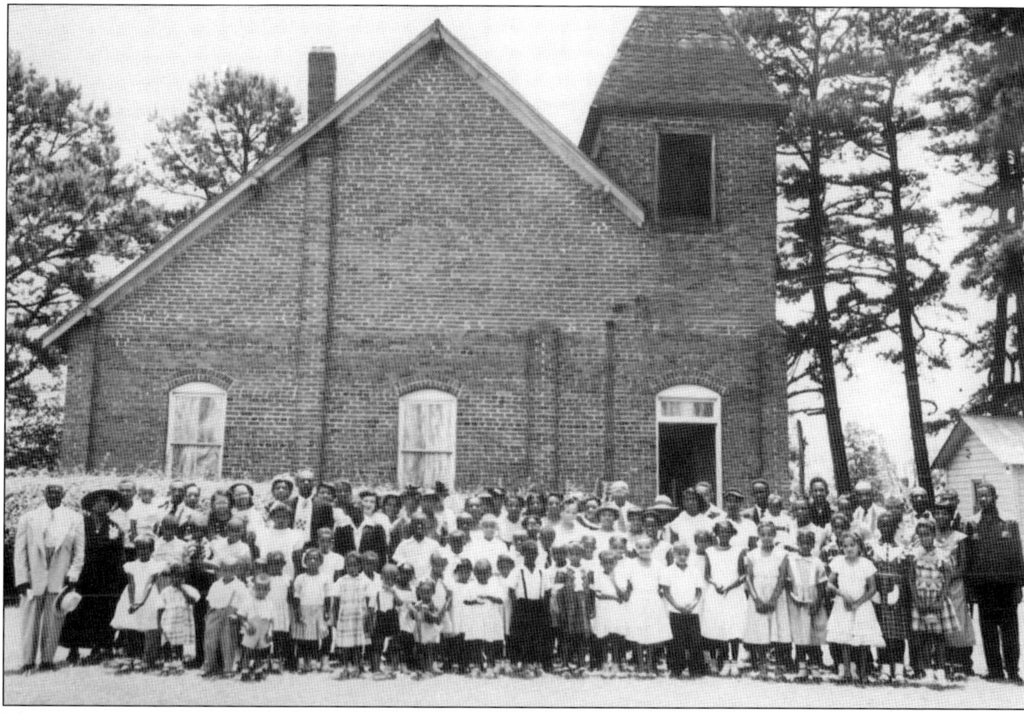

Elon First Baptist Church in Morgan Place has served the African American community in Elon since it was founded in 1922 by John McMullen. He built a small building on his land on Ball Park Avenue. The church met the third Sunday of each month. Rev. Sandy Gilmer led the church from 1925 to 1956. Rev. Weaver Davis came in 1958 and led renovation of this building. (Elon First Baptist Church.)

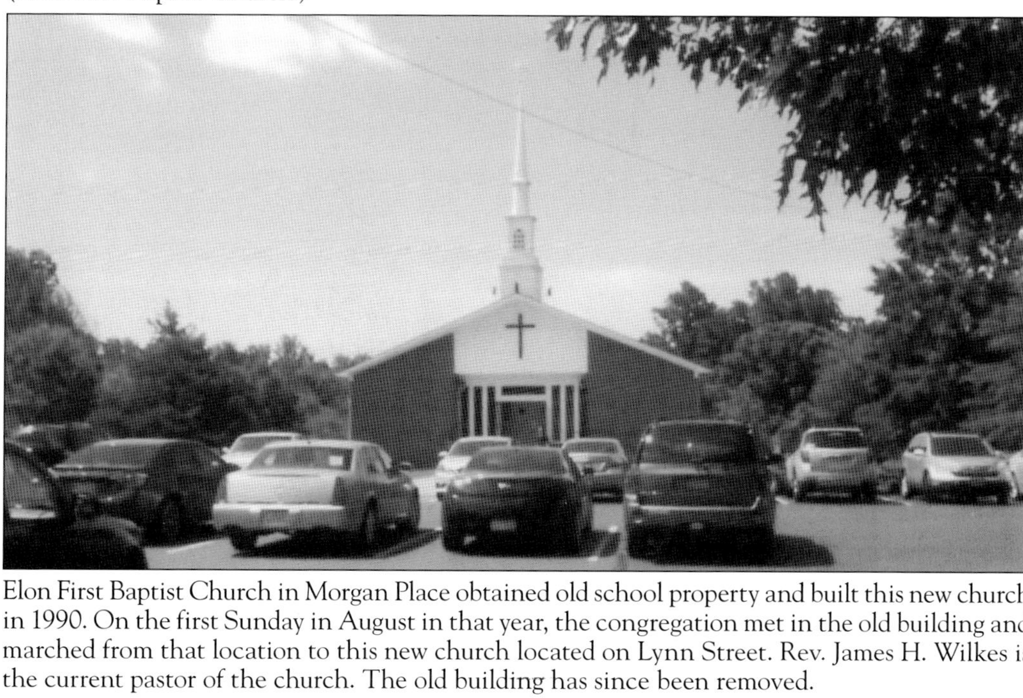

Elon First Baptist Church in Morgan Place obtained old school property and built this new church in 1990. On the first Sunday in August in that year, the congregation met in the old building and marched from that location to this new church located on Lynn Street. Rev. James H. Wilkes is the current pastor of the church. The old building has since been removed.

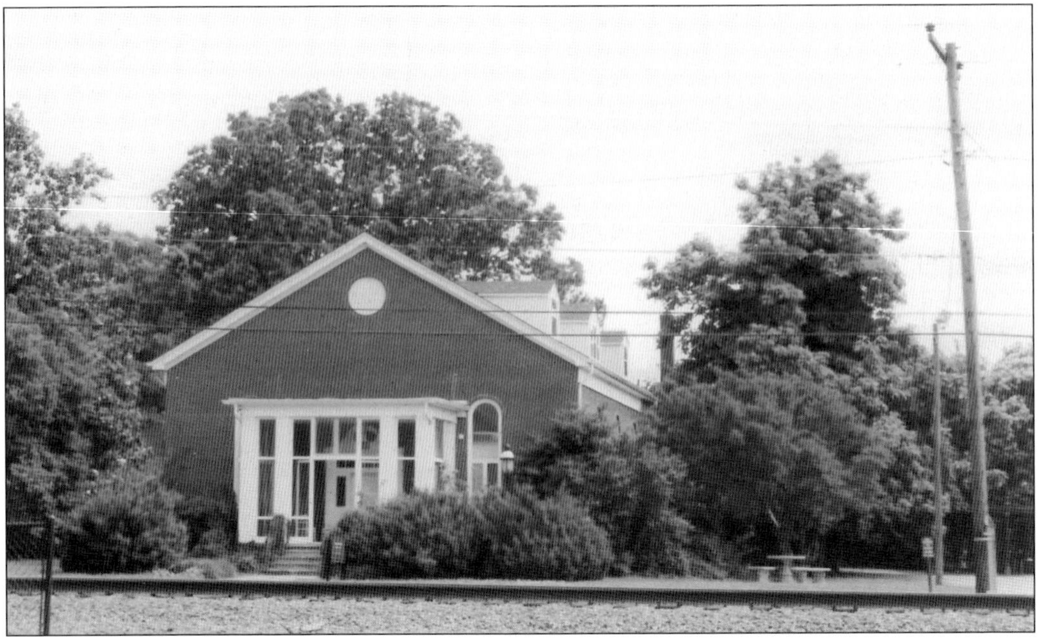

First Baptist Church of Elon first met in the old Grange Hall on South Williamson Avenue, but in 1948 constructed this building on West Trollinger Avenue at South Holt Avenue facing the railroad tracks. After 20 years, growth brought the need for new space, so land was purchased on Lawrence Avenue at Haggard Avenue and new facilities were erected. This building has been converted to apartments.

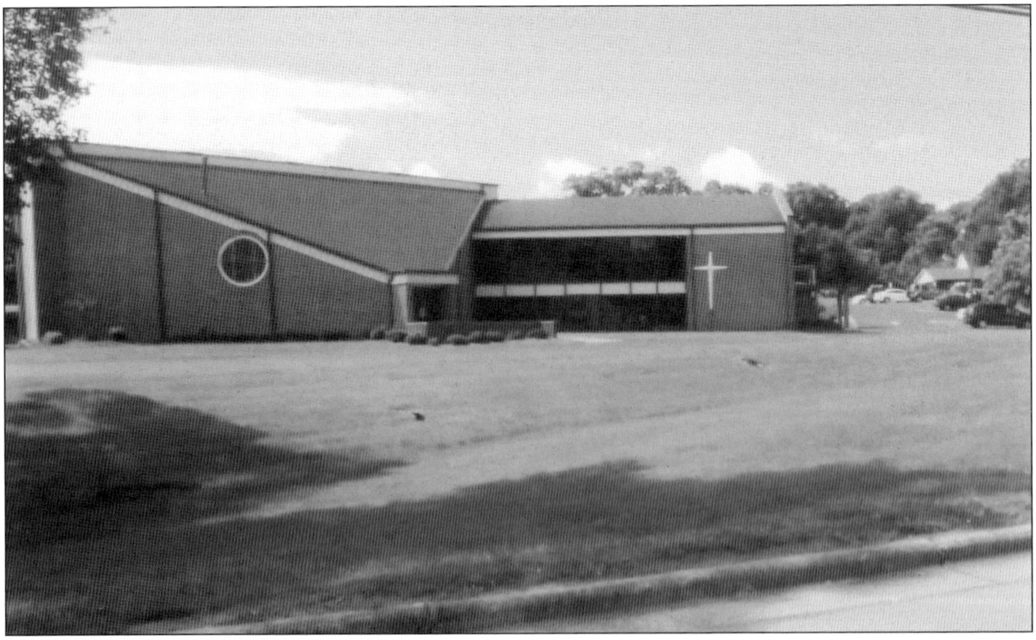

When First Baptist Church of Elon moved to its new location, it first erected an education building that was opened in September 1968. The church had Sunday school rooms and related facilities, and the auditorium in that building was used for worship services. The new worship facility was constructed later.

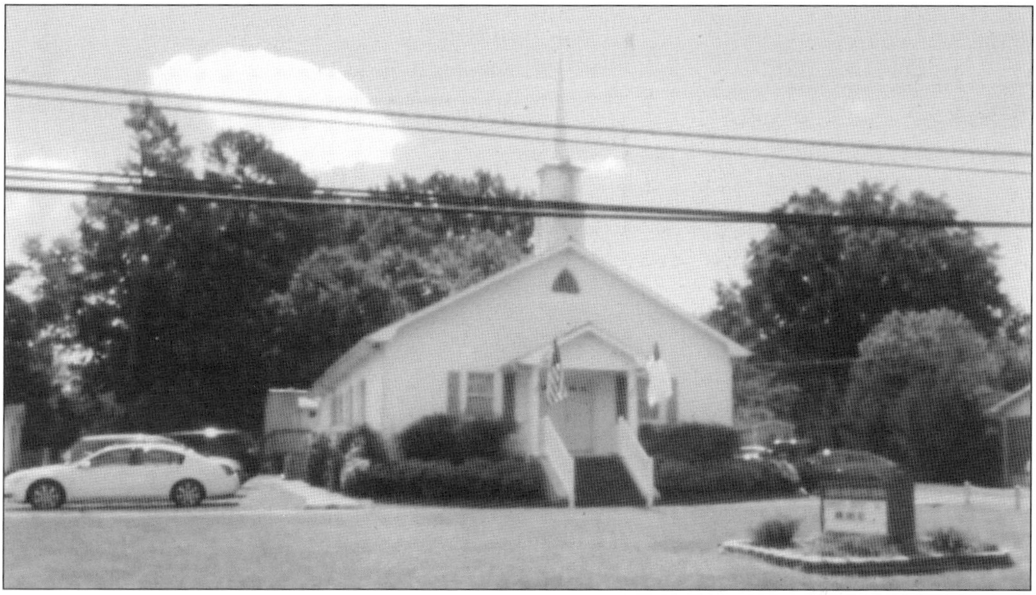

The Guiding Light Baptist Church is located on South Williamson Avenue and is one of several churches that have been located in that area as the town of Elon has grown to the south. This building served originally as the Grange hall, but it found new life when the first meetings of First Baptist Church of Elon were held there.

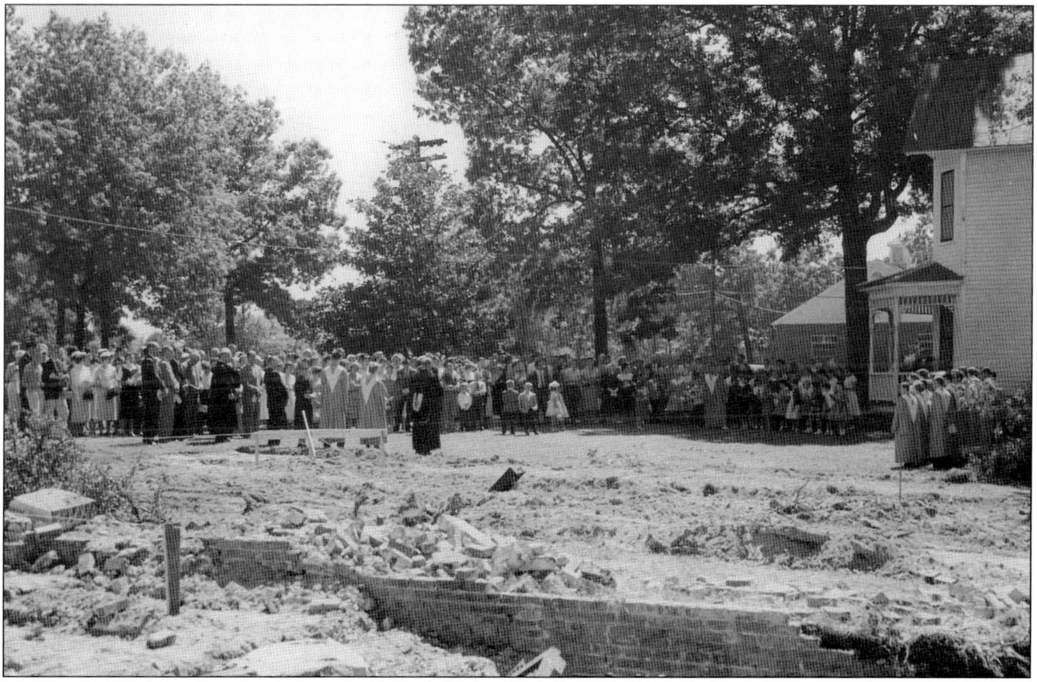

On September 14, 1958, members of the Elon College Community Church gathered on property at the corner of North Williamson Avenue and Haggard Avenue and broke ground for a new house of worship. Prior to that, the church, originally the Elon College Christian Church, had used college facilities for worship dating back to 1891. The location is directly across from the Elon University campus.

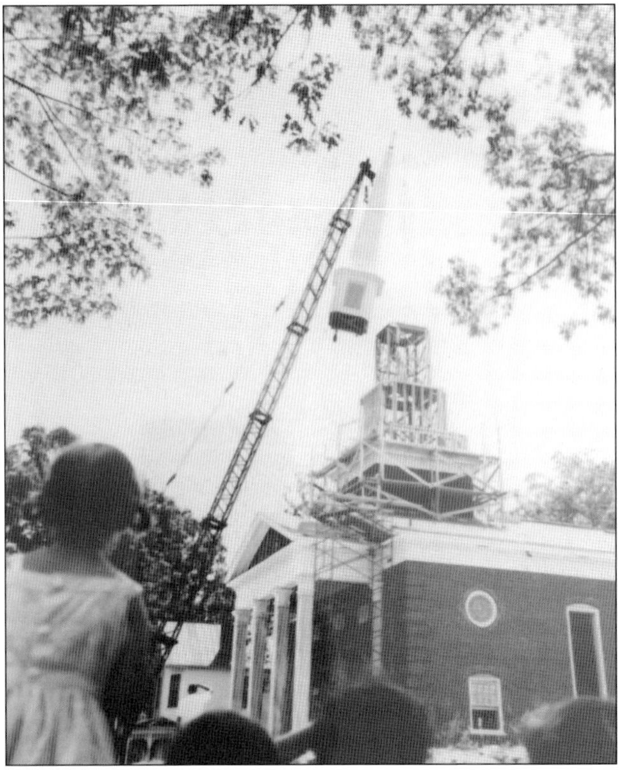

It was a big day in 1959 when a tall crane hoisted the steeple atop the Elon College Community Church and set it in place. The congregation had waited many years for its own home, and the steeple work signaled that work on the facility was near its end. The work was completed and the congregation was in its new home later that year. (Kathleen Patterson.)

This building was the parish house of the Elon College Community Church for many years. It was the site of dinners, parties, and other special events for the church and community. It remained in place as the church built a new education building in 1975 and became something of a community landmark. It was removed when the church built its new community life center in 2012. (Kathleen Patterson.)

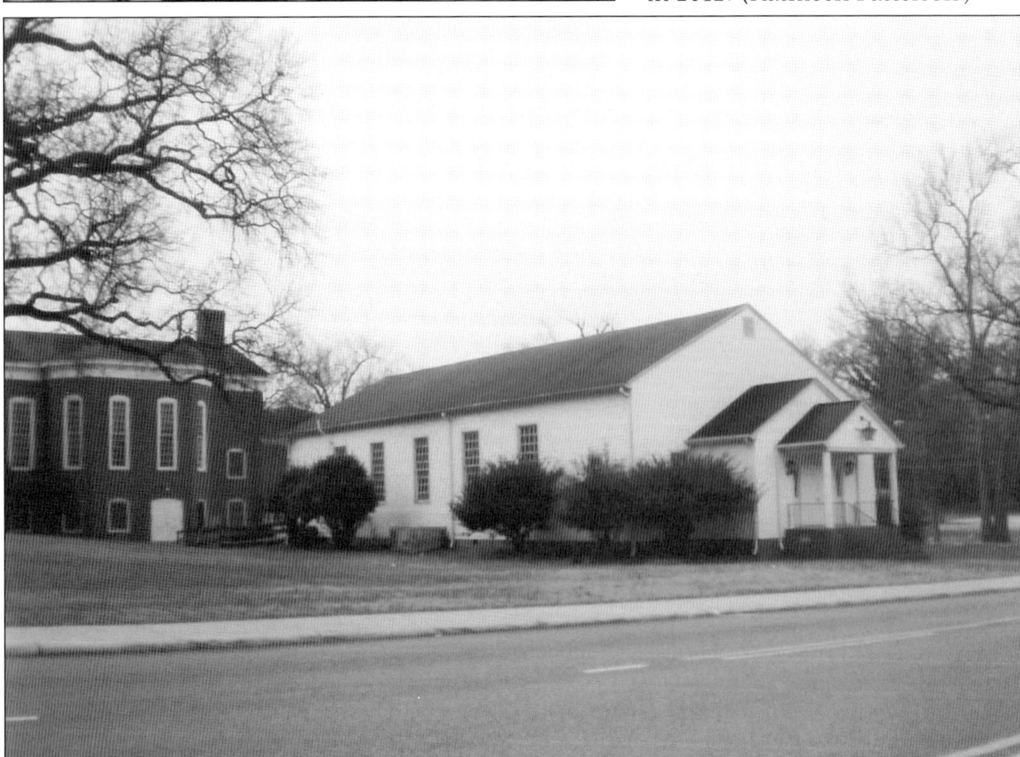

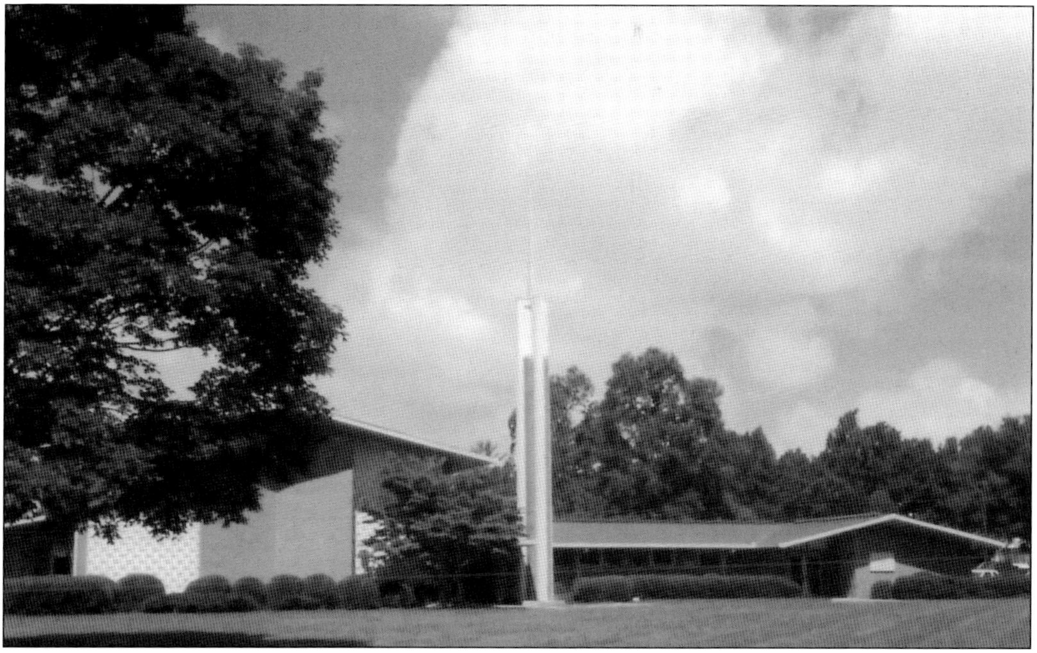

Another Elon church is the Church of Jesus Christ of Latter-day Saints on South Williamson Avenue. This sanctuary was built in 1970. The presence of this church is reflective of the variety of denominations that have grown up in the past several decades in the area. Represented in addition to the Mormons are members of Baptist, Methodist, Presbyterian, United Church of Christ, Nazarene, and independent congregations; Catholics have mass on campus and in Elon Community Church.

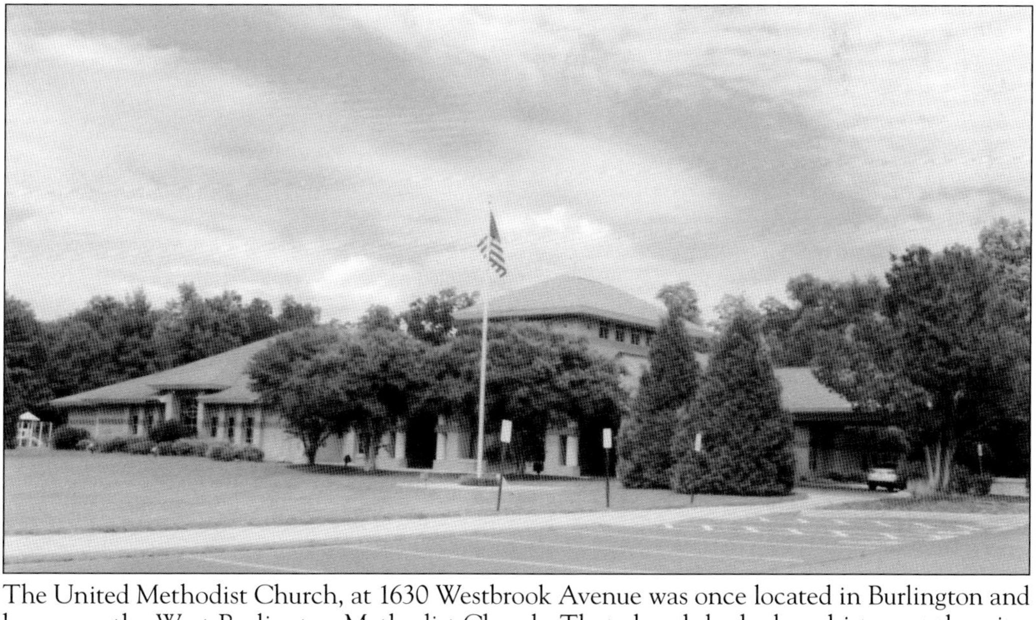

The United Methodist Church, at 1630 Westbrook Avenue was once located in Burlington and known as the West Burlington Methodist Church. That church had a long history at that site, but when it was destroyed by fire, the congregation decided to not rebuild there but to look for a new location. On April 12, 1992, the cornerstone was set at the new Elon home for the church.

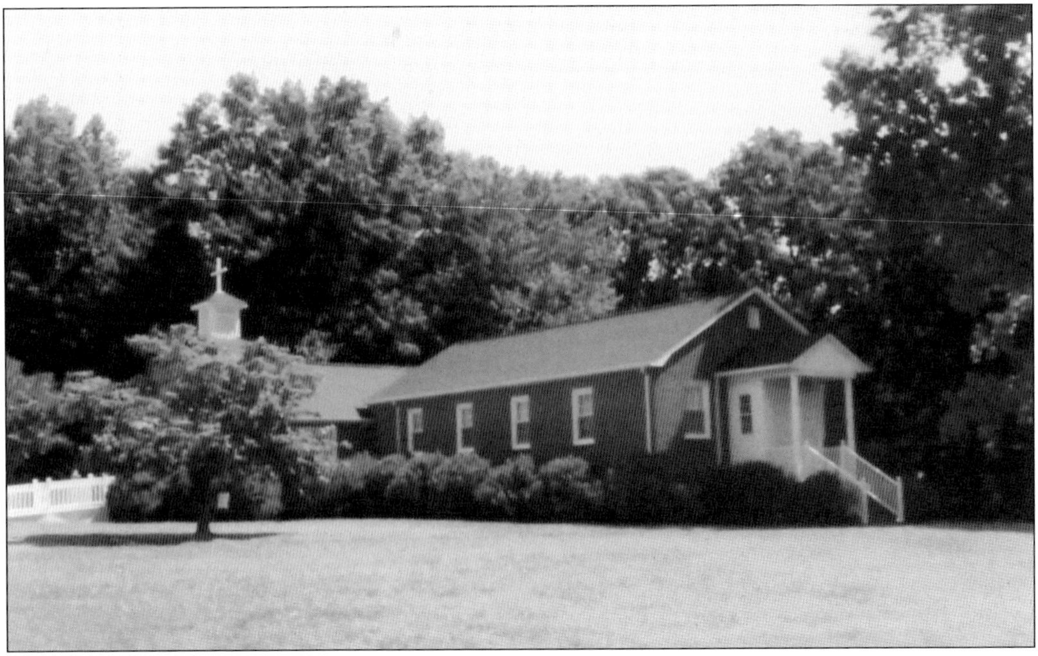

Trinity Presbyterian Church has been a part of the Elon community since 1954. It was organized on October 10 that year, and it is located at 101 Eastgate Drive and can be seen from South Williamson Avenue. The church sits amid an area of heavy residential growth that has occurred in the area where Burlington and Elon come together.

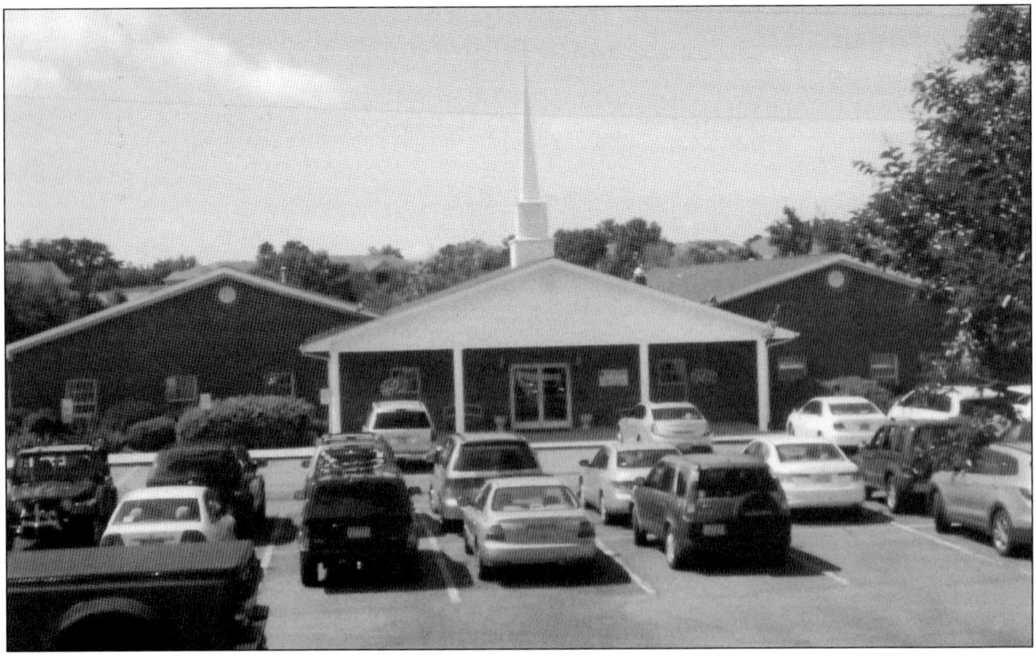

Antioch Community Church sits on the eastern side of the town of Elon in a site once occupied by Powerline Church of the Nazarene. It is a nondenominational church organized in 1987, and from 1993 to 2002 met on the campus of Elon University. In 2002, the church moved to its present location on Powerline Road.

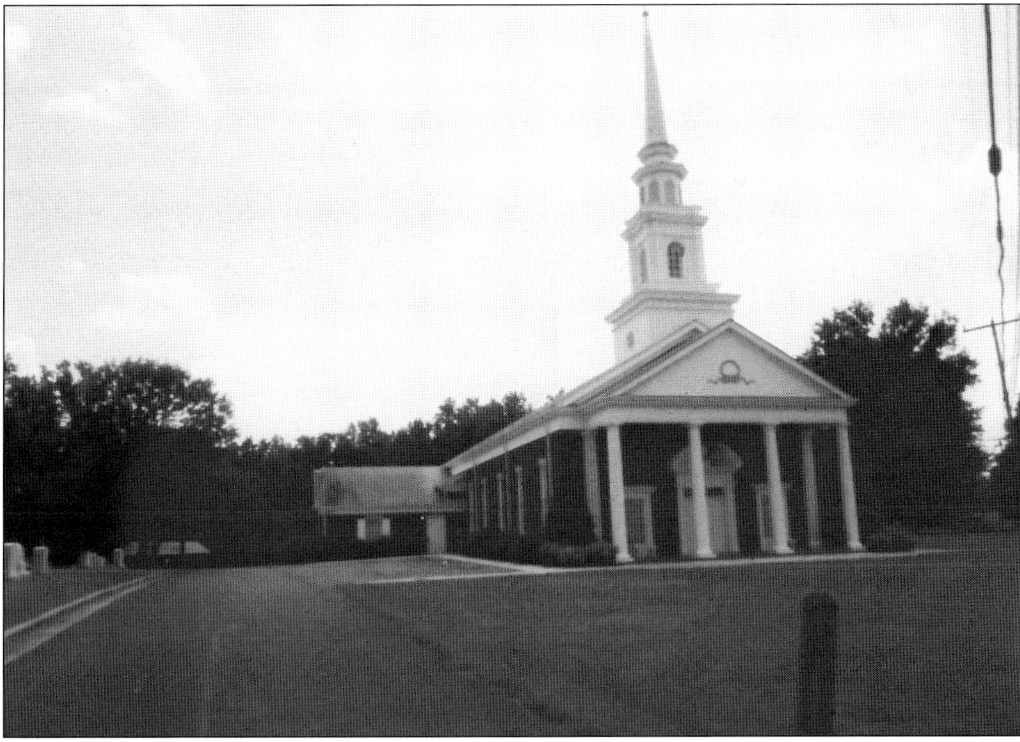

Shallow Ford Christian Church sits just north of the town of Elon, and it is one of the oldest in the area, organized in 1832. That was 17 years before Alamance County was formed and 61 years before the town of Elon was incorporated. A large cemetery where many early residents of the area are buried is located next to the church.

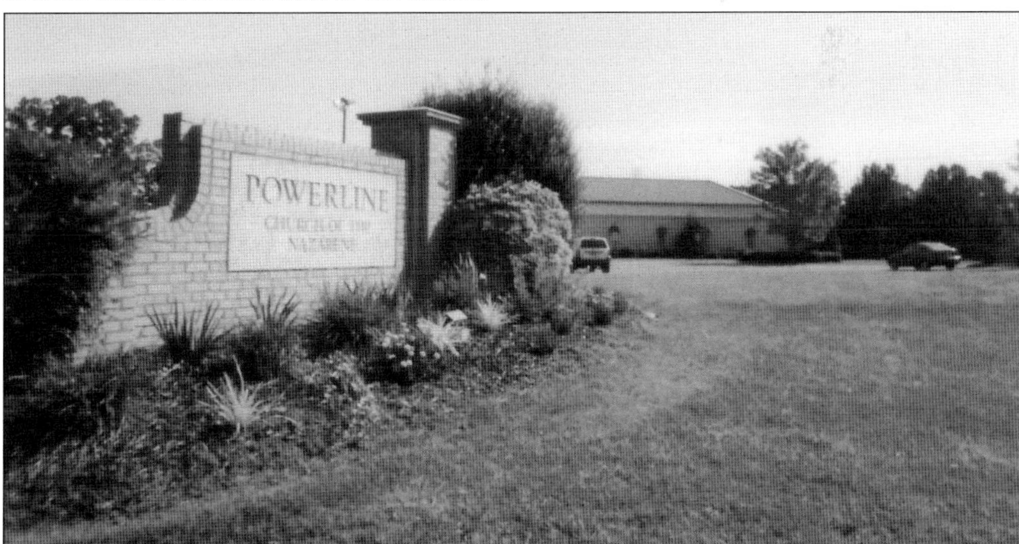

Powerline Church of the Nazarene had its beginning as West Burlington Church of the Nazarene on Markham Street in Burlington in 1965. It moved to Powerline Road in Elon in 1992 and changed its name at that time. In May 2002, the church moved into these new facilities on North Manning Avenue in Elon.

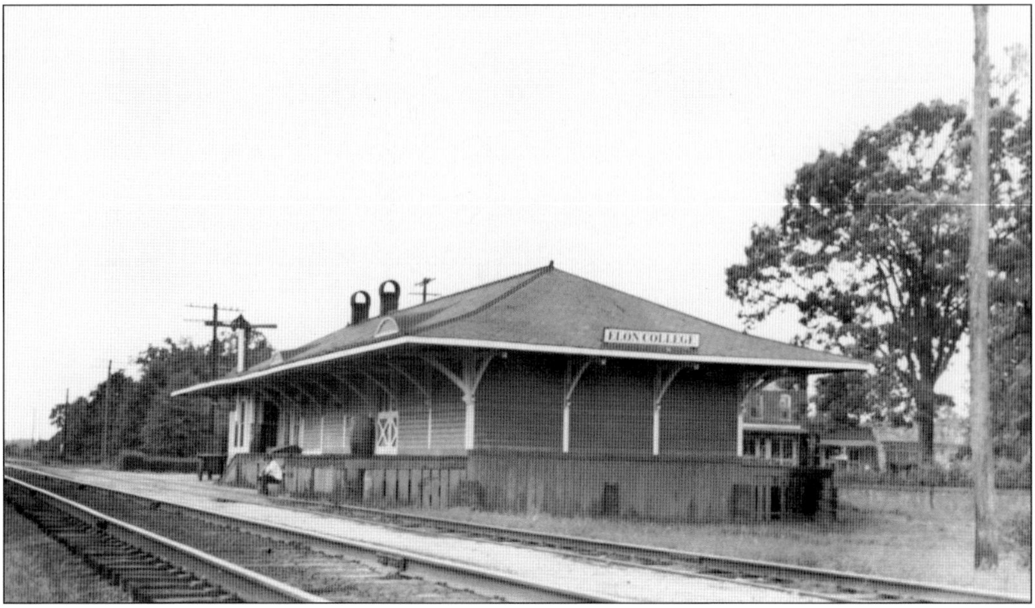

The depot at the town of Elon College was still in full use in 1944 handling freight, still serving mills in the area, and providing passenger transportation for the community. The depot was on the north side of the tracks, and on the right side buildings along the 100 block of North Williamson Avenue are visible. (Elon University.)

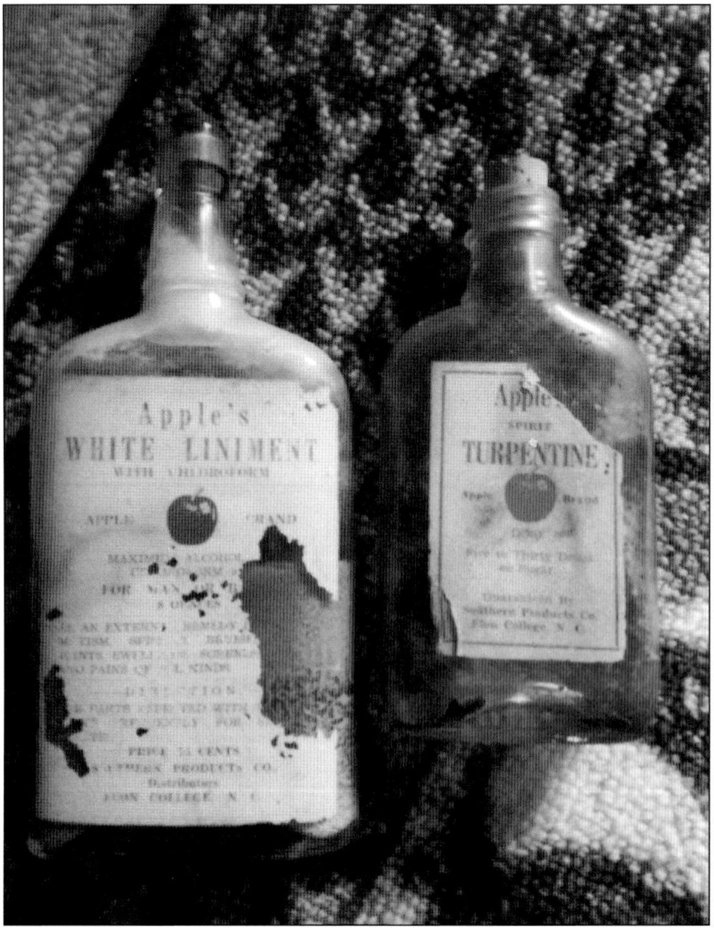

Over the years, there have been Elon businesses that have faded into history. One produced products aimed at improving one's health. Apple's White Liniment, at left, was for joints and muscle pain, and directions for the turpentine at right note a dose is five to 30 drops on sugar but do not state its use. Distribution was by Southern Products Company of Elon College. (Brannock Page.)

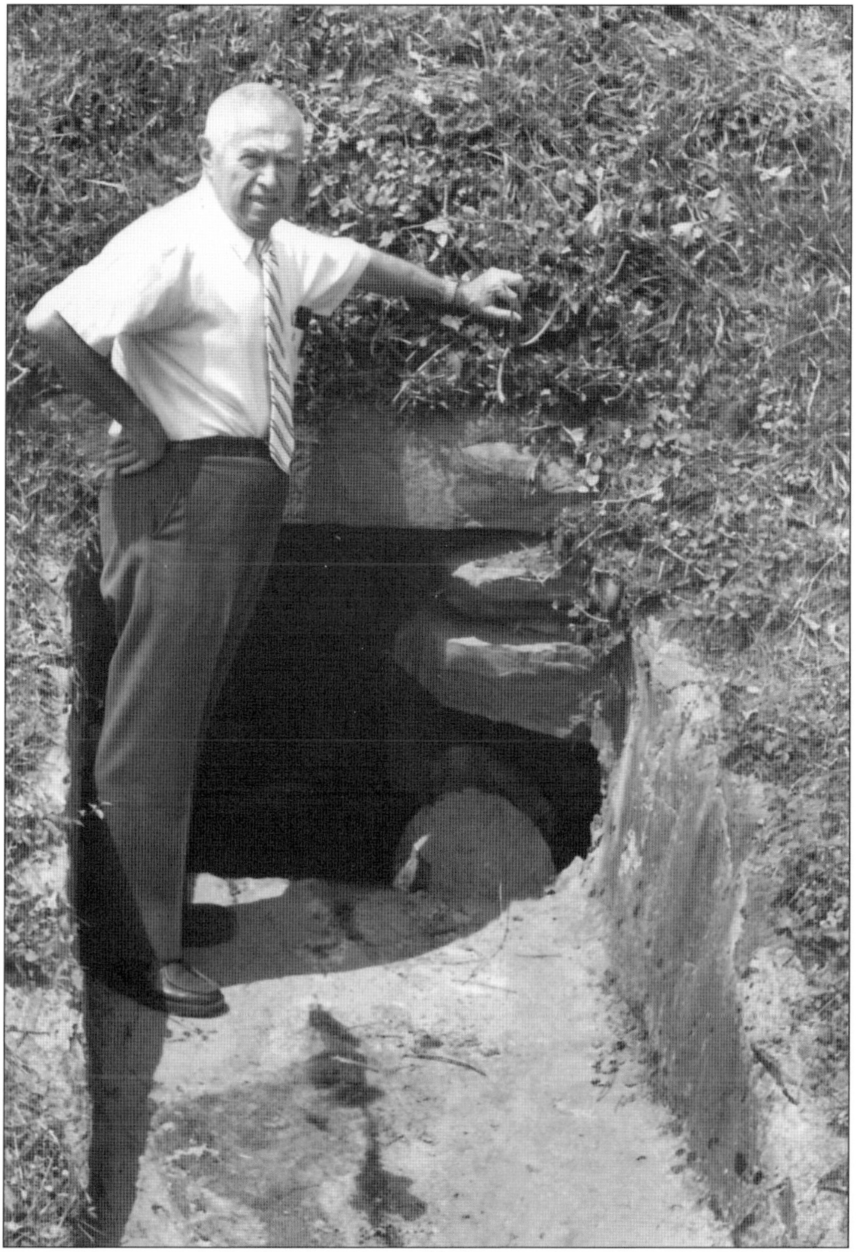

Larry Alley was an engineer and a member of Alley, Williams, Carmen & King, a well-known firm in Burlington. He also did engineering work for the Town of Elon, and it was in that role that he was on the site of what looks like a tunnel under the railroad tracks between Oak Avenue and Antioch Avenue. Actually, this is the oldest man-made structure in Elon. It is a culvert built in 1856 when the North Carolina Railroad was ending work on its line from Goldsboro to Charlotte. Apparently, it was built to allow a flow of water. Trains began moving along that line in early 1856. That culvert remains open today under the tracks with no apparent use other than as the home for some groundhogs that have been seen frequenting the site over the years. At one time, there was a piece of concrete at the site onto which had been written the date and text that labeled the site as the "first man-made structure" in Elon.

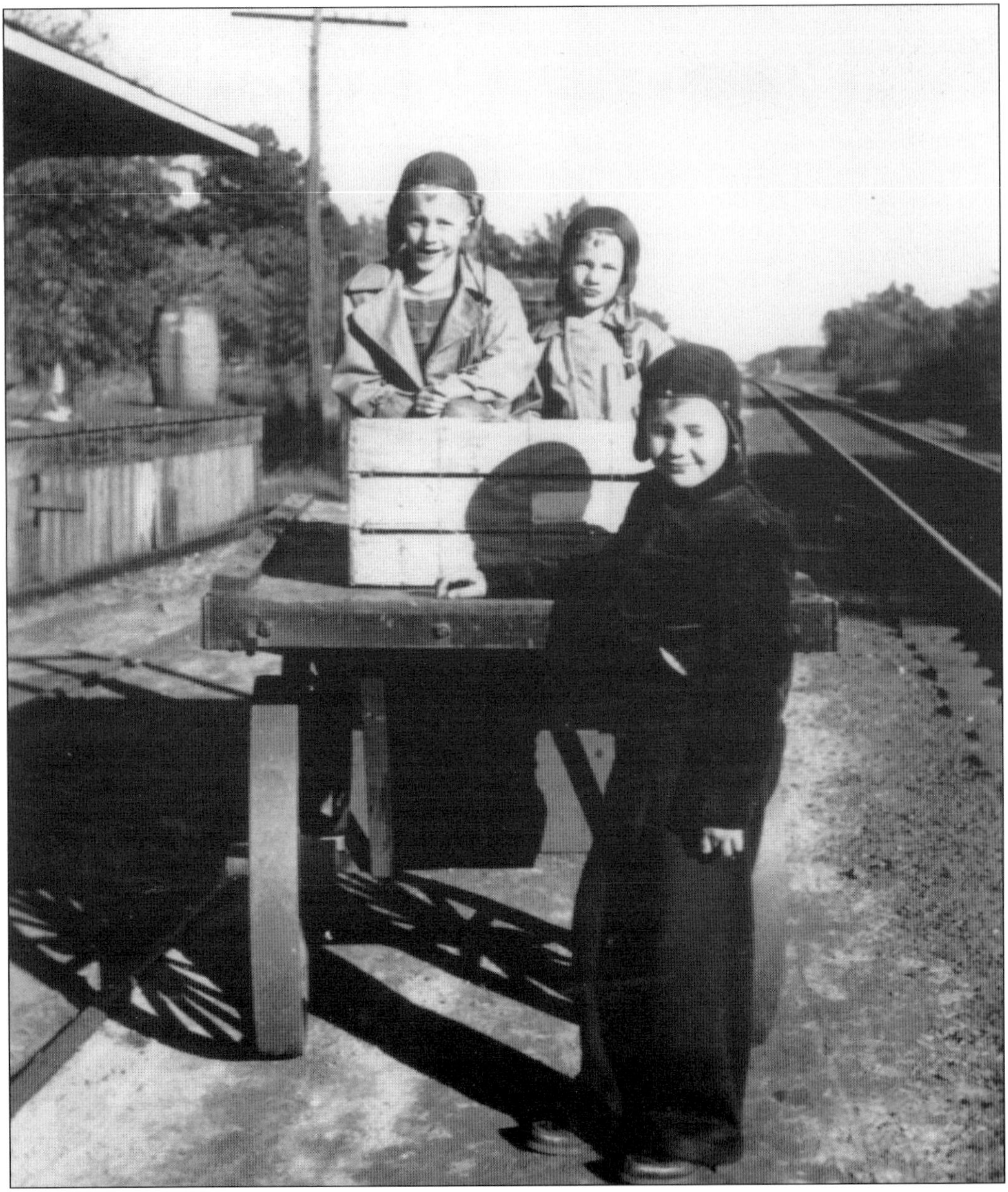

Young boys always seem to be attracted to trains, and that was true for these three young men who lived in Elon College in the 1940s when this photograph was made. They are, from left to right, John, Jim, and Ed Powell, the sons of Dr. Thomas E. Powell Jr. Dr. Powell was a graduate of Elon College, and upon graduation he began teaching biology and geology at the college. In 1927, while still teaching, Powell started his own company, Carolina Biological Supply Co., to supply materials needed in the teaching of the sciences in high schools and colleges across the nation. That operation was located just outside Elon College at its eastern town limits. Carolina Biological Supply Co. continues operations today. Ed later succeeded his father at the head of the company, Jim started a medical testing laboratory that later became LabCorp, and John was an attorney who was involved at times with both his brothers in their work over the years. (Dr. James B. Powell.)

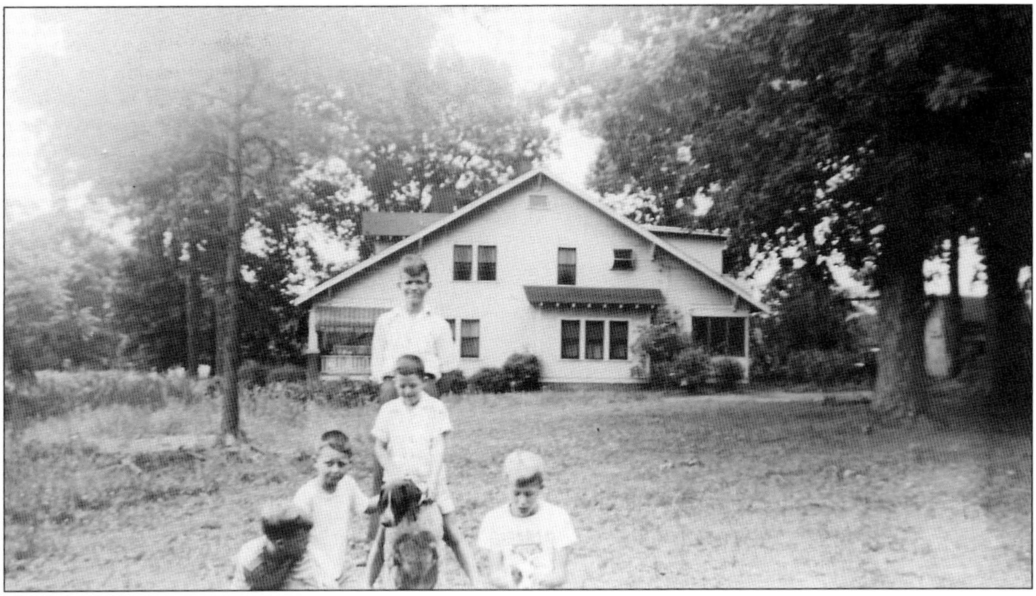

Playing in the big area beside the Powell home, from left to right in the foreground are Jim Powell, Wes and Brad Reynolds, and John Powell. Jimmy Scott is standing behind them. This was in the late 1940s. The house was located on Haggard Avenue near the Elon Public School but was later moved to East College Avenue and is now used by Elon University. (Dr. James B. Powell.)

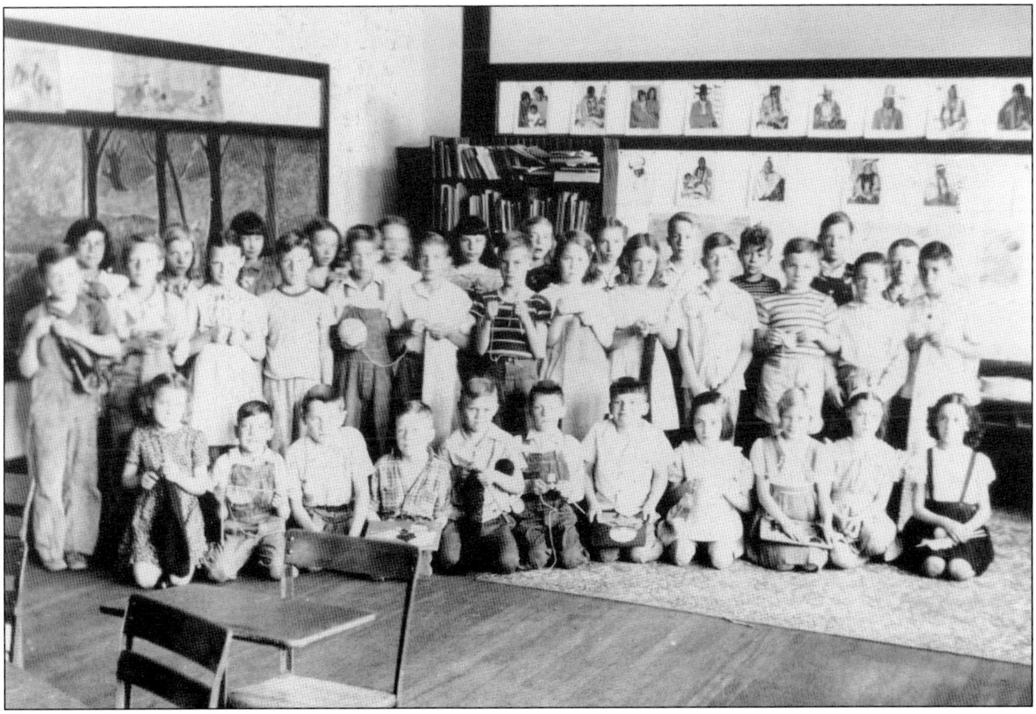

These young students at the Elon College Public School are displaying the results of one of their school activities in Miss Brown's third grade. This was in the 1946–1947 school year, and as strange as it might seem, the students had been receiving instruction in how to knit. They are showing the things they had knitted in class. (Dr. James B. Powell.)

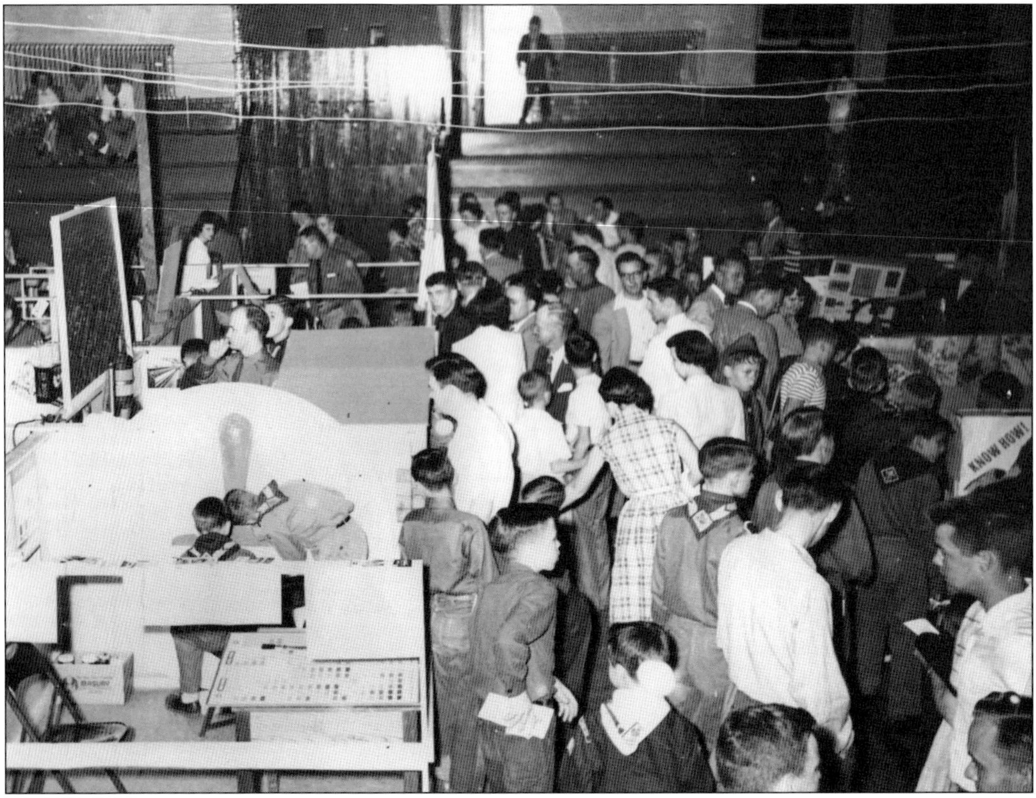

The gymnasium area in the Elon College Public School was the site of many varied activities during the school year. In this particular photograph, the local Boy Scouts are having a show to display the work they were doing in Scouting. Scouts prepared their projects, set them up in the gym, and invited families and town residents to the annual show of their work. (Dr. James B. Powell.)

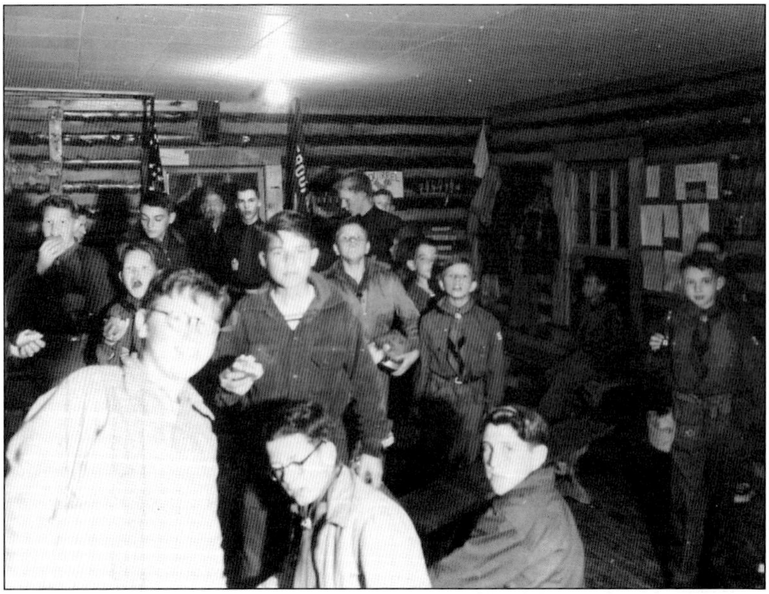

Members of Boy Scout Troop No. 51 are shown together in their meeting place around 1950. The troop was sponsored at that time by the Elon Exchange Club, which continues to meet today. The Exchange Club has a number of projects that benefit the community. A popular Brunswick stew sale funds those projects. (Dr. James B. Powell.)

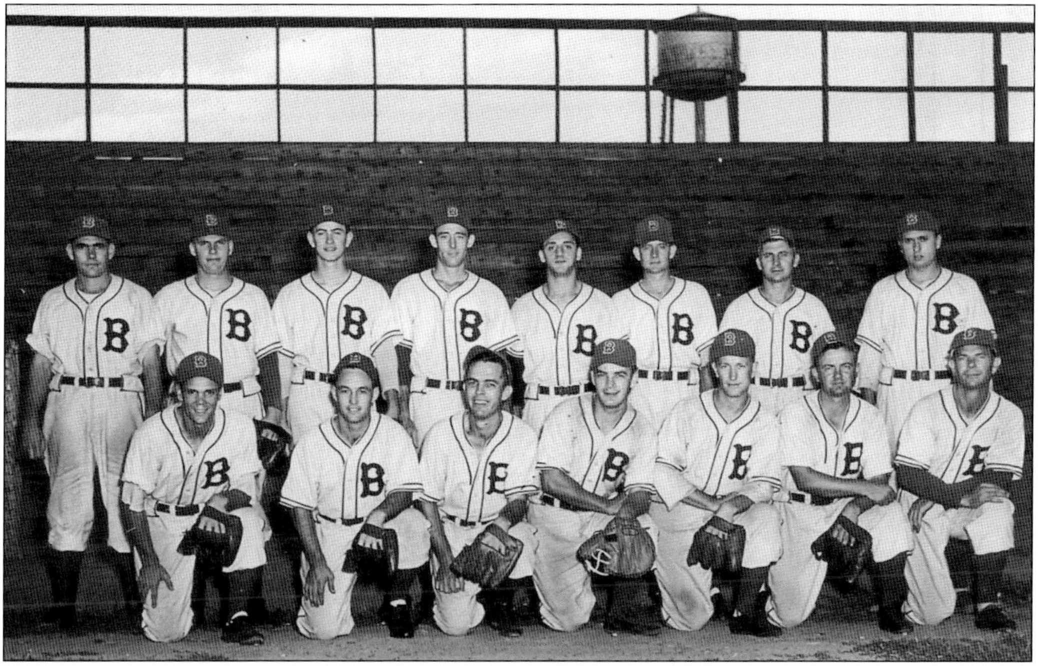

The Burlington Bees were a professional team playing in the Carolina League in the late 1940s. The team played in the old baseball park just off South Williamson Avenue in Elon College and won the league championship in 1949. Crowds were so large at times that some fans had to sit on the outfield grass along the fence in order to see the games.

The girls are in their evening dresses and the boys in their Sunday suits as they attend a dance at the Elon College High School gym in the late 1940s. Here, they are gathered around the refreshment table, and it appears that cookies and bottles of Coca-Cola were on the menu for the night. (Dr. James B. Powell.)

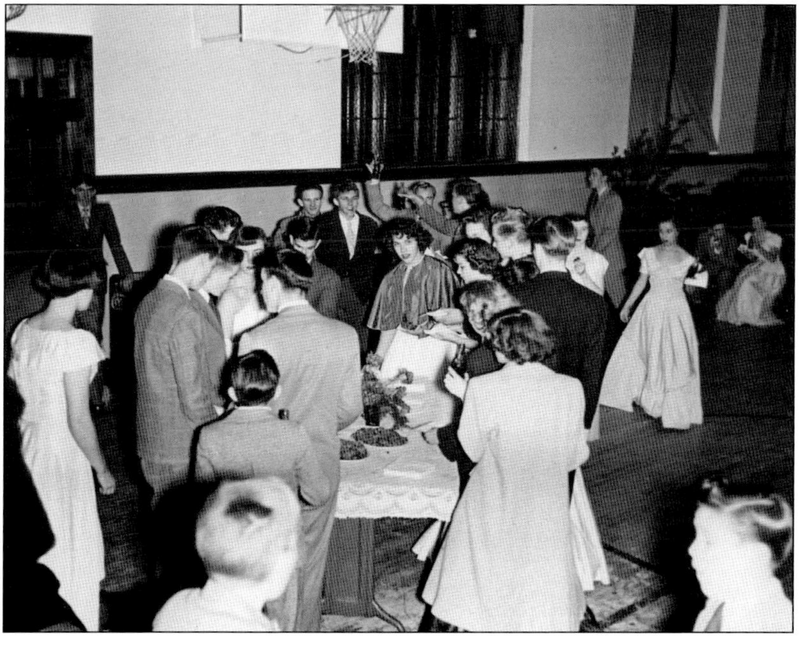

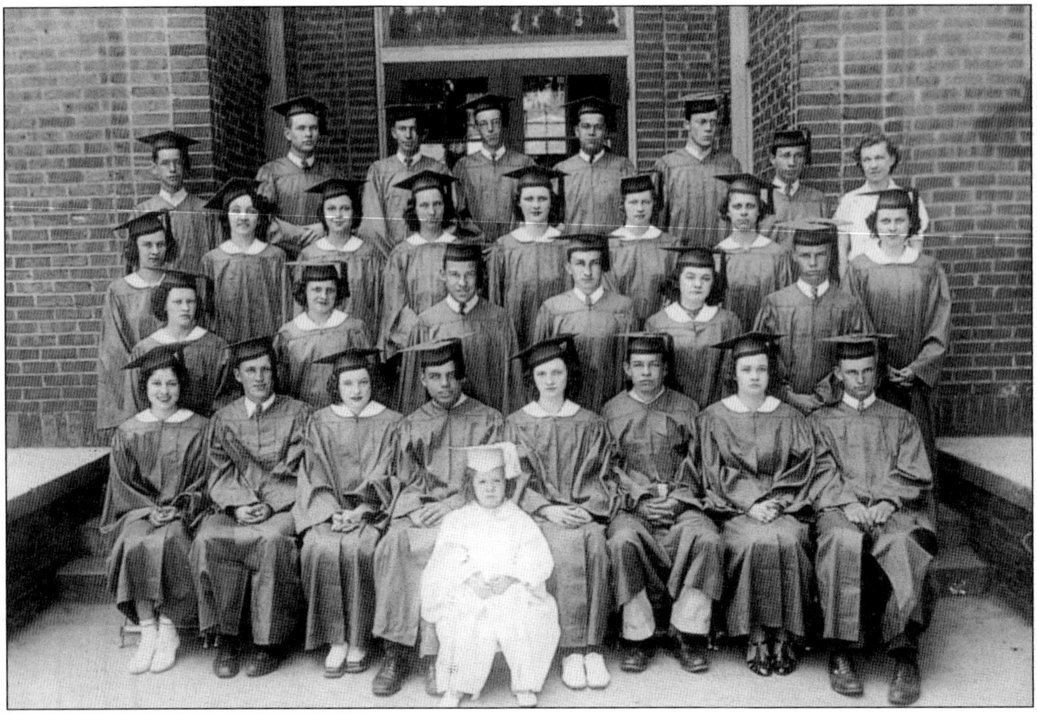

It was graduation time at Elon High School in the 1940s, and students gathered on the steps with their mascot and teacher for the official class photograph. It was not a particularly large class, but it was typical of those at other high schools in the Alamance County Schools. Each community had its own high school before consolidation and small classes were the rule. (Dr. James B. Powell.)

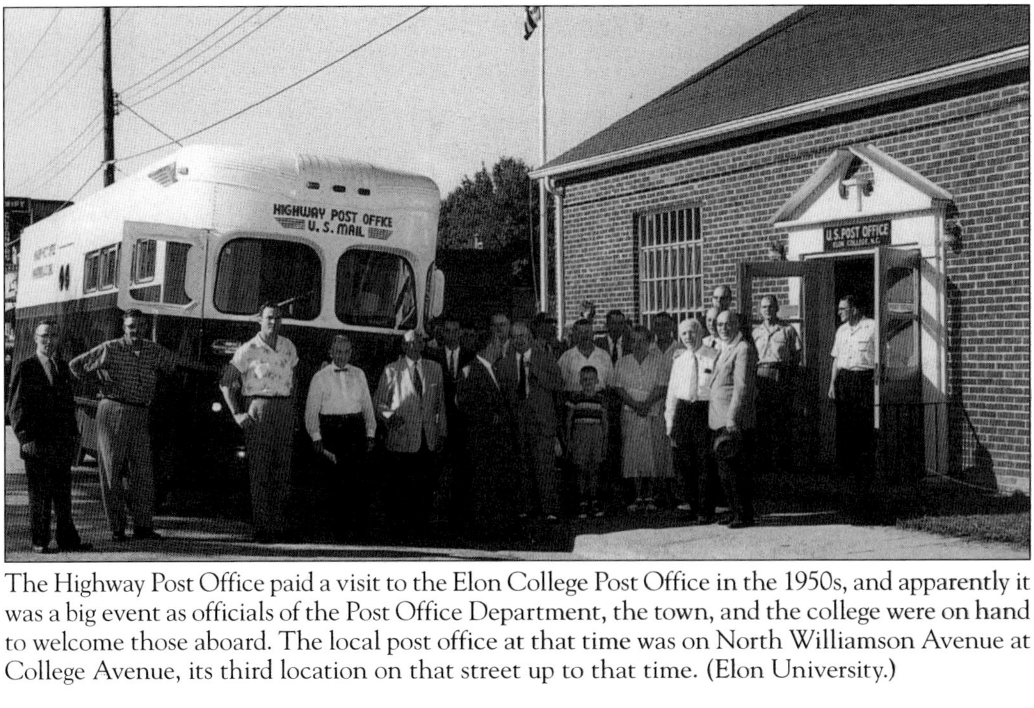

The Highway Post Office paid a visit to the Elon College Post Office in the 1950s, and apparently it was a big event as officials of the Post Office Department, the town, and the college were on hand to welcome those aboard. The local post office at that time was on North Williamson Avenue at College Avenue, its third location on that street up to that time. (Elon University.)

It is Easter Sunday in 1957 and little Sheree Atkinson, the daughter of Dee and Mona Atkinson, enjoys the sunshine in the yard of the Veteran Apartments on North Williamson Avenue. In 1946–1947, the Federal Housing Authority built the barracks-like apartments to be used by World War II veterans and their families while the veterans attended school. (Mona Atkinson.)

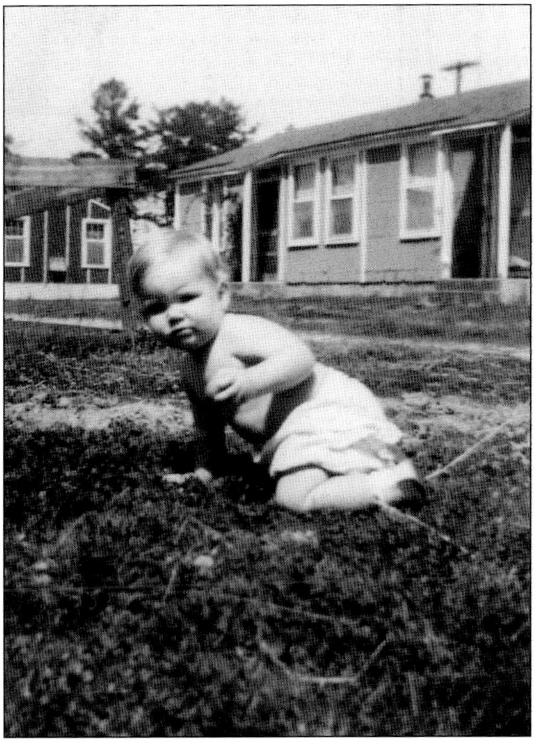

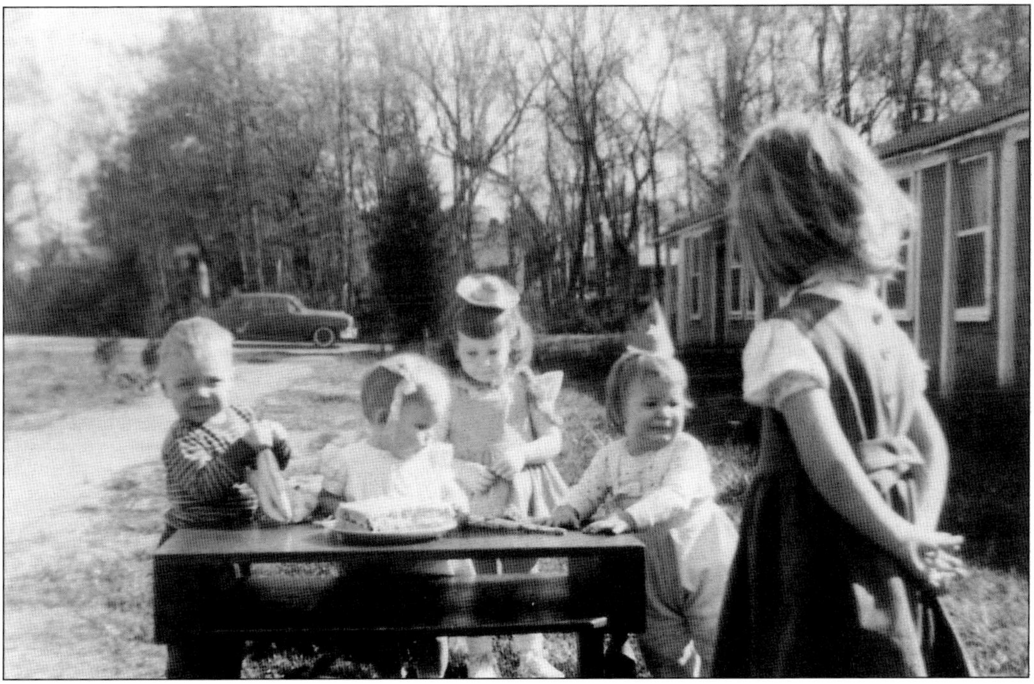

Sheree Atkinson and her friends enjoy a birthday party in 1957 with the Veteran Apartments in the background. The FHA built 66 apartments—one-, two-, and three-bedroom units—for the use of World War II veterans attending Elon College. The apartments stood on the site now occupied by the Oaks residence complex on North Williamson Avenue. (Mona Atkinson.)

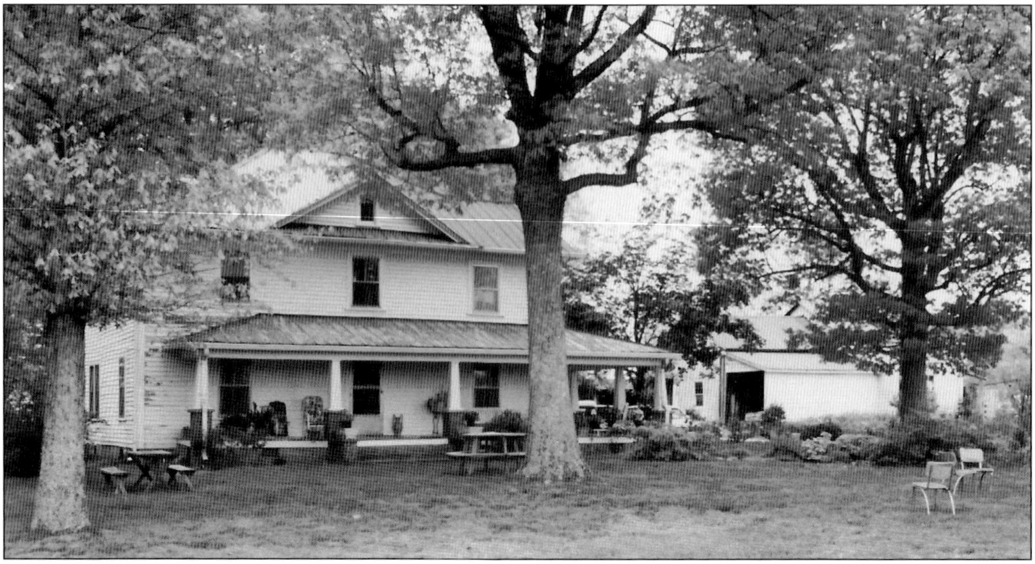

This was the home of William E. Loy and Betty Ann Westmoreland Loy that stood for many years on the eastern limits of Elon. There is a wall marker there recognizing the Loy Farm that is now a part of Elon University. William Loy farmed a large area east of Magnolia Cemetery between the railroad and Oak Avenue–West Front Street. (Jean Loy Toms.)

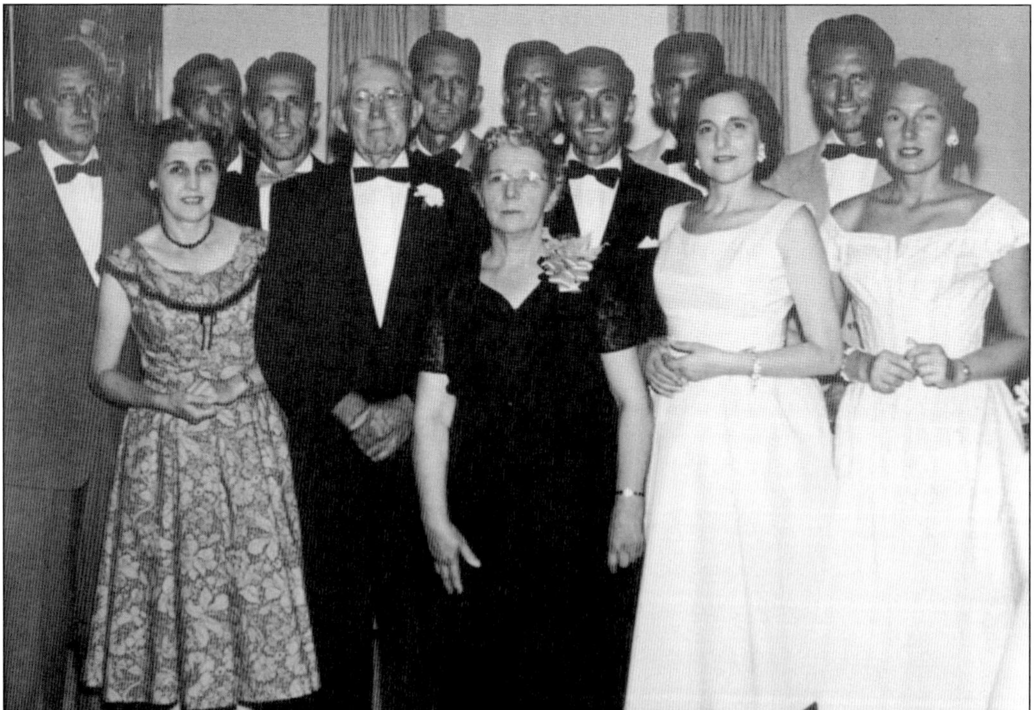

In 1957, the Loy family came together to celebrate the 50th wedding anniversary of William E. and Betty "Mama" Loy, seen in the middle of the front row with daughters (from left to right) Josie L. Huey, Leola Loy, and Janice L. Newman. Sons are, from left to right, Howard, Eugene, Freeman, Ervin, Leon, Keith, Durwood, and Bill. (Jean Loy Toms.)

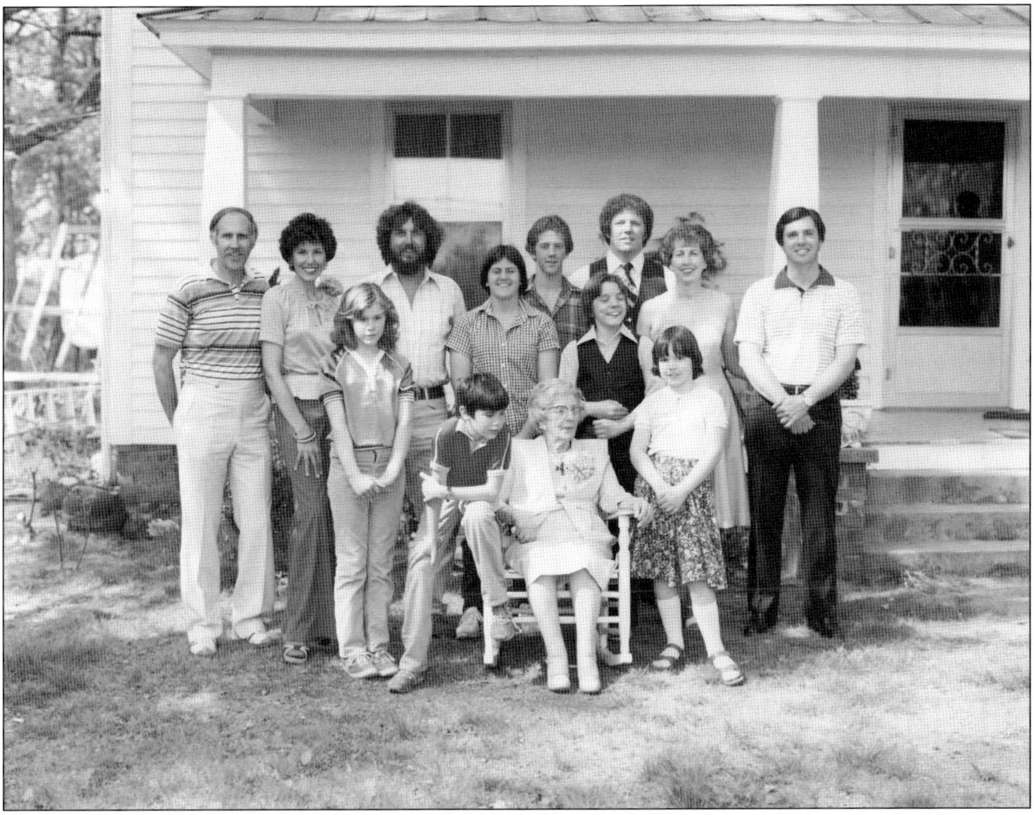

The grandchildren of Mama Loy pose with her on her 91st birthday in 1979. At left is Paul Huey, restaurant operator in Elon, and next is his cousin Jean Loy Toms. When Elon University obtained the property in 2006, officials developed a sustainability program featuring a greenhouse, gardens, and a solar farm with 10,000 panels that can provide power for 415 homes. (Jean Loy Toms.)

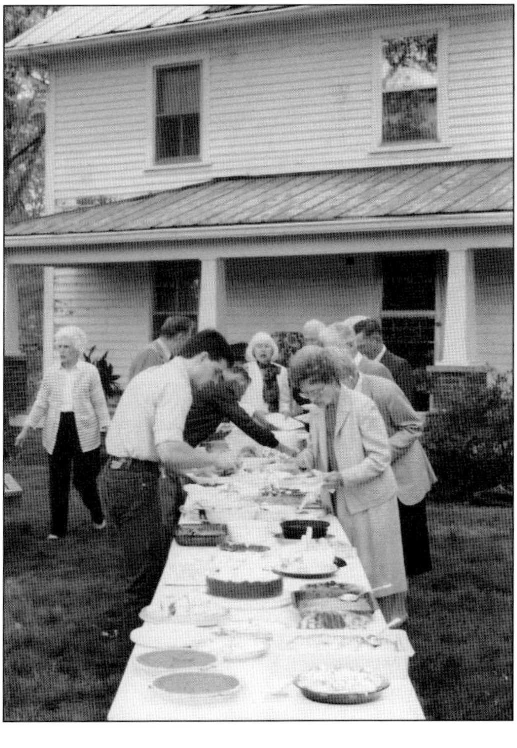

One of the traditional parts of Loy gatherings was dinner in the front yard, an occasion that was part of family events all across the South in years past. This was in 1989, when Mama Loy was 101. She lived to be 103. In 2000, Elon University bought the property, with lifetime rights for Loy family members there. Elon accessed the property in 2006. (Jean Loy Toms.)

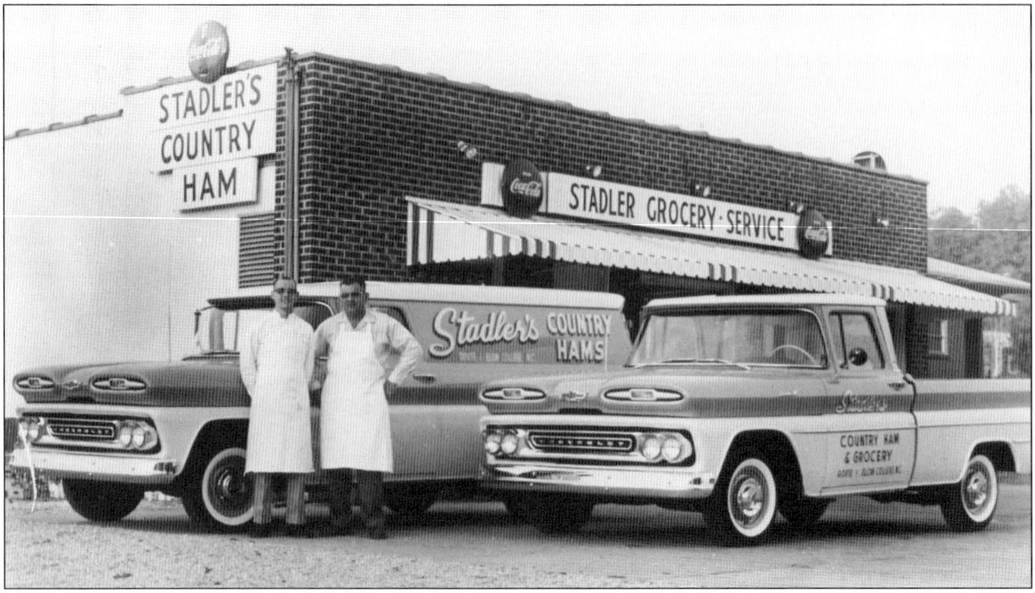

In the 1950s, Charlie Stadler (right) operated this little grocery store on East Haggard Avenue. His son Virgil worked with him. They had a love for country ham, raised a few hogs, and sold some ham in the store. Virgil went to school to better learn how to produce quality country ham and came back with an eye to expanding the sale of that ham. (Virgil Stadler.)

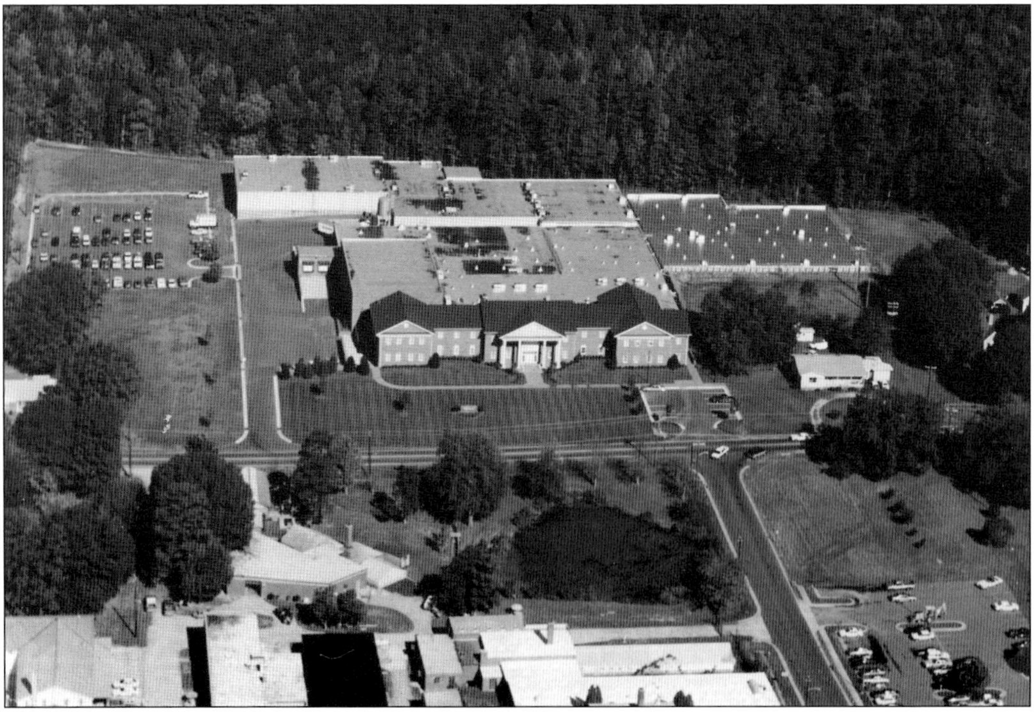
From that little store in the 1950s grew this huge facility where country hams would be processed for sale over the eastern United States for many years to come. It was one of the major business success stories in Alamance County. Smithfield later bought the company, and it would sell the property to Elon University, which now uses the site for its School of Health Sciences. (Virgil Stadler.)

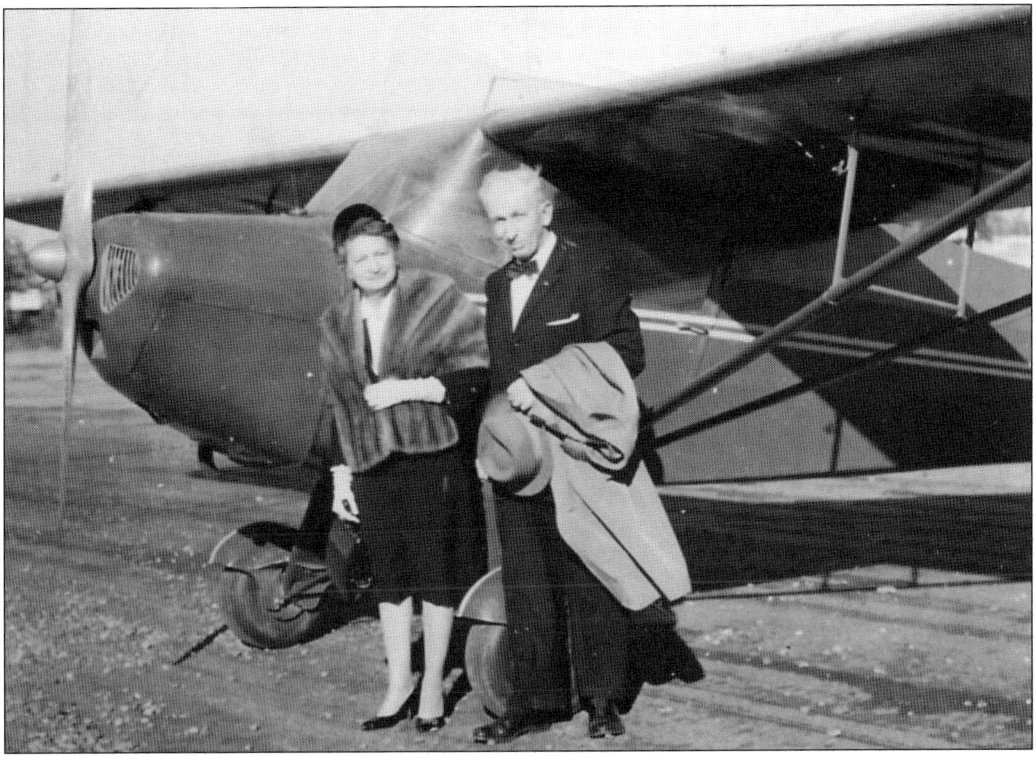

Dr. Alonzo Hook is an Elon College legend. He graduated in 1913 and joined the faculty in 1914. He remained on the faculty 69 years. Hook founded the Physics Department and was dean of the college on two occasions. He attended every graduation from 1910 to 1982 and died on commencement day in 1983. Here, he and wife, Jessie Hook, prepare for flight from an area airport. (Mona Atkinson.)

Dr. Alonzo Hook earned his pilot's license in 1939 and headed the Elon College Civilian Pilot Training Program during World War II. He liked to take aerial photographs of Elon and send them as Christmas cards to friends with the homes of those friends marked on the photographs. Hook was also a pioneer in the college's athletic programs and is in the Elon Sports Hall of Fame. (Mona Atkinson.)

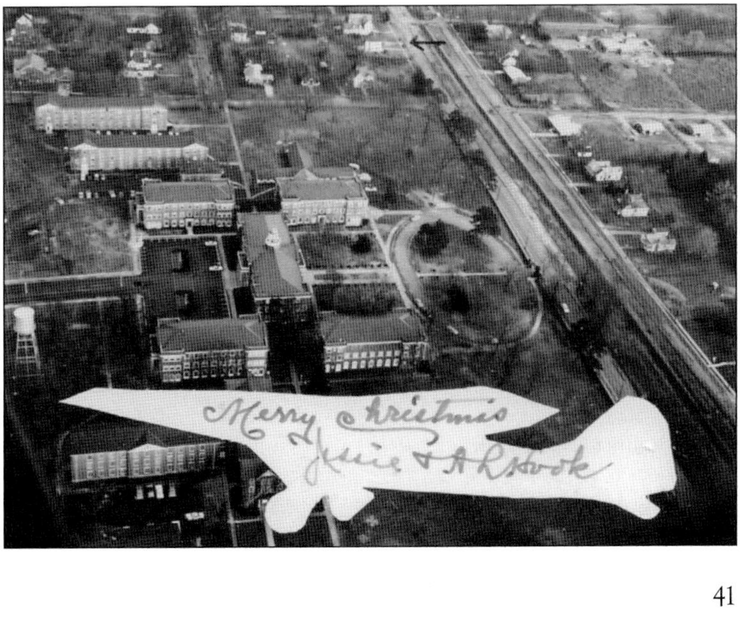

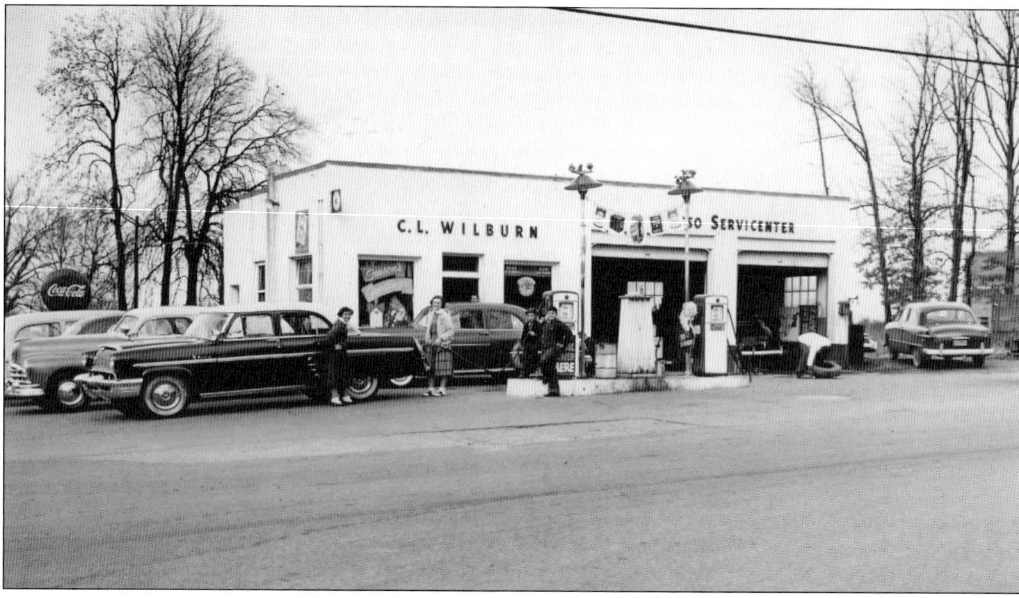

One of the major landmarks in Elon College for many years was the C.L. Wilburn Esso Service Center at East Haggard Avenue and North Williamson Avenue. It was right on the corner, and down the block on Haggard was Alumni Gym. Wilburn's service center is gone now, and the area is part of the landscaped approach to the gymnasium. (Jean Loy Toms.)

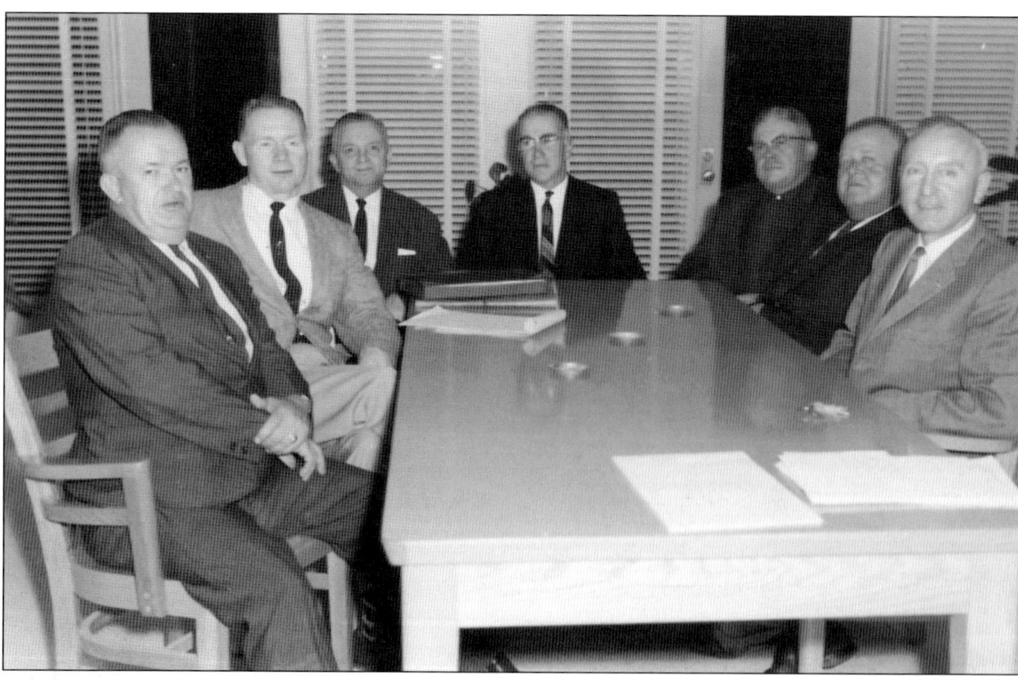

When Western Alamance High School opened in 1962, this committee chose A.M. Primm as principal. Members are, from left to right, Russell Taylor, Jim White, Nimrod Harris, Mark McAdams, Harold Rascoe, Dan Ireland, and Principal Primm. Elon students moved to the new school, and Elon High School became a middle school at that time. (Dr. Eugene and Jo Grimley.)

Mona Atkinson and her children, Sheree and Del, display the big snowman they built during a snowstorm that provided this winter wonderland in January 1962. The Atkinson house and the one in the background were built in the early 1900s along Lebanon Avenue. The homes are gone now, and the university Academic Village occupies this location. (Mona Atkinson.)

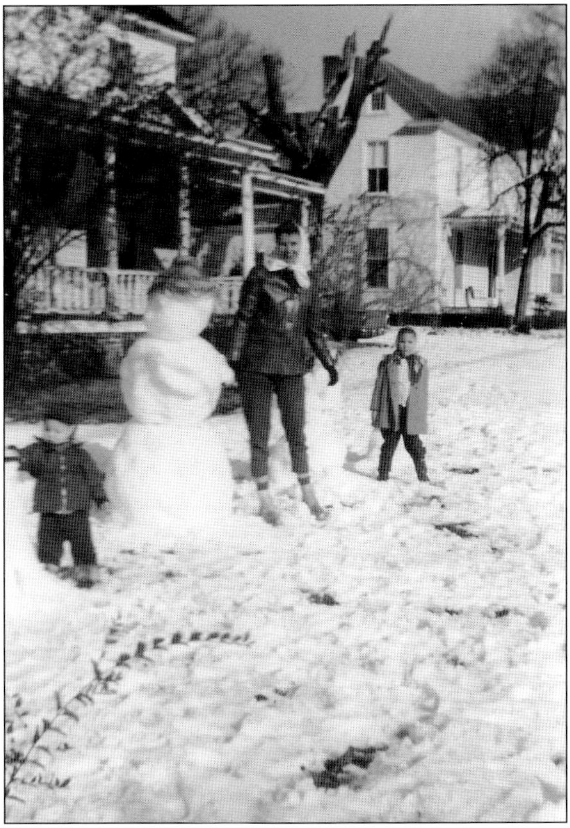

These children are kindergarten students at the Elon Community Church, and they are participating in a program for parents and friends in the church and community. From the appearance of the walls, it is likely that the program is being held in the old white frame parish house building that adjoined the church until 2012, when the new community life center was opened. (Jane Shutt.)

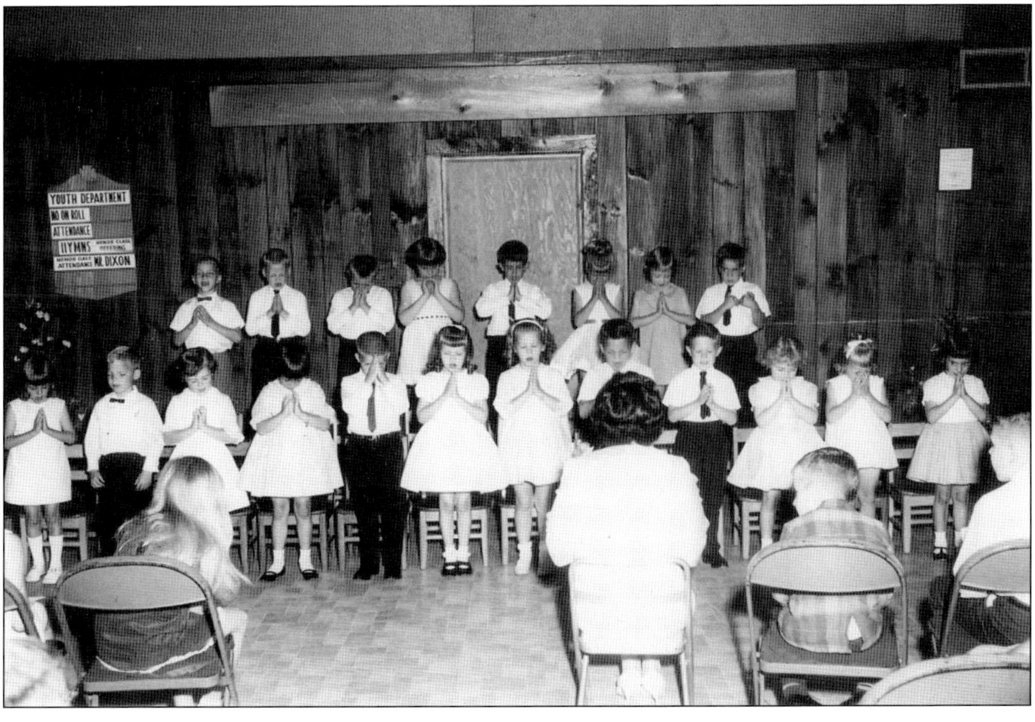

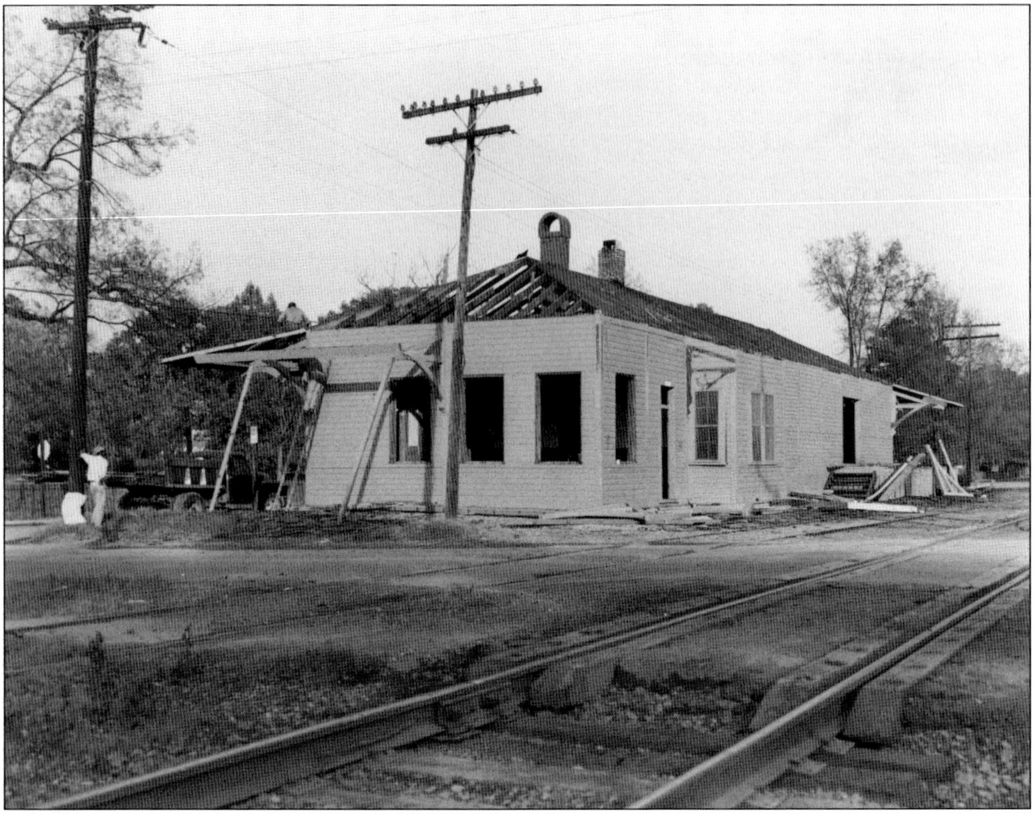

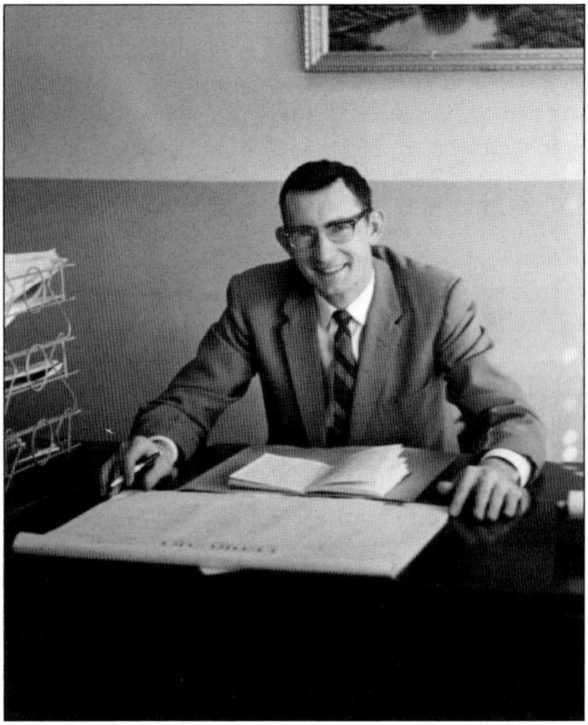

In the 1960s, the world of transportation had changed and the depot in Elon College was no longer in service. Built in the 1880s, it had served the passenger and freight needs of the community through two world wars and the Great Depression. In 1961, however, the railroad decided the depot was no longer needed and it was demolished, removing the link to the town's birth. (Elon University.)

Dee Atkinson was the only principal of Elon College Middle School. When consolidation came in 1962, Elon College High School became a middle school. Atkinson served until Western Alamance Middle School opened in the late 1970s, and Elon students moved there. He retired in 1987 after 30 years in education. An Elon College graduate and basketball star, Atkinson served two years as athletic director at the college. (Mona Atkinson.)

The children of Dr. J. Earl Danieley are dressed up for Easter and are posing beside the Holland House, home of the Elon College president from 1963 to 1992. Pictured from left to right, Mark, Jane, and Ned grew up with Elon College as it grew under the leadership of their father from 1957 to 1973, when he retired as president and returned to the chemistry classroom. (Jane Shutt.)

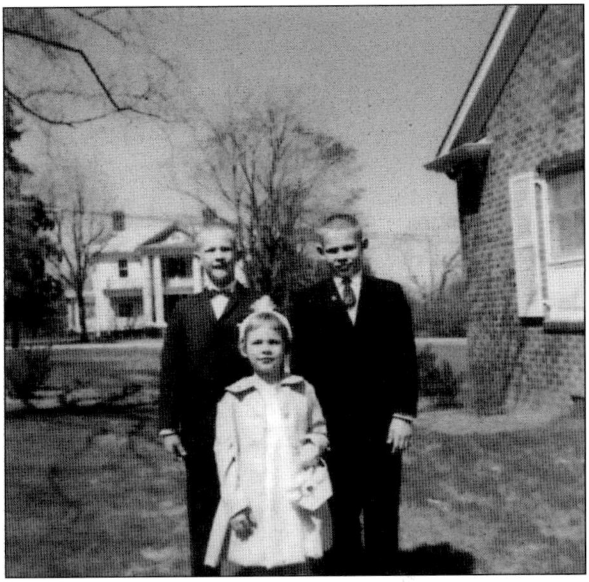

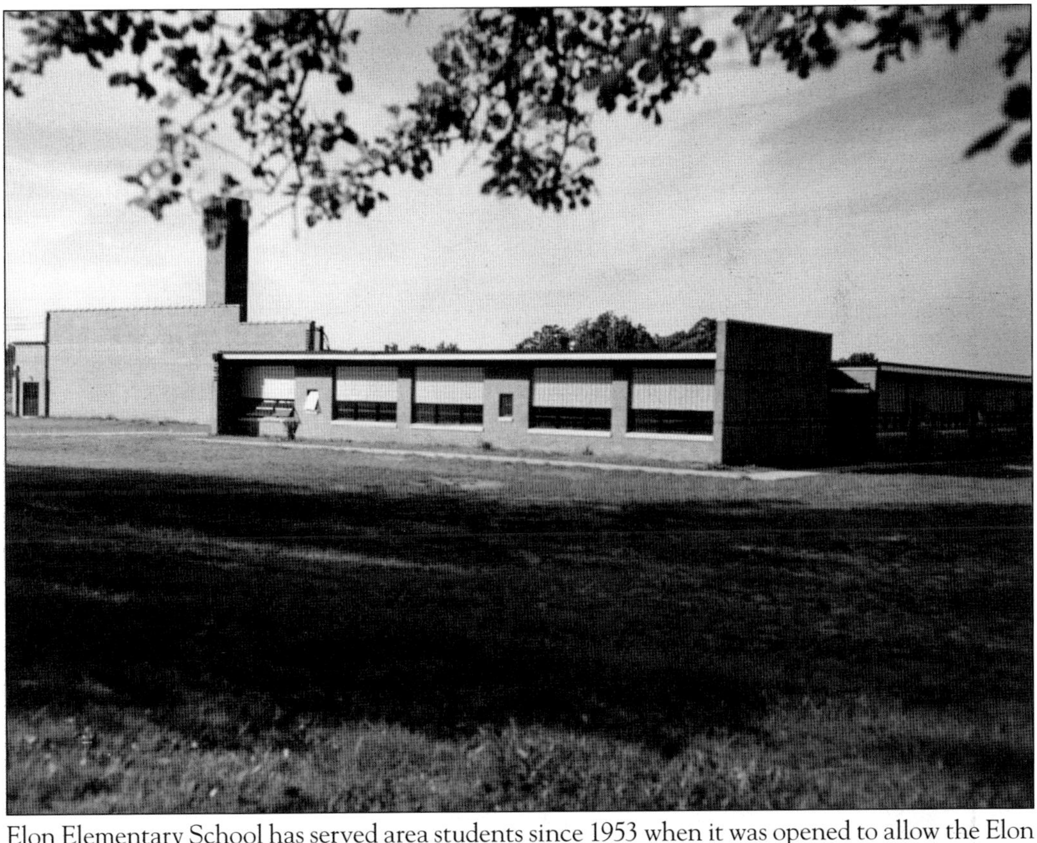

Elon Elementary School has served area students since 1953 when it was opened to allow the Elon College Public School to serve only higher classes. The elementary school was last renovated in 1987 and in 2017 was home to 724 students. It has been announced that Elon University will build a new elementary school and take the old school property for university needs. (Elon University.)

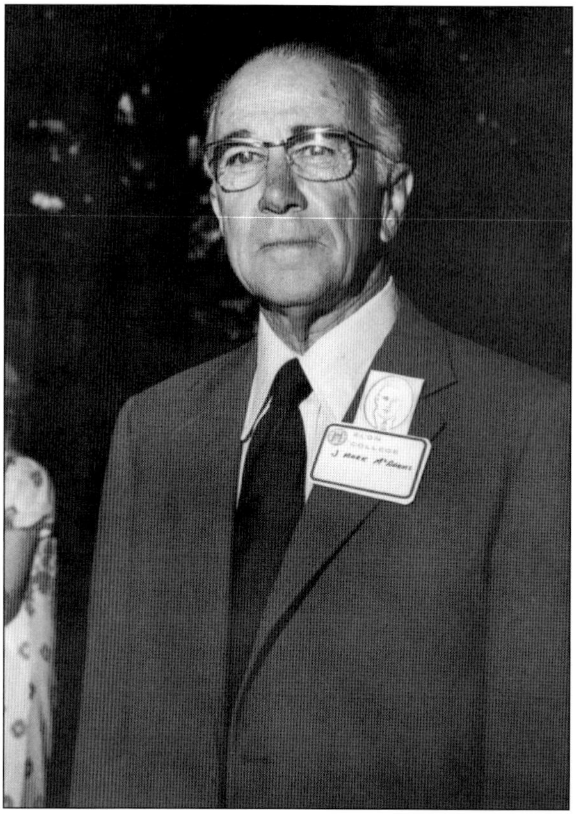

Mark McAdams was a 1924 Elon graduate and played three sports and captained the football team. After graduation, he made his home in Elon and in the 1950s served as mayor. McAdams also served a number of years as the Alamance County surveyor. He often said his top achievement as Elon mayor was getting Southern Bell telephone service to the town. (Elon University.)

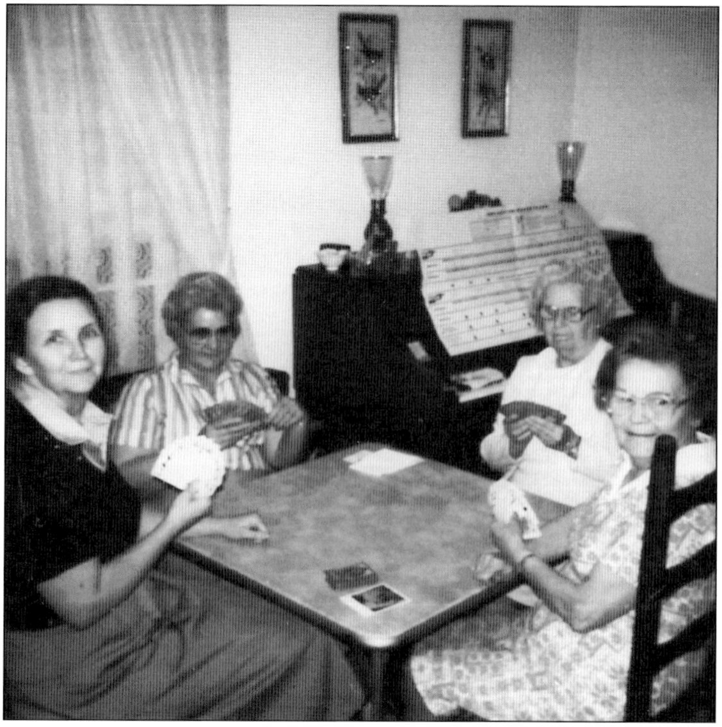

Amid all the activity in Elon College over the years, residents still found time to enjoy their friends and share good times. These four ladies did that in a bridge club that met regularly over the years. From left to right are Mona Atkinson, Virginia Richardson, Jackie Matlock, and Gladys Vickers. (Mona Atkinson.)

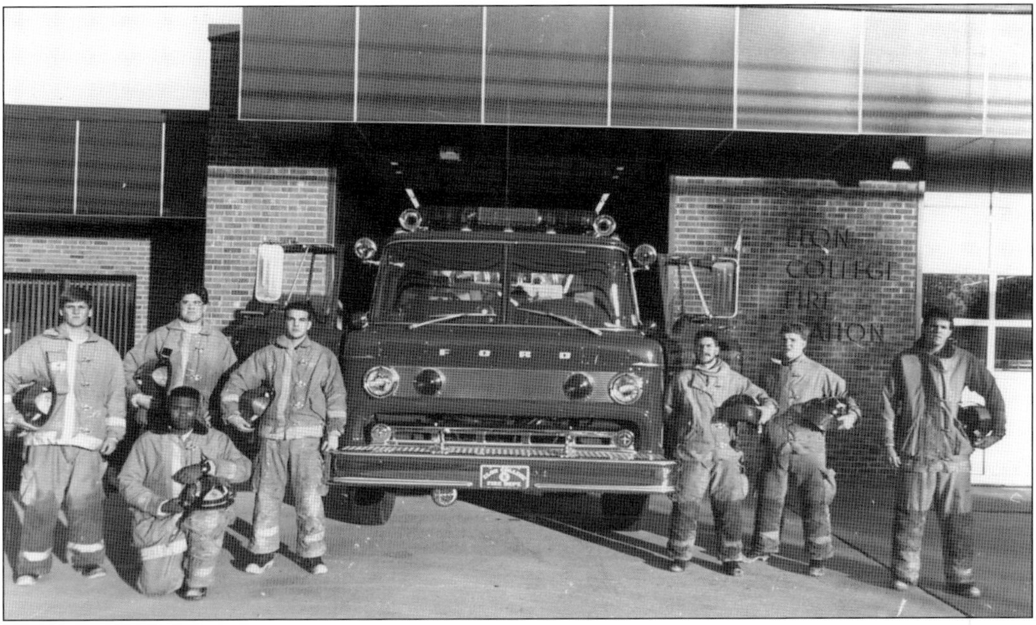

The first fire service in Elon College was an Alamance County volunteer fire and rescue department formed in 1947. It was located on North Holt Avenue. In 1972, a bond issue was approved and this station was opened in February 1973 on South Williamson Avenue a short distance south of the railroad. The town officially formed its own department in 2015. (Elon University.)

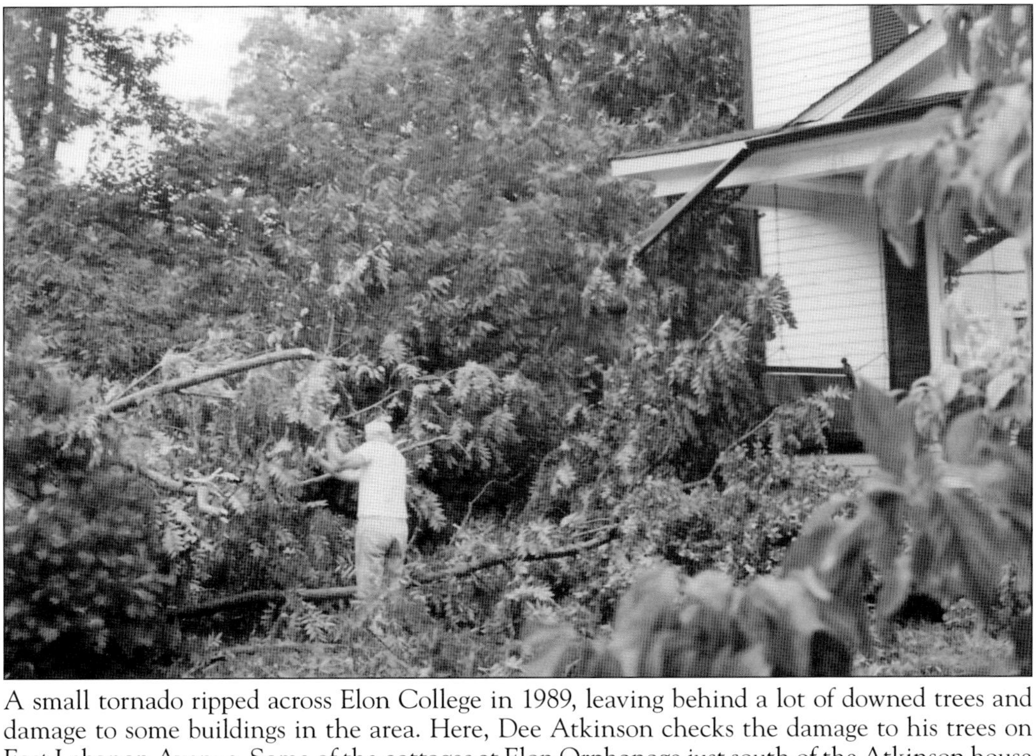

A small tornado ripped across Elon College in 1989, leaving behind a lot of downed trees and damage to some buildings in the area. Here, Dee Atkinson checks the damage to his trees on East Lebanon Avenue. Some of the cottages at Elon Orphanage just south of the Atkinson house suffered heavy damage, but no injuries occurred. (Mona Atkinson.)

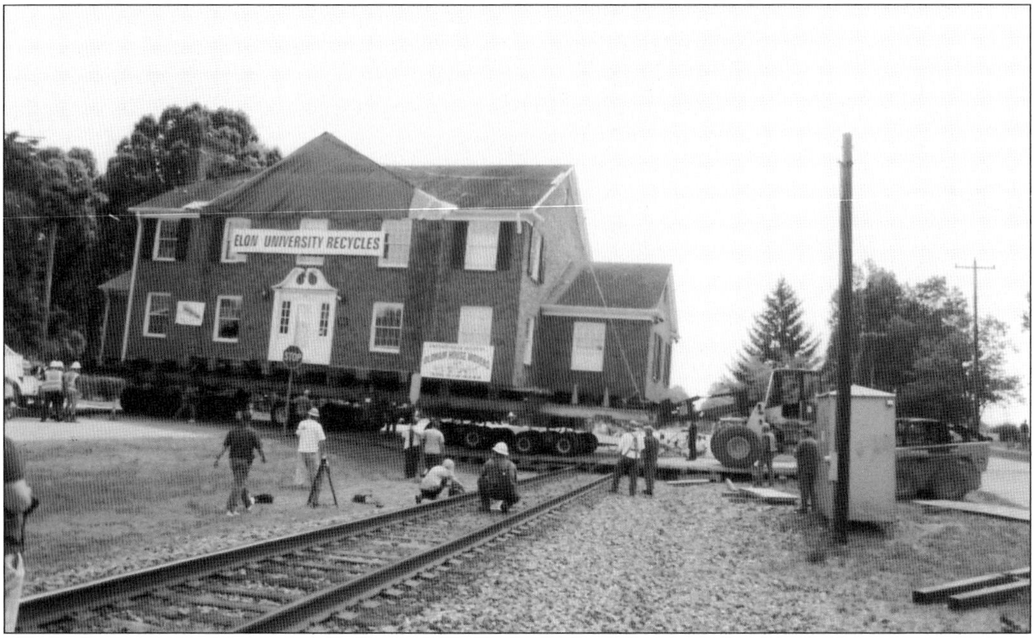

The Holland House was built in 1963 as the residence of the college president and family. After another residence came into use in the 1990s, Holland House found a new life as home for the Newman Center, the Catholic campus ministry. That required a move for the house across the railroad to the south campus, where it now stands in front of Holt Chapel.

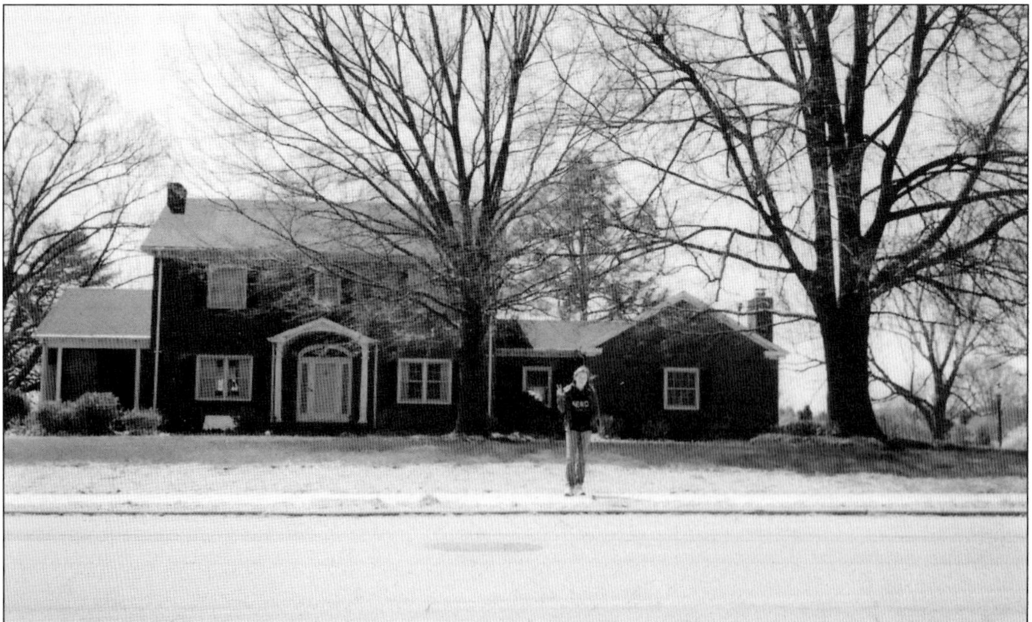

In the 1950s, the Elon Orphanage built a home on Oak Avenue as the residence of the orphanage superintendent and family. Dr. John G. Truitt Sr was the first resident, and Dr. Wally Snyder later lived there. Dee and Mona Atkinson moved there in 2000 from Lebanon Avenue, where Lindner Hall was to be built. Rachel Atkinson is shown in front of the house. (Mona Atkinson.)

One of Elon's best-known residents in 2018 is Jack McKeon. He is a graduate of Elon College and was a major-league baseball manager who in 2003 led the Florida Marlins to the World Series Championship over the New York Yankees. The second-oldest major-league manager in history, McKeon had a long career before finally retiring to his Elon home in 2011 at the age of 80.

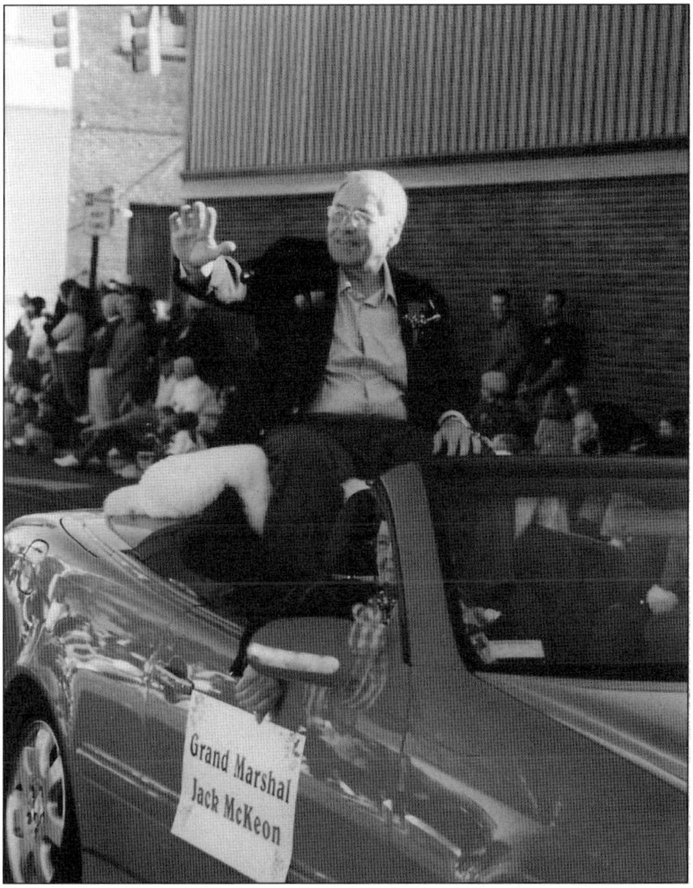

Elon's much-traveled post office finally found a more permanent home when in 1965 it was moved to this facility on South Williamson Avenue at the intersection with East Trollinger Avenue. The post office was formerly located in several locations north of the railroad, three of them in the 100 block of North Williamson Avenue.

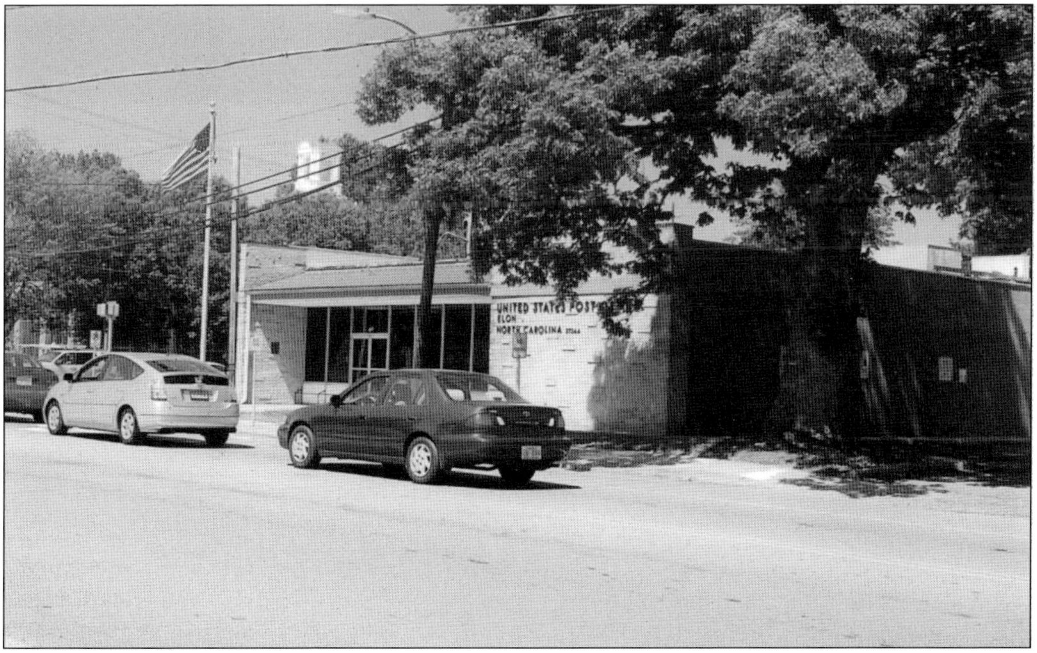

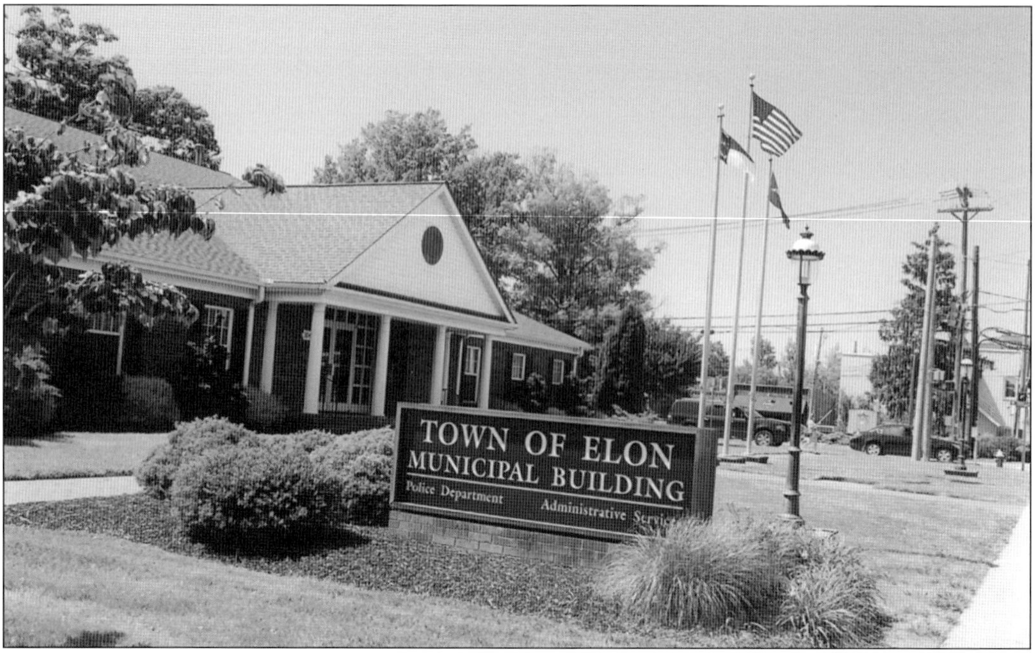

The site of Elon's government has moved more often than the post office. Over many years, the town board met in homes, businesses, classrooms, the town depot, a former dry cleaning site, and a former fire station. On September 17, 1984, a new town hall was dedicated at 104 South Williamson Avenue across from the post office.

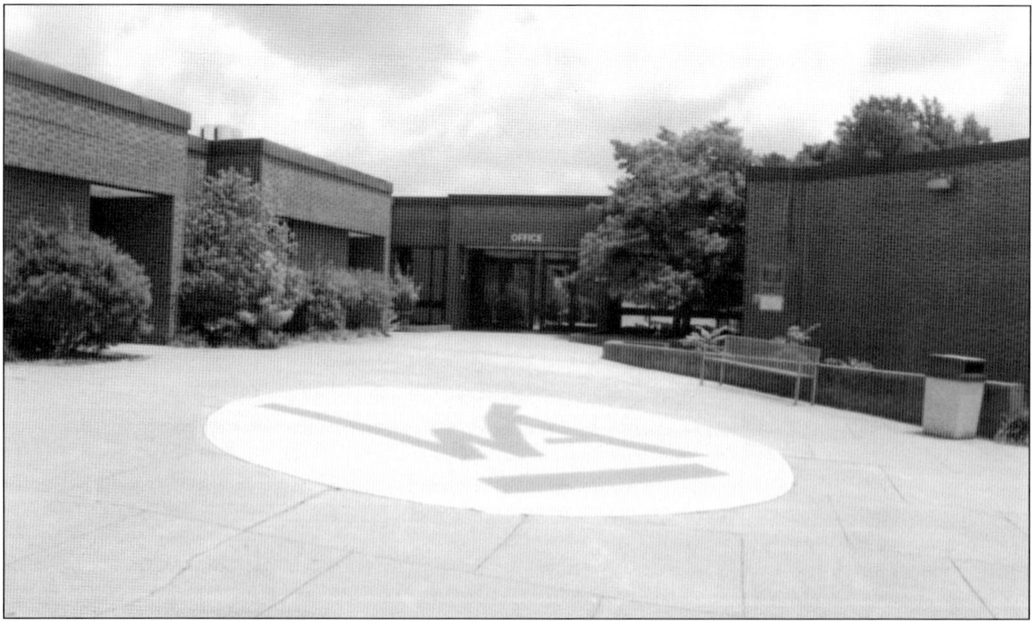

Western Alamance Middle School now serves students from the Elon Community. It was opened in the late 1970s and brought together students from both the Elon school and Altamahaw-Ossipee school. Western Alamance Middle School is located on Highway 87 north of the town of Elon. When this school opened, the old Elon school building was closed and was later obtained by Elon College.

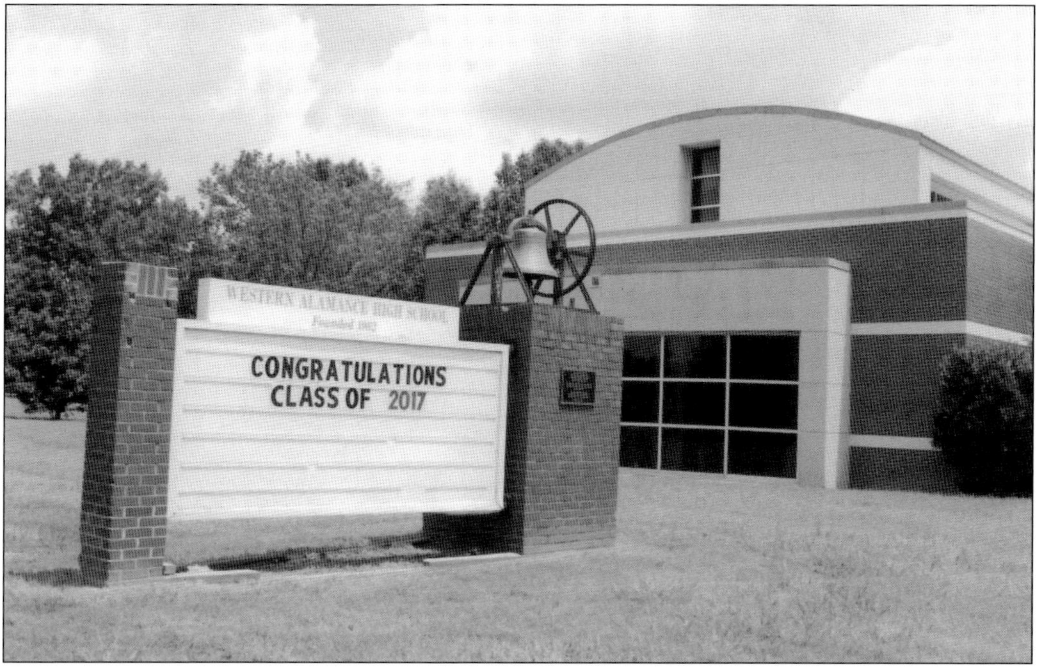

Alamance County schools went through consolidation in the 1960s, and Western Alamance High School was one of the new high schools. It was opened in 1962 and serves the northwestern quarter of the county, involving students previously attending Elon College and other schools. When this school opened, Elon High School became a middle school until Western Alamance Middle School opened in the late 1970s.

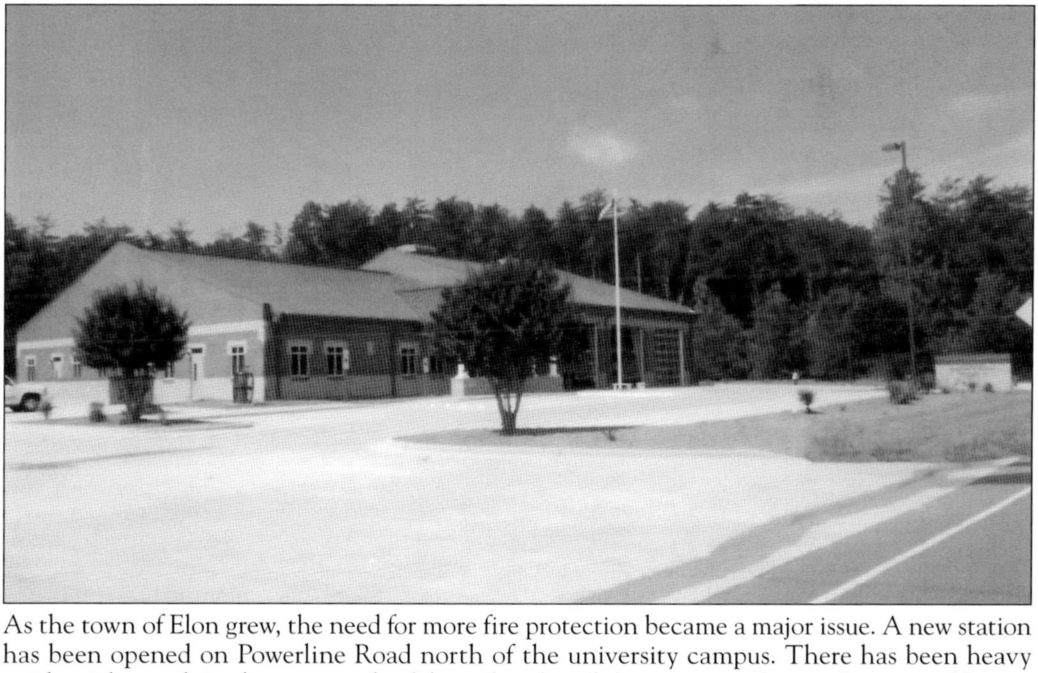

As the town of Elon grew, the need for more fire protection became a major issue. A new station has been opened on Powerline Road north of the university campus. There has been heavy residential growth in the area north of the railroad, and the university has made major additions and built new facilities in recent years, adding to the protection needs.

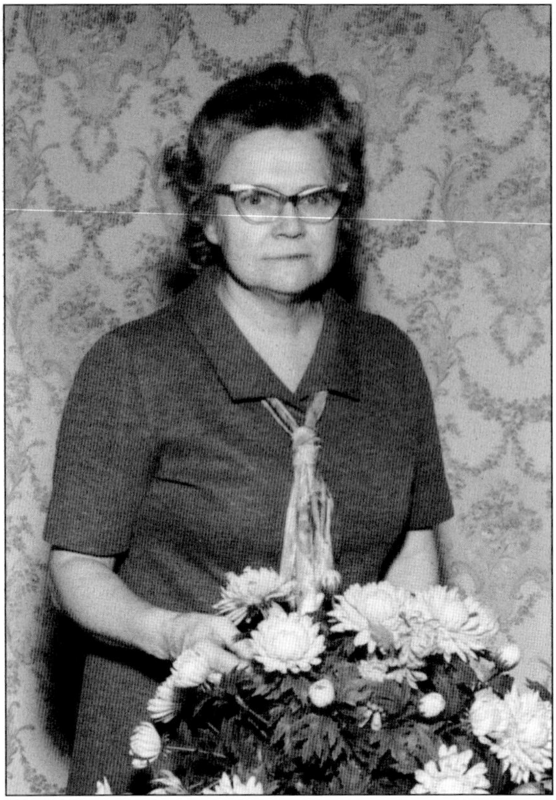

Another of Elon's well-known citizens is Edith Brannock, daughter of Prof. Ned Brannock, an 1899 Elon graduate and longtime chemistry professor. Miss Brannock was a high school home economics teacher in Burlington schools, and she joined the Elon faculty in 1962 and taught home economics until 1980. She passed away in 2017, but not before celebrating her 99th birthday. (Elon University.)

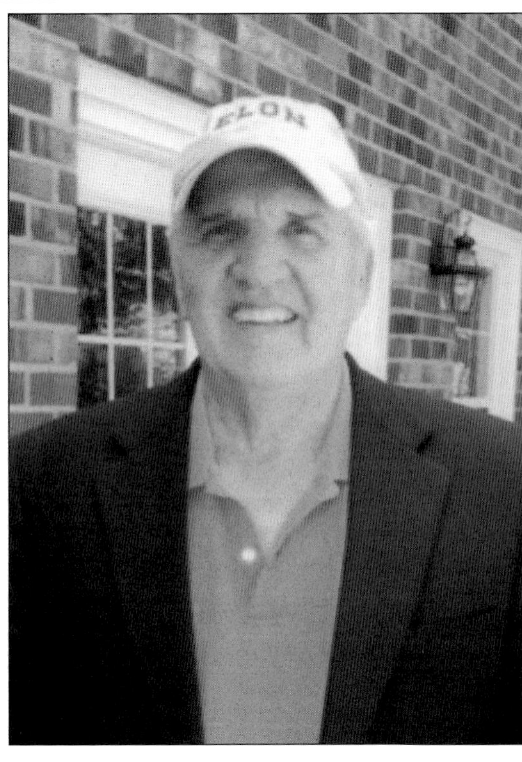

One of Elon's most recognized citizens is Mayor Jerry Tolley, pictured here in his familiar Elon cap. Dr. Tolley was Elon College football coach from 1977 to 1981 and won national NAIA championships in 1980 and 1981. He retired then and worked for LabCorp and later the university. Tolley was elected to the town board in 1983 and as mayor in 1989. He took two terms off, returned, and is in his sixth term as mayor.

Two

The 100 Block of North Williamson Avenue

There are not many places in the town of Elon to which all residents in its 125-year history can relate.

But there is at least one: the 100 block of North Williamson Avenue. When the town was incorporated in April 1893, the first businesses had already taken their place in that block, and it quickly became the town's business center. In 2018, the town's 125th year, it is still the business center, although there has been a lot of turnover among the names and types of businesses over the years.

It started with a store building constructed at 100 North Williamson Avenue just about the time Elon College opened in 1889. That store, built by railroad station agent Walter L. Smith, burned in 1891 but was soon rebuilt as a two-story unit—a store on the ground floor and living quarters upstairs. Dr. W.T. Herndon and A.F. Young operated a drug and general merchandise store there. Over the years that followed, buildings were added down the block, and they were home to such operations as barbershops, the town offices, the Elon Grill, Garrison's Soda Shop, Brown & Company restaurant, a furniture store, a bank, a hair salon, and at least three locations of the Elon College Post Office. This strip of businesses is just across the street from the western limits of the college campus, and many remember cutting class to go to the Elon Grill, grabbing lunch at the soda shop, or just hanging out between classes.

In recent years, a more modern look has come to much of the block with the Elon Town Center and its Barnes & Noble bookstore and a restaurant in its corner section at West College Avenue. There are other new businesses toward the railroad. Though change has come over so many years, that building erected in the 1890s remains at 100 North Williamson Avenue, still a part of Elon in 2018.

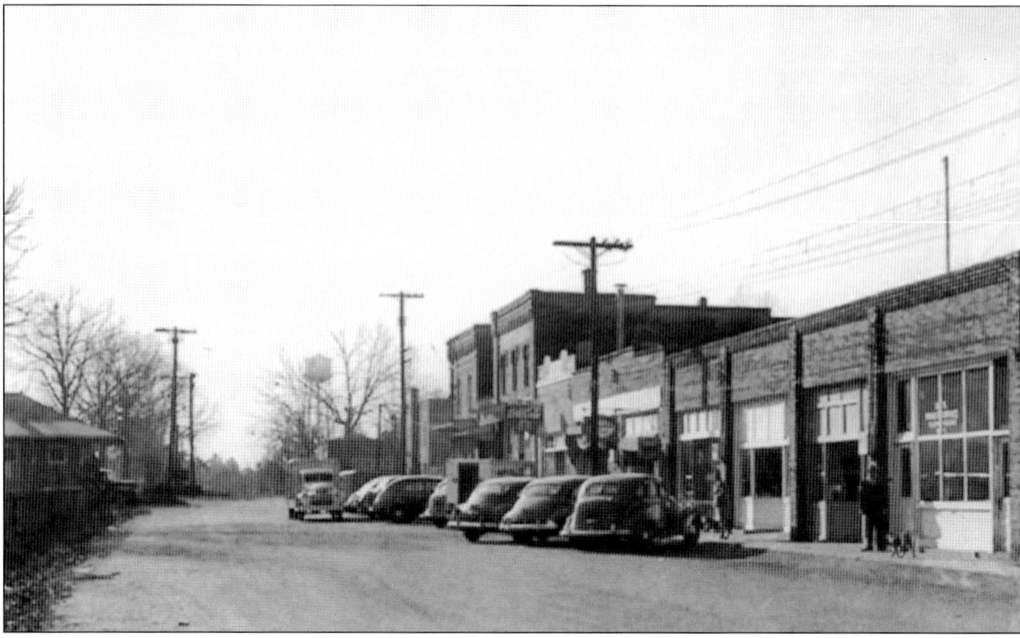

This is the 100 block of North Williamson Avenue as it appeared in 1940. The view is looking south toward the railroad. The end of the depot is visible at left. There is little to identify the businesses on the right, although there is a Coca-Cola sign near the far end, indicating a café or a soda shop. (Elon University.)

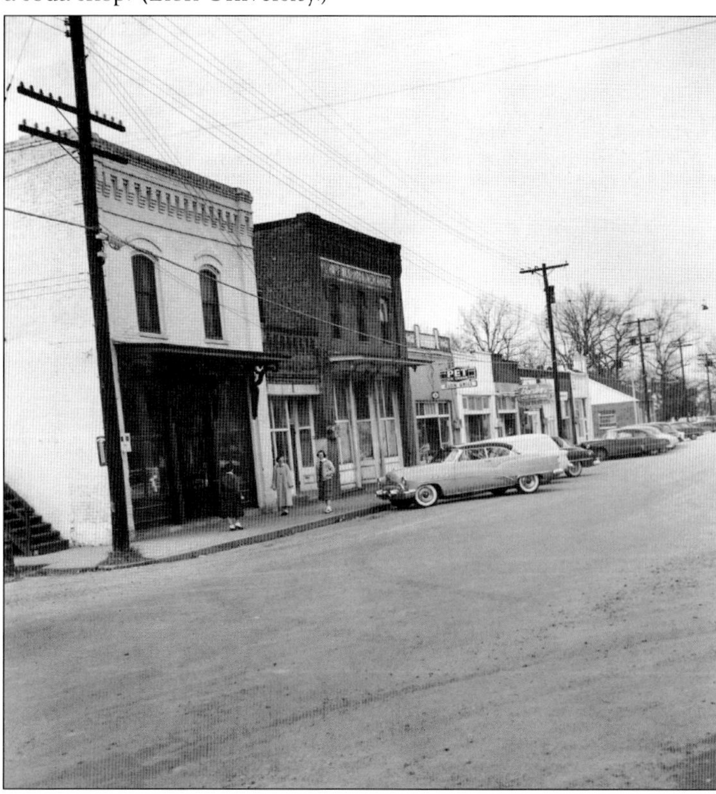

This photograph shows the block from the railroad, looking north in 1957. The building at left is 100 North Williamson and is the site of the first business building in town. That structure burned in 1891, and this building was erected soon after. The bottom of an outside staircase is seen at lower left, but early photographs of this building show no stairs. (Jean Loy Toms.)

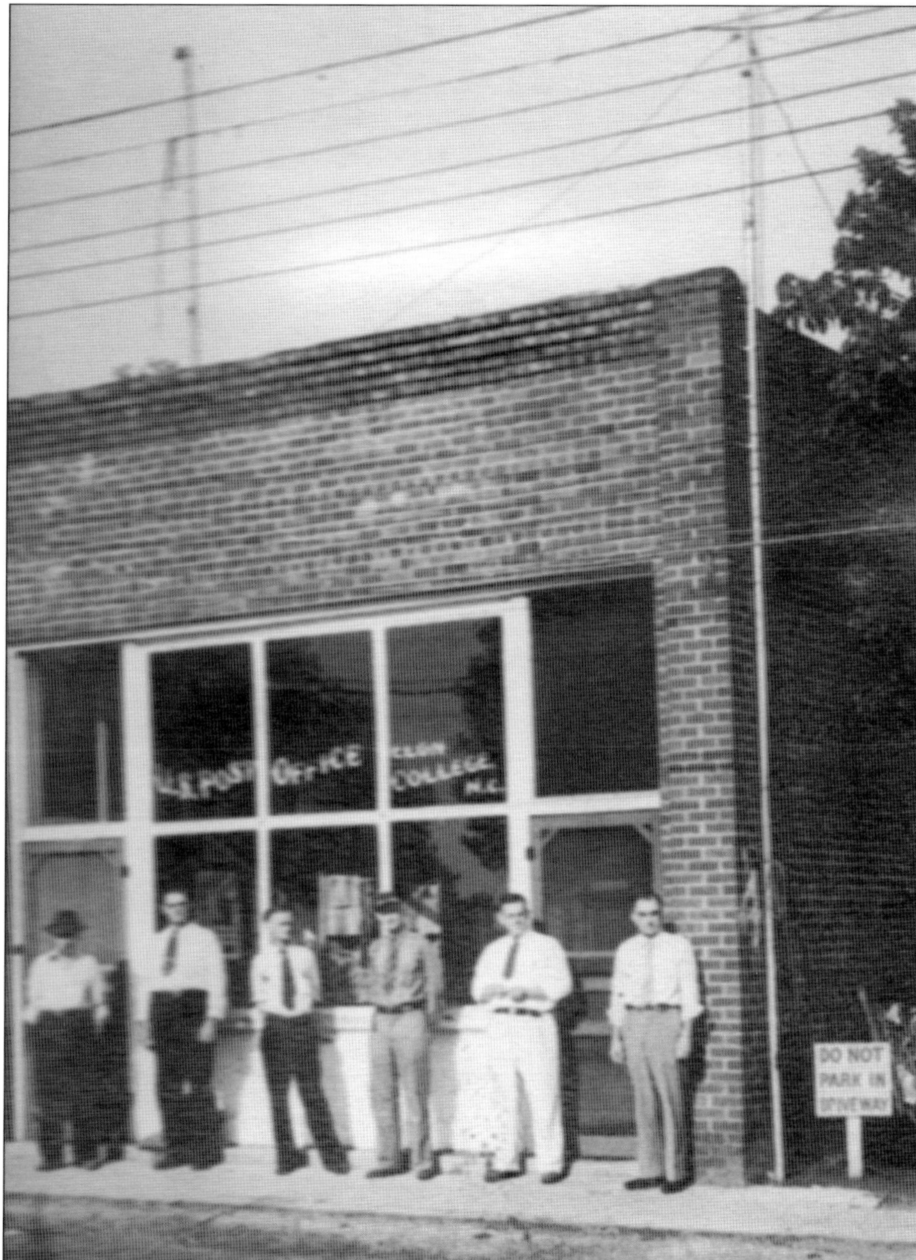

This building was at the north end of the line of businesses in the 100 block of Williamson Avenue in the 1940s. This was the second location of the post office in this particular block. It was at 102 North Williamson Avenue before moving to this site. This building served as the post office prior to 1948, when it again moved to a new building up the block at the College Avenue corner. Members of the office staff are seen here in front of the building. This building would be used later by Jim Haynes, who operated a furniture store there for several years. A driveway runs beside the post office, but in later years buildings would be erected all the way to the end of the block. The post office would stay in this block until it moved to the present building in 1965. (Earl Vickers.)

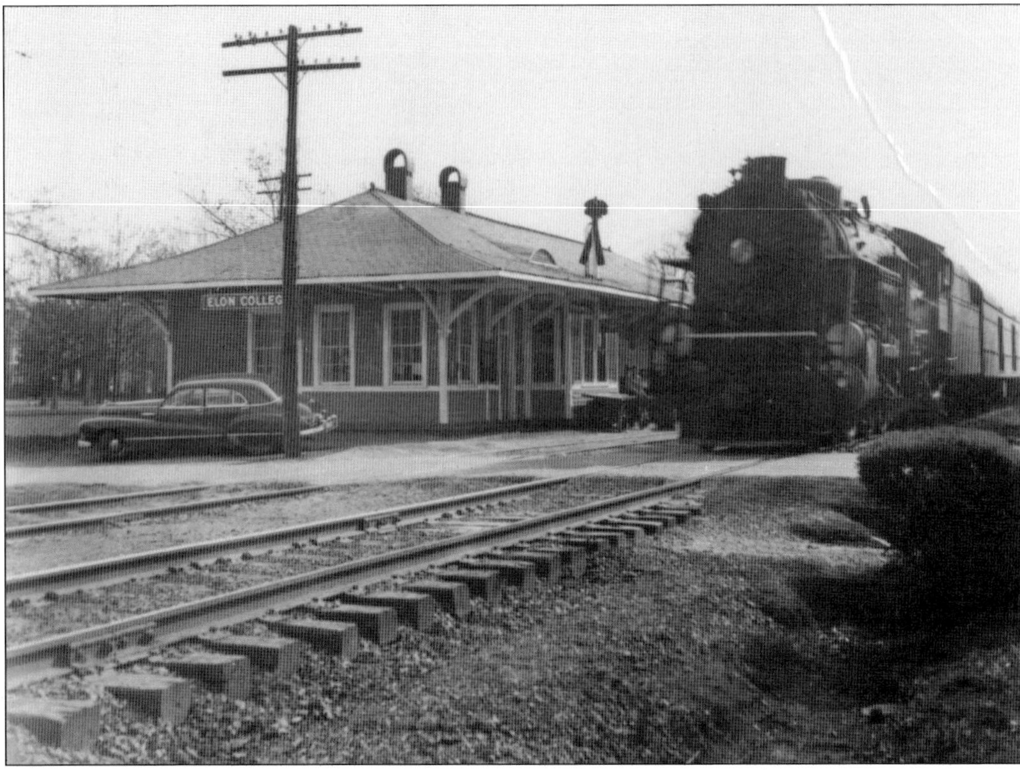

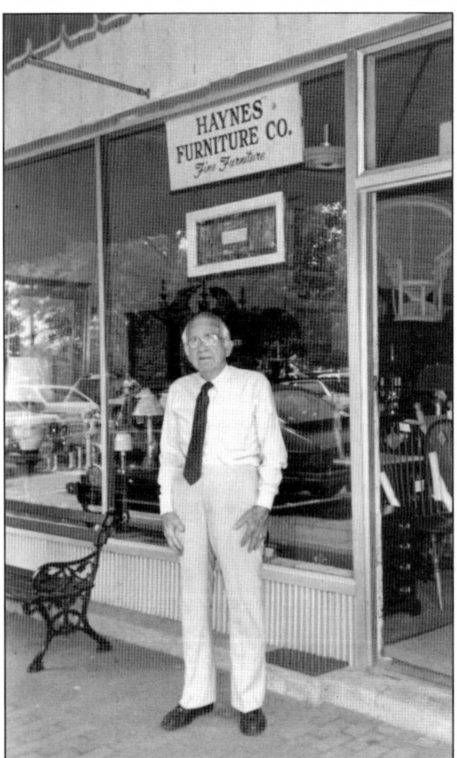

The Elon College depot was a part of the 100 block but on the side of the college opposite the business buildings. A train sits at the depot in this photograph from about 1950. The depot was still a major freight stop at that time, serving textile mills to the north of town and a growing number of other businesses surrounding Elon College. (Elon University.)

Jim Haynes was a fixture for many years at 118 North Williamson Avenue. He operated a very popular furniture shop there. Haynes did not have a large showroom, but he specialized in ordering direct from furniture manufacturers for individual customers. This building had previously been home to the Elon College Post Office.

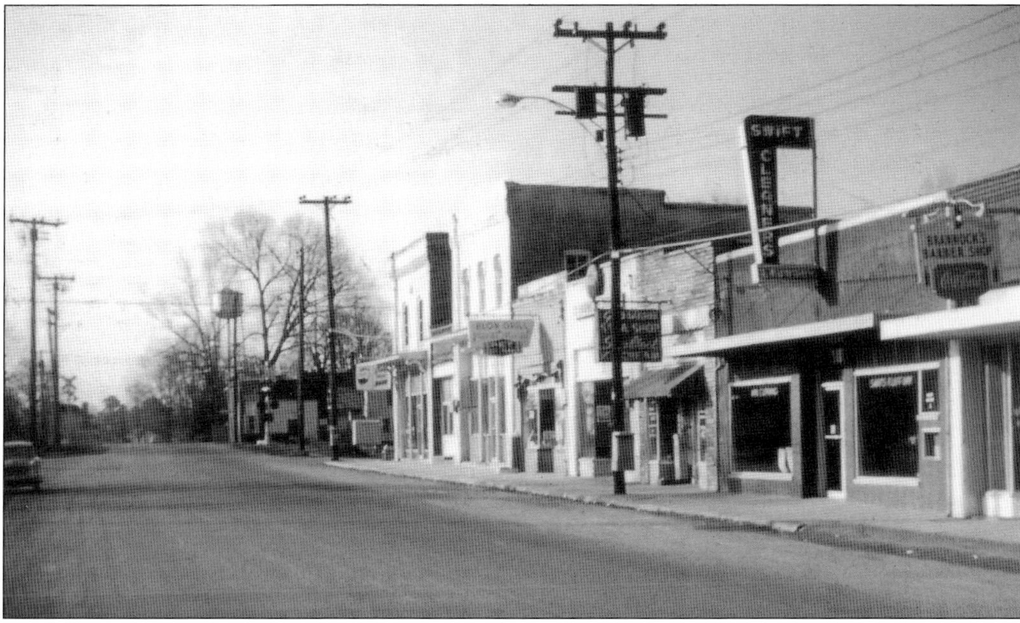

By 1962, the 100 block of North Williamson Avenue was a more active place with several new businesses in operation. Brannock's Barber Shop is there along with Swift Cleaners and two very busy locations—Garrison's Soda Shop and the Elon Grill. There is also a Pepsi sign hanging in front of the building at 100 North Williamson, indicating another eating establishment. (Elon University.)

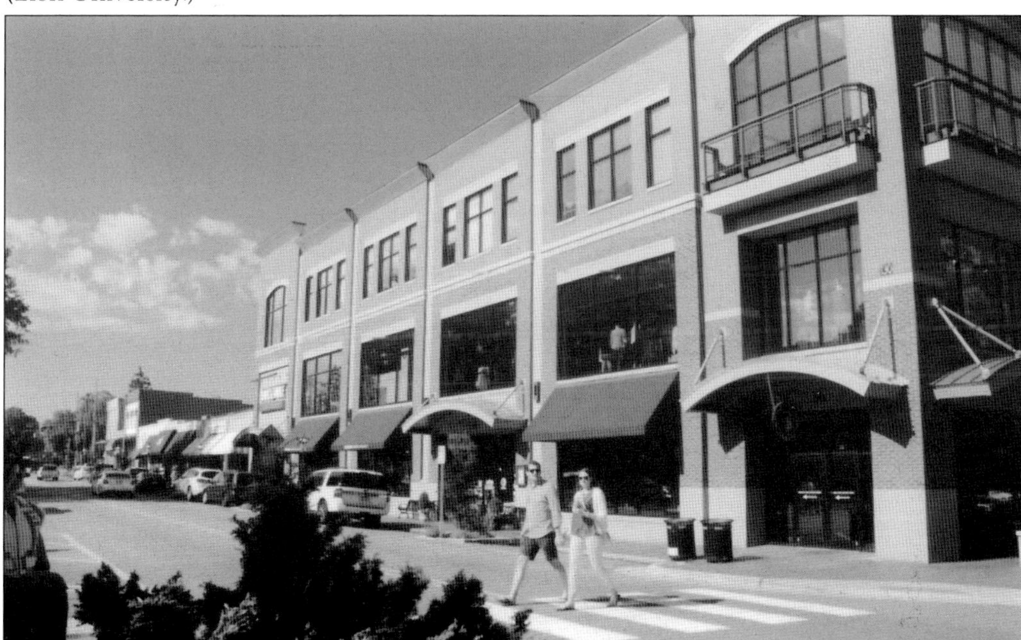

This picture was made in 2017 and shows a similar view as the prior image. The block is filled from corner to corner with a variety of businesses. On the corner is the Town Center with Pandora's Pies, a popular restaurant featuring pizza, sandwiches, salads and ice cream. Barnes & Noble is next, followed by the Acorn Coffee Shop and the Oak, another food and beverage operation.

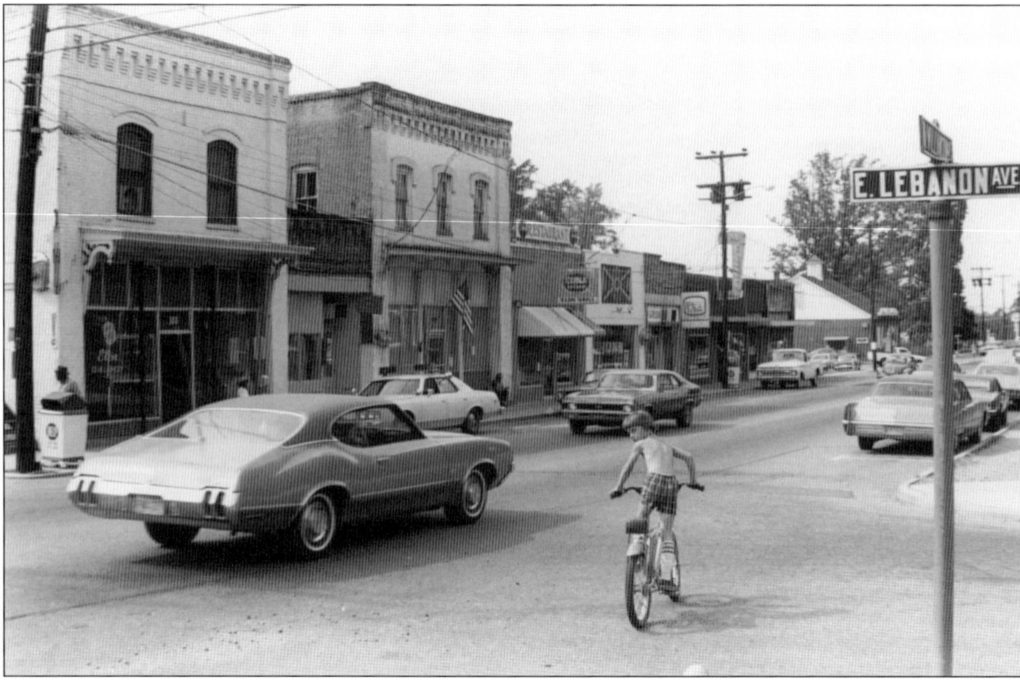

The 100 block is seen from the railroad in another late-1960s photograph. The Elon Grill is halfway down the block, and Garrison's Soda Shop is a few more stores down. The Swift Cleaners sign is there, and at the end is a building alone at the corner. In this photograph, it is a bank, as there is a drive-through window on the side. The post office had been there previously.

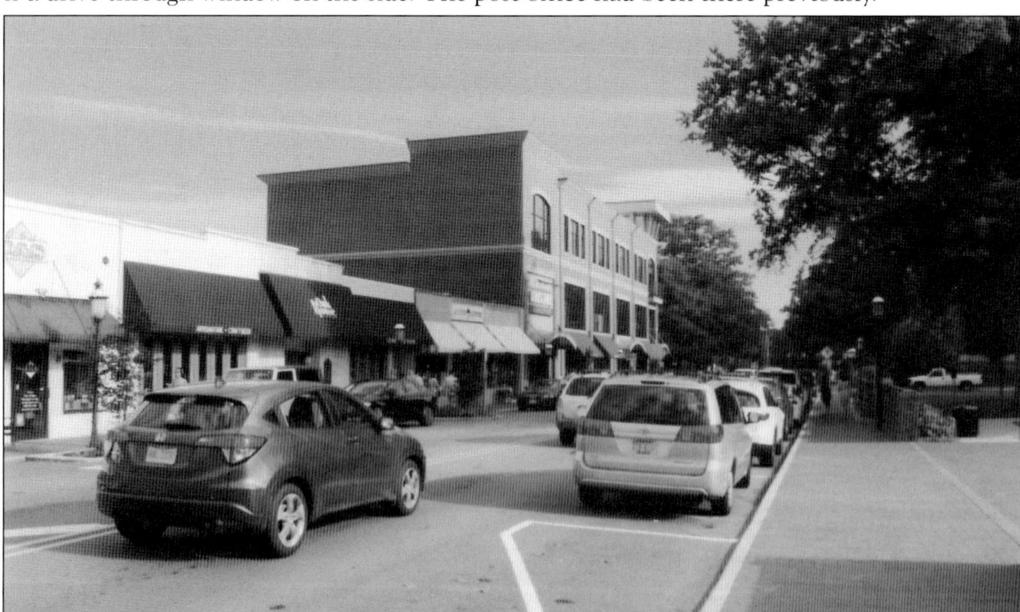

This photograph is from 2017 and shows part of the block in the previous image. Modern storefronts line the street, and at the end are Barnes & Noble and Pandora's Pies in the large three-story Town Center. The street is a busy spot in Elon today, and the business area turns the corner at Lebanon Avenue and offers more restaurants and retail businesses.

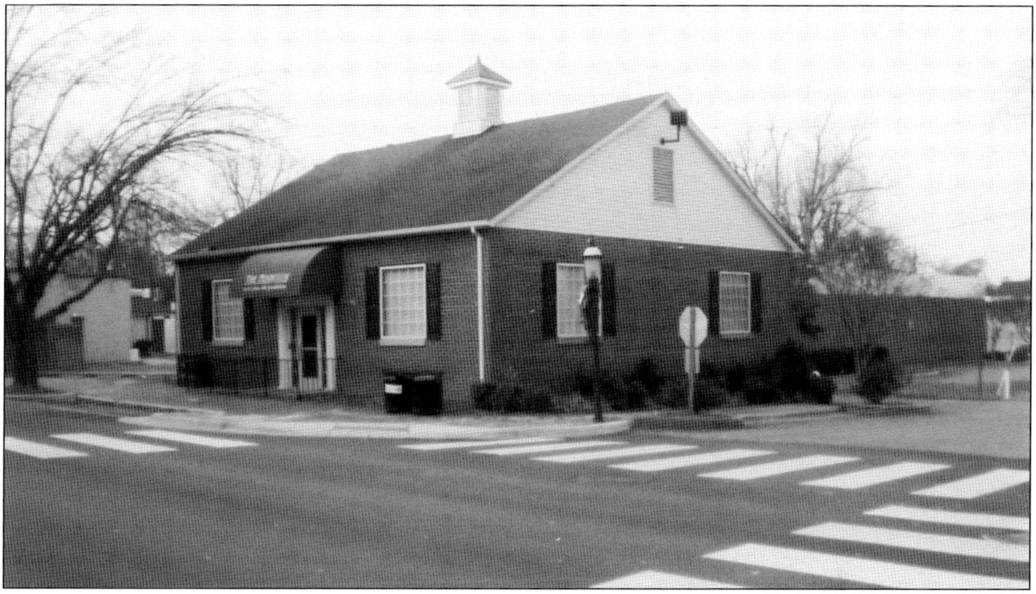

This building was constructed as the third North Williamson Avenue location of the Elon College Post Office. The post office remained here until it was moved to the south side of Williamson Avenue in 1965. At that time, a bank moved into the building. When this photograph was made, the building was home to the *Pendulum*, the Elon University student newspaper. The Elon Town Center now occupies this entire area. (Elon University.)

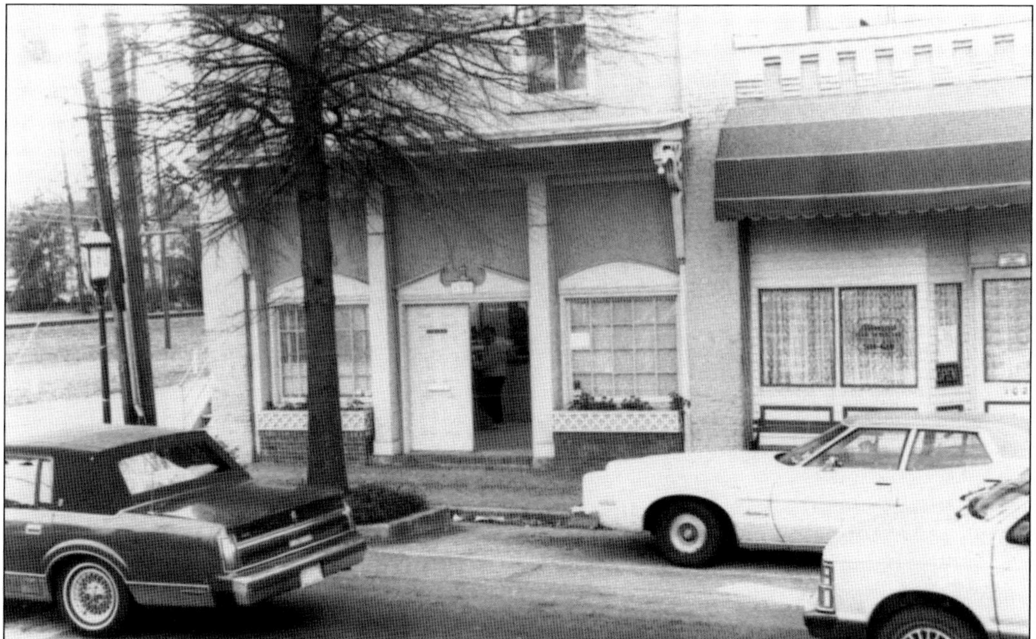

This photograph from the 1990s shows the front of the building at 100 North Williamson Avenue. A number of businesses have operated in that location since it was built in the 1890s, and in more recent years the Elon School of Communications has used it. The location next door was a barbershop for many years and is now a beauty salon.

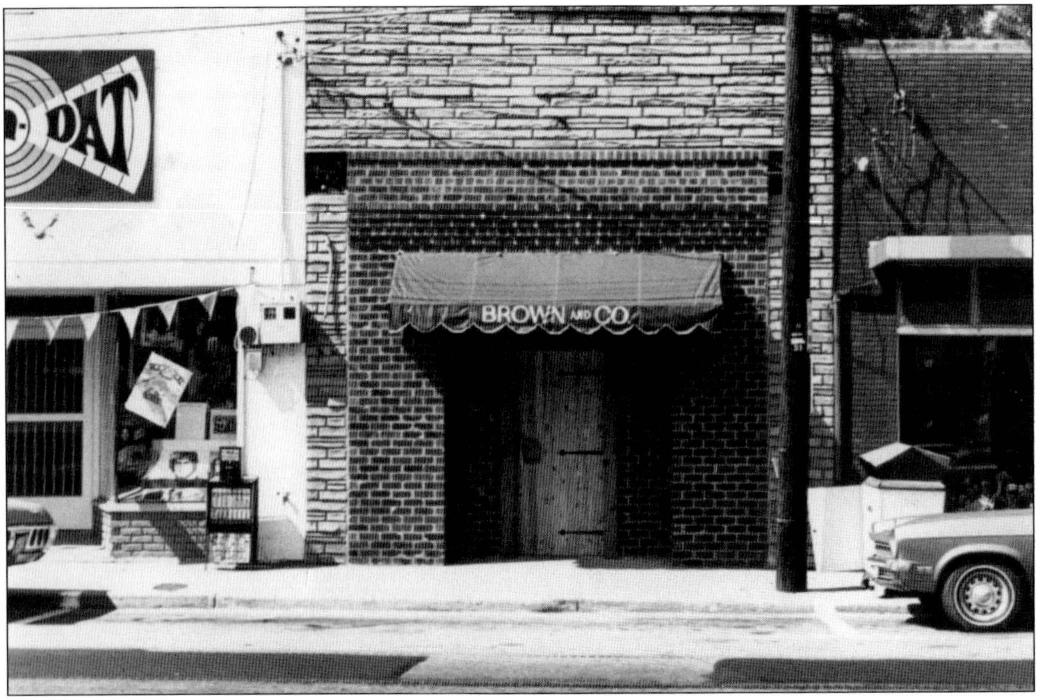

For many years, one of the most popular eating spots along the 100 block of North Williamson Avenue was Brown and Co., located near the middle of the block. It was started by Joel Brown and his wife, Beverly. They sold it and a few years later opened another popular spot, Sidetrack Restaurant, around on Lebanon Avenue. That restaurant later became the Root. (Elon University.)

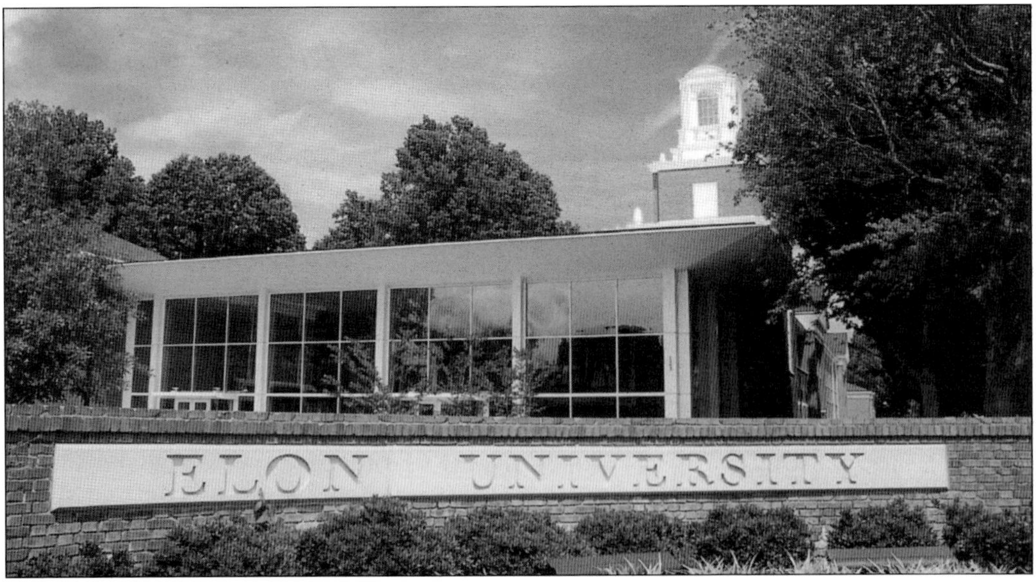

While most of the photographs show the west side of this street, this one shows the School of Communications building that opened in 2016 on the east side, giving an entirely new look to that side of Williamson Avenue. The wall surrounding the university for many decades was opened in front of this building to allow free access from the street, adding a new dimension to the 100 block of North Williamson Avenue.

Three

The Christian Orphanage

In 1907, a 14-year-old girl from Durham, Lela Mae Canada, walked through the door of a building across the railroad tracks from Elon College and became the first resident of the Elon Christian Orphanage.

The orphanage had long been a dream of some in the Christian Church. There had been talk of such a facility for more than 30 years in the church organization. Finally, in 1892, Mrs. J.P. Barrett, the former secretary of the Children's Mission programs, was at a meeting of the church conference in Elon College, where she put life to the idea. Barrett made an offering of 65¢ during the conference, the money to be used to launch an orphanage program. The proximity to Elon College was no accident. The college was also formed by the Christian Church.

It took several years to get the project moving, but finally in 1907 the orphanage became a reality and would be home to orphans and half orphans. For many years, the orphanage operated a farm on a large tract of land south of the railroad, and the children had chores in the farm operations. They went to school at the Elon Public School just north of the railroad tracks.

It was in 1964 that the facility became known as the Elon Home for Children, Inc. As time passed, the mission of the orphanage began to change to meet the needs of a changing population of children. A private school was opened and much attention was given to foster care in the piedmont of North Carolina. The facility closed its Elon operations in the first decade of the new century and now operates as the Elon Homes and School for Children in Charlotte.

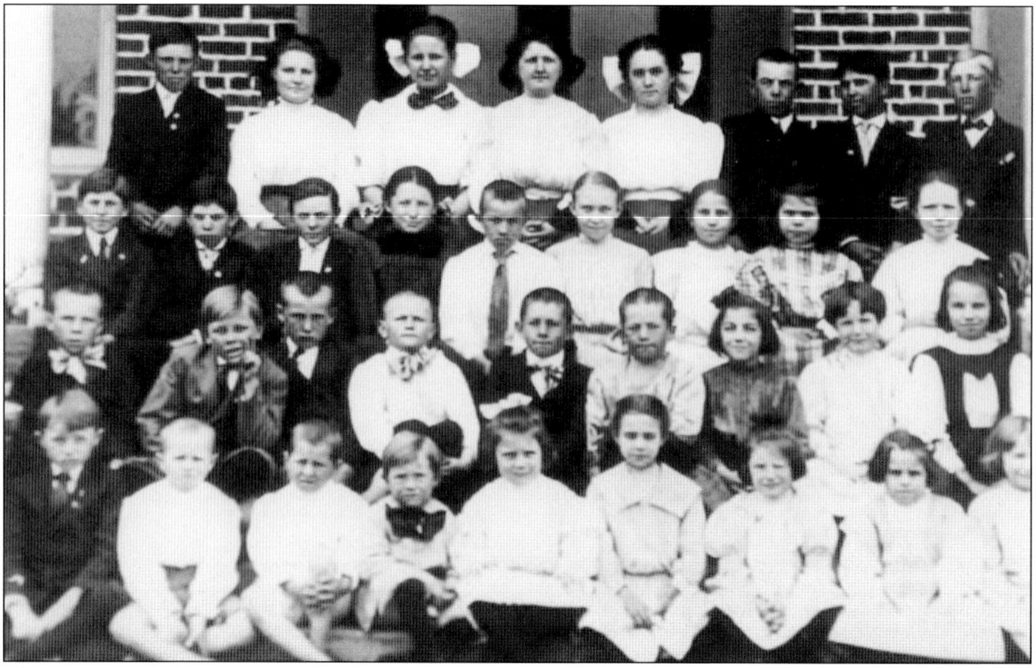

This is a group of young boys and girls who were early residents of the Elon College Christian Orphanage that opened in 1907. Lela Mae Canada, fourth from left on the back row, was the first resident of the orphanage. The orphanage was located on what is now the South Campus of Elon University, and some of the buildings are still in use by the university.

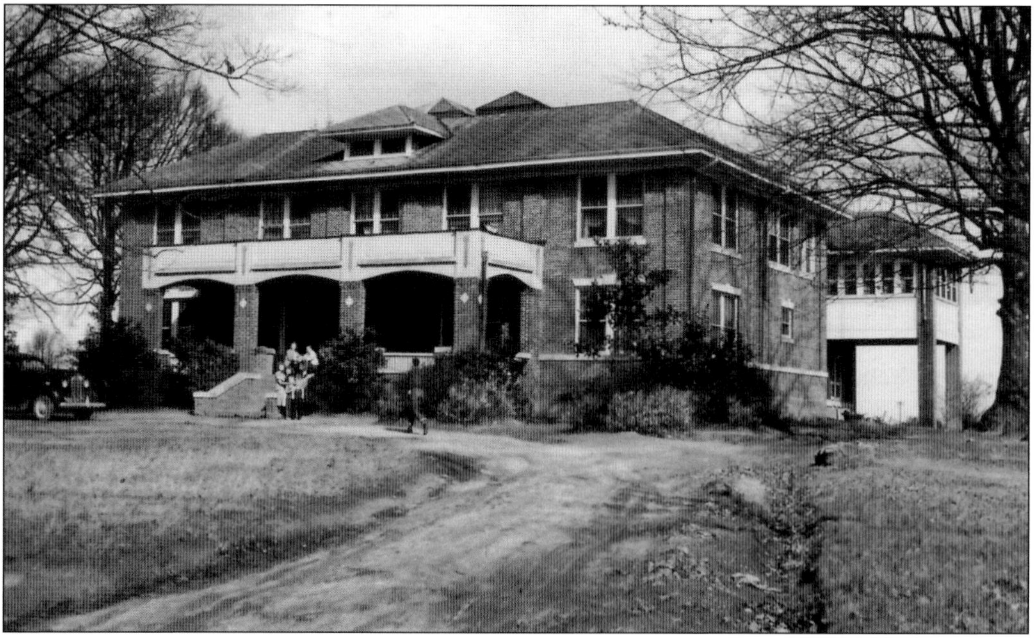

In the early 1920s, the orphanage was quite crowded with youngsters, so a new facility was needed. Johnston Hall was dedicated on the campus on July 19, 1928. It was named to honor Charles Johnston, who had been superintendent since 1916. Timber was cut from the orphanage property to be used in construction. Today, the building is home to the Elon University development offices.

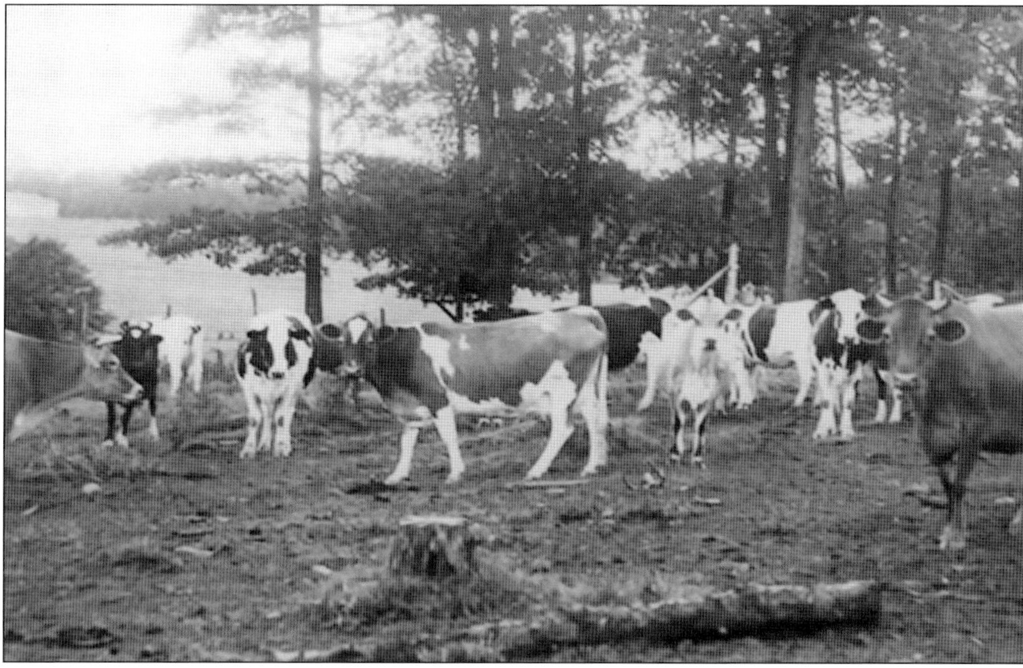

In its early years, the orphanage operated a farm to provide food for the children living there. A herd of cattle was kept in a dairy operation, and the children shared in the operations of the farm—the boys tending to the cattle, helping in the gardens, and cutting hay; and the girls preparing food and handling kitchen chores.

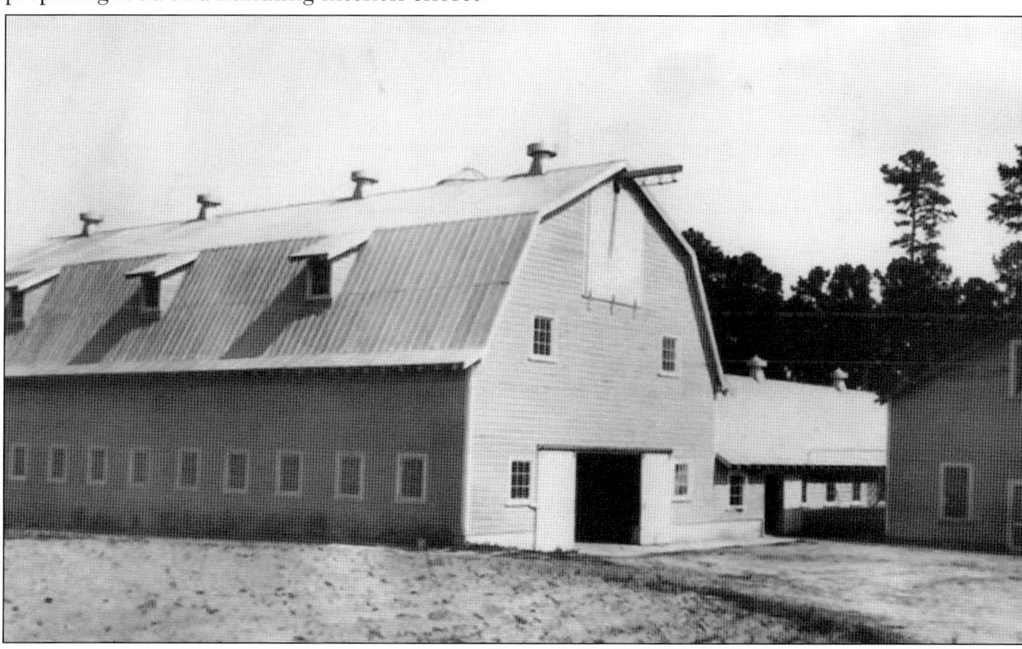

This large barn housed the dairy cattle and equipment used on the farm. Boys in residence spent a lot of hours in the barn helping with the milking and feeding the cattle. That was done around the hours they spent in school at the Elon College Public School just across the railroad tracks from the orphanage.

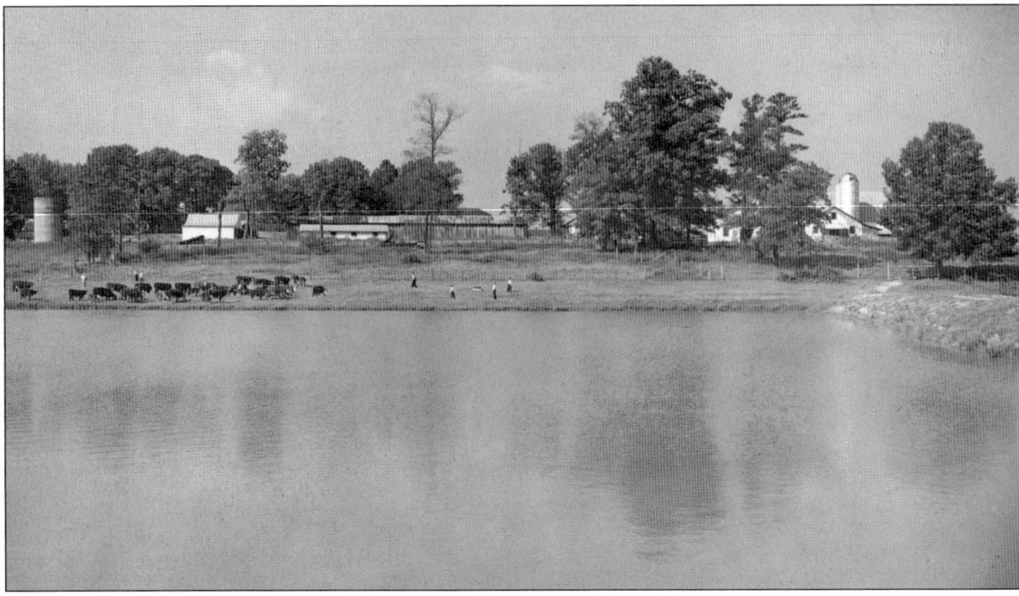

A large lake was part of the orphanage property for many years. Farming operations surrounded the lake. Later, the farming operations had to be closed, partly because regulations regarding the ways in which the children could work had changed drastically. The orphanage, however, continued to serve children for several decades to come.

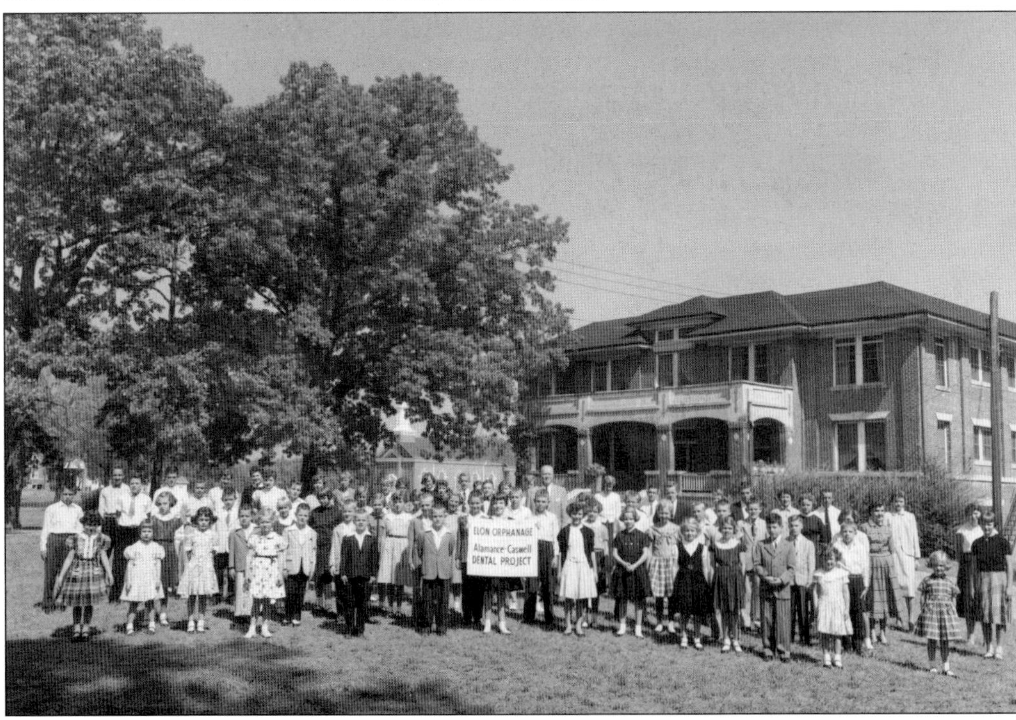

In the 1950s, the children at the orphanage were honored for their part in an Alamance-Caswell Dental Project. Here, the entire population of the orphanage is gathered on the campus in front of Johnston Hall for a photograph denoting their participation in the project. The children are dressed in their Sunday best. (Elon University.)

The celebration for participation in the dental project included lunch for all the orphanage children in Johnston Hall. Dr. John G. Truitt Sr., superintendent of the facility, is seen at right at a table in the back. Various groups in the area often held special events for the children, and in the early years they were taken to Burlington by train for some such happenings. (Elon University.)

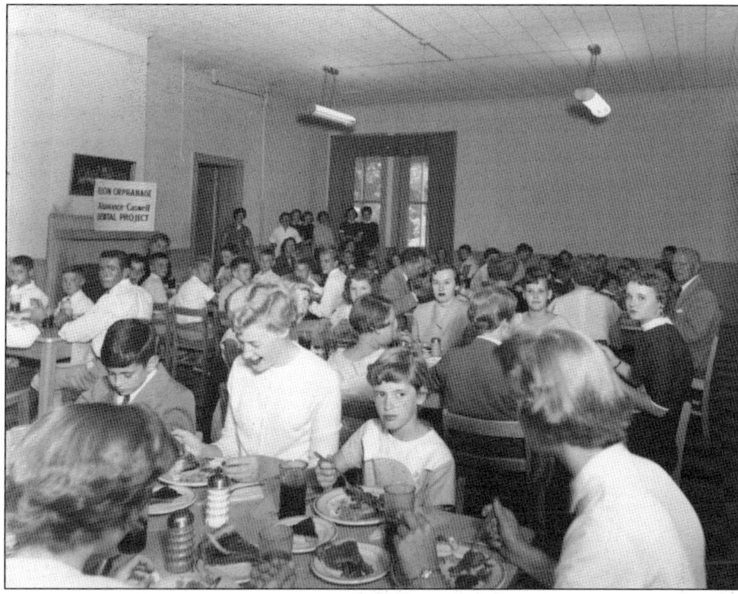

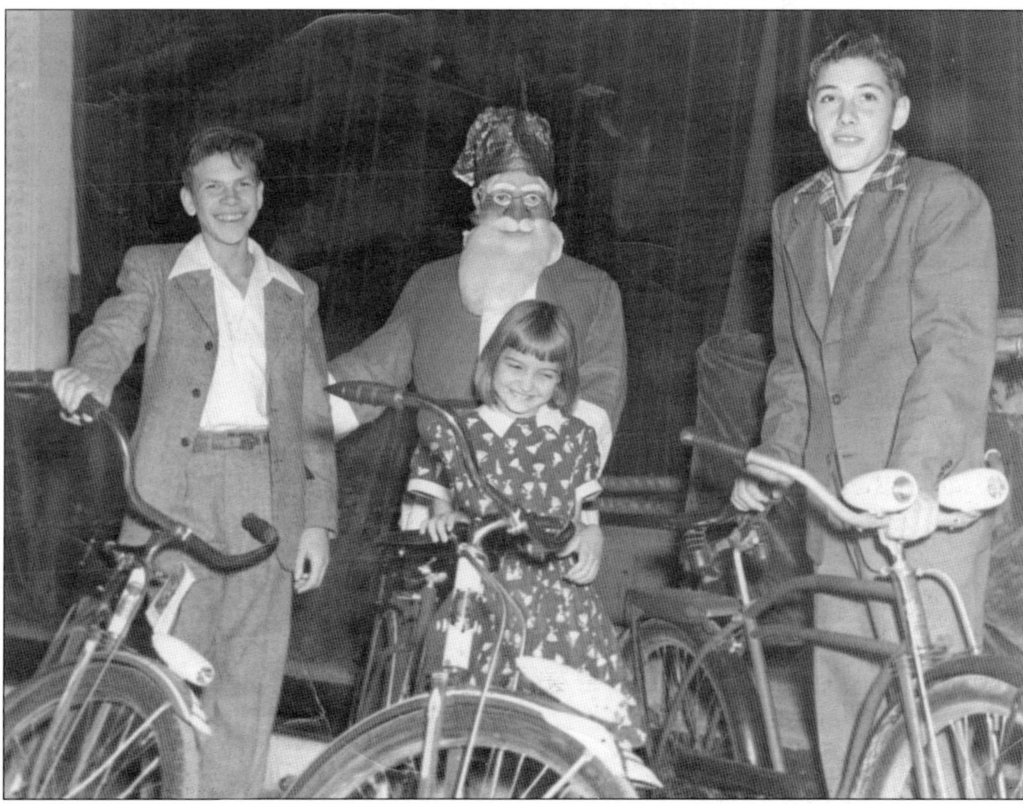

Santa Claus always made special trips to the orphanage at Christmas. He made these three young people quite happy by giving them bicycles, and there were gifts for every child to make sure Christmas would be happy for them. Area civic clubs often took part in such events and provided gifts. Many area residents took the children into their homes to spend Christmas with them. (Elon University.)

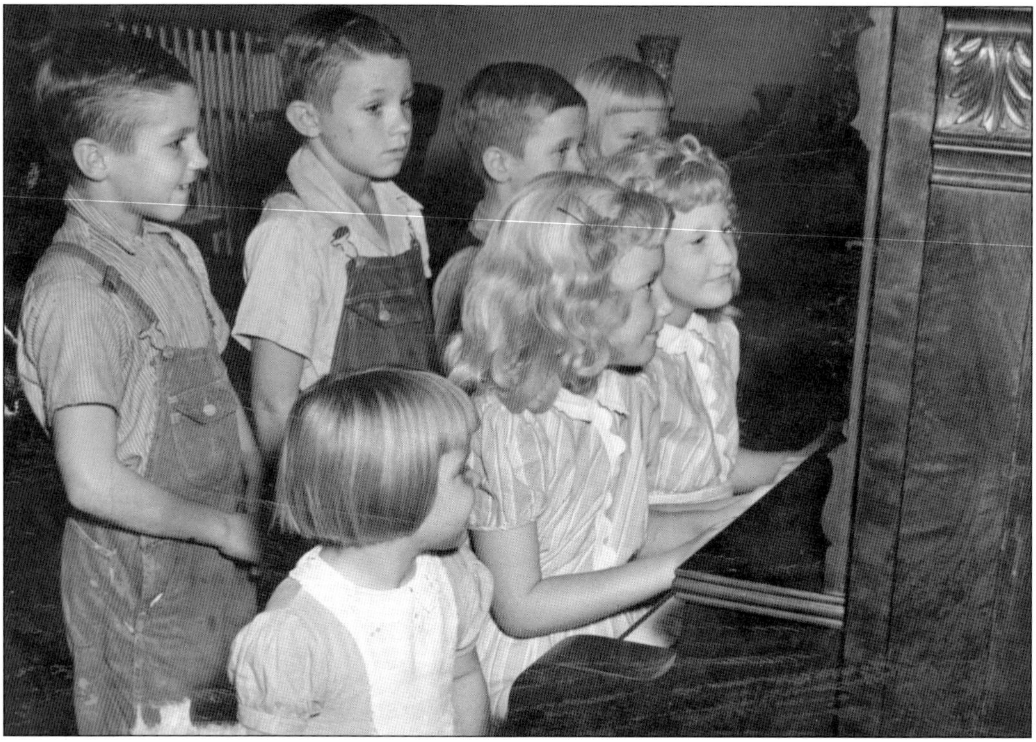

The orphanage children often found many ways to entertain themselves when homework and chores were done. A piano and two little girls who could play it were all that was needed for a bit of singing and laughing with their friends on this occasion. Early orphanage children ranged in age from babies to high schoolers.

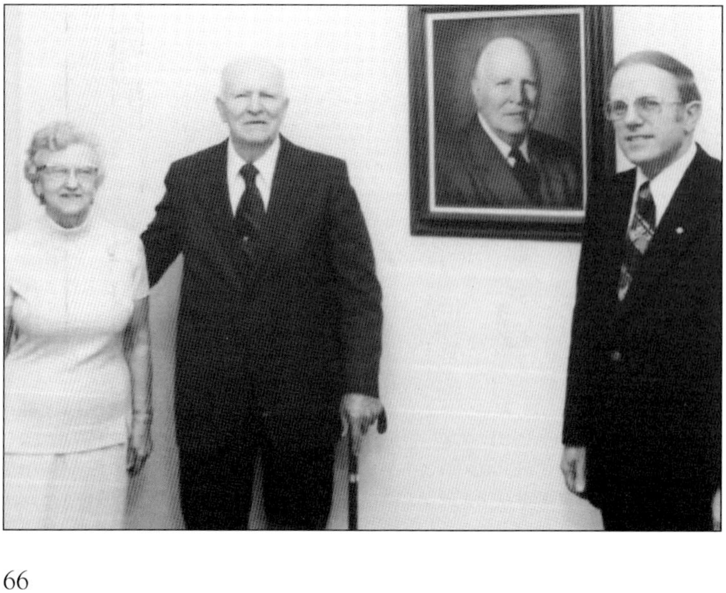

Dr. John G. Truitt Sr. was recognized after his retirement from the orphanage with the naming of the administration building on campus in his honor. He served from 1949 until 1960. His wife, Delia, is pictured with Truitt as Dr. Wally Snyder (right), who succeeded him, displays his portrait in the Truitt Building. Elon University now owns that building, and the Truitt name remains.

Holt Chapel was constructed on the campus of the Elon Orphanage in1957 to honor William Kirkpatrick Holt and his wife, Maude May Holt, both of whom had been strong supporters of the orphanage and its work. For more than 49 years, it was used by the orphanage for services on Sunday morning and Wednesday night, and for weddings and special community events. It is now owned by Elon University and is still in use.

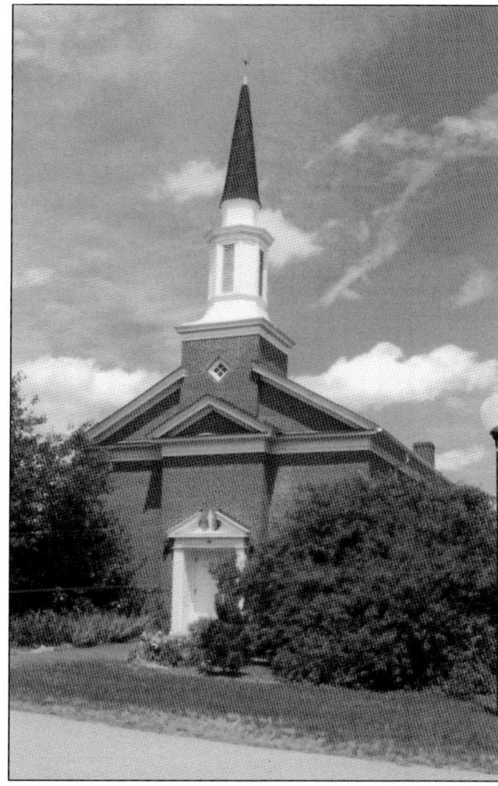

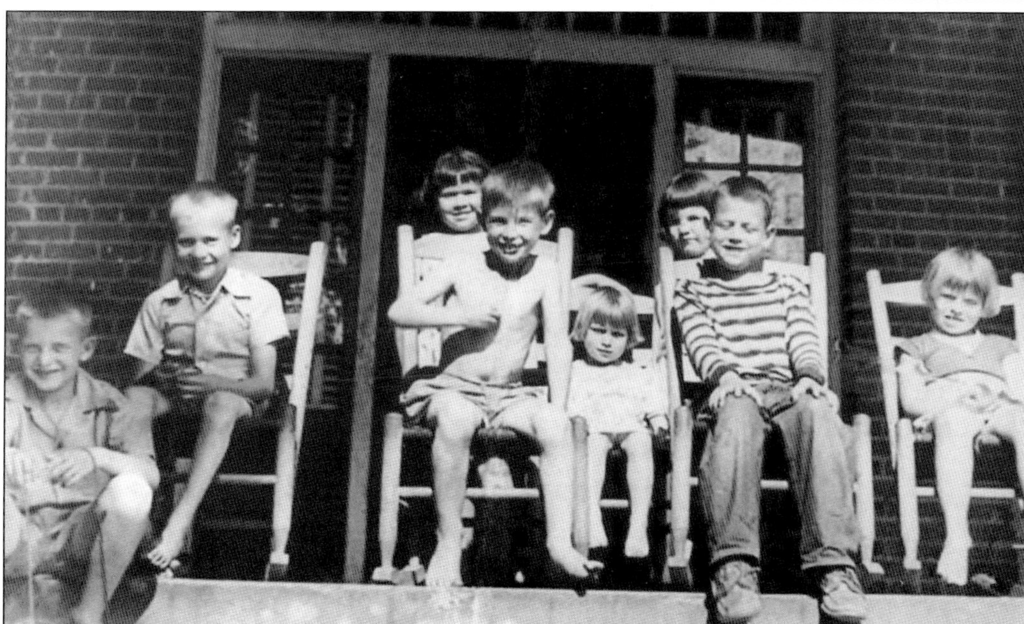

Young residents of the Elon College Christian Orphanage enjoy a summer day on the front porch of Johnston Hall, rocking in the sunshine and laughing with their friends. The children were orphans or half orphans and were from the local area as well as from distant locations in North Carolina and Virginia.

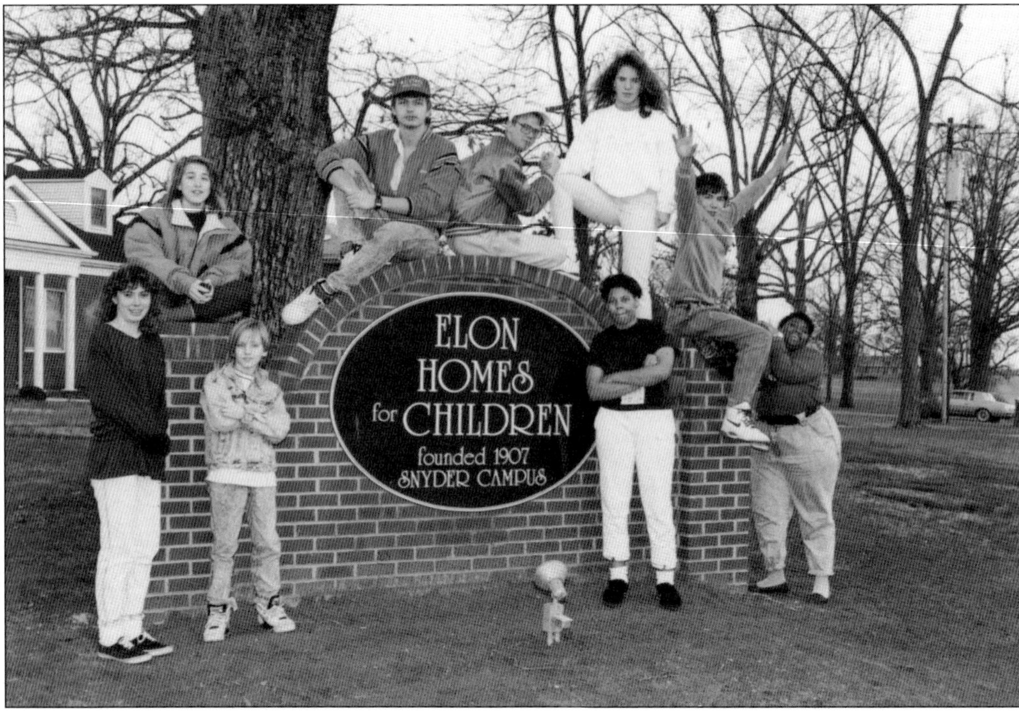

In later years, the operations of the orphanage changed due to a number of reasons, one being the role of the government in childcare. Such changes brought new operations to the Elon campus, and no longer was care confined to orphans. The name became Elon Homes for Children. Eventually, local operations ended and moved to Charlotte. (Elon University.)

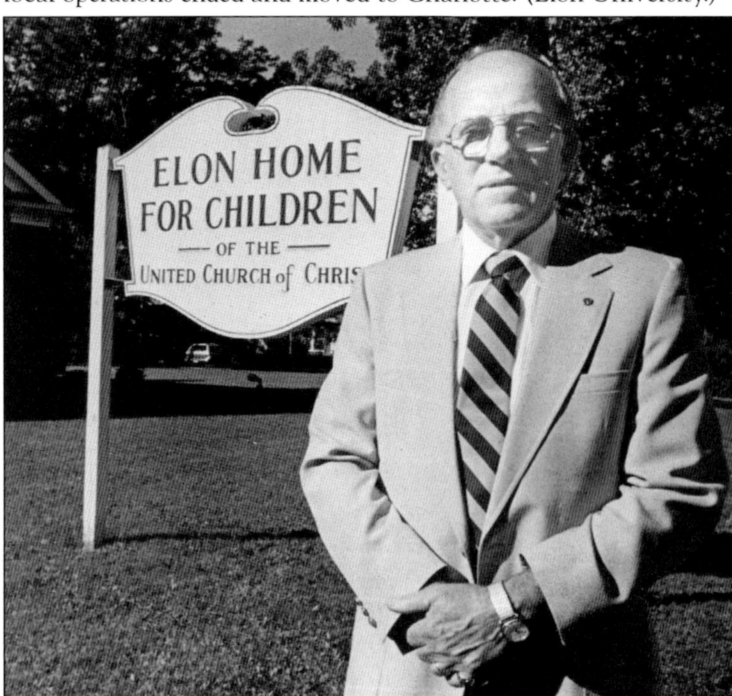

Dr. Wally Snyder was superintendent of the orphanage and then the Elon Homes for Children for 30 years, beginning in 1960. During his tenure, the population of the facility grew and new facilities were built to accommodate the growth. Dr. Snyder, like Dr. Truitt before him, was a retired minister, having served churches in several areas, including Burlington, before joining the orphanage. (*Burlington Times-News*.)

Four

THE UNIVERSITY

In the years since its founding in 1889, Elon University has risen from a small college in a remote area of piedmont North Carolina to a position as one of the most respected universities in the United States. Today, Elon is a university of more than 6,000 students studying in fields including communications, business, education, law, and the arts and sciences. And it is a university recognized as a leader in several areas in which such schools are ranked.

In 2017, it was ranked No. 1 among regional universities in the South by *U.S. News & World Report,* and it continues to be a leader in study abroad programs. More than 70 percent of all Elon students study abroad during the Elon experience. Elon is also recognized for its teacher-student ratio and is No. 1 in academic experiences, a category in which eight areas that promote student success are ranked by that same organization. For several years Elon University has been recognized as having the prettiest campus in the United States. In 2017, it was recognized as one of the 25 most beautiful campuses in the world by BuzzFeed.

Its athletic teams participate in the Colonial Athletic Association with schools along the East Coast and into New England.

Elon University had its beginning in 1889 when it was formed by the Southern Christian Convention, a forerunner of today's United Church of Christ. Over the years, the school battled through a number of difficult periods: World War I, the 1918 flu epidemic, a 1923 fire that destroyed its administration and classroom building, the Great Depression, and World War II. It survived, however, and experienced growth as the years passed.

For many years, Elon drew students primarily from North Carolina and eastern Virginia, but today they come from all over the United States and from many foreign countries as well. Most still come from North Carolina, but large numbers now come from Massachusetts, Connecticut, New Jersey, and other northeastern areas.

On June 1, 2001, Elon College became Elon University, as its leaders felt the new name would better reflect the school's governance, earn it greater credibility, and place it in a better position with its admissions competitors. Since then, Elon has enjoyed tremendous growth and earned its place among the nation's elite educational institutions.

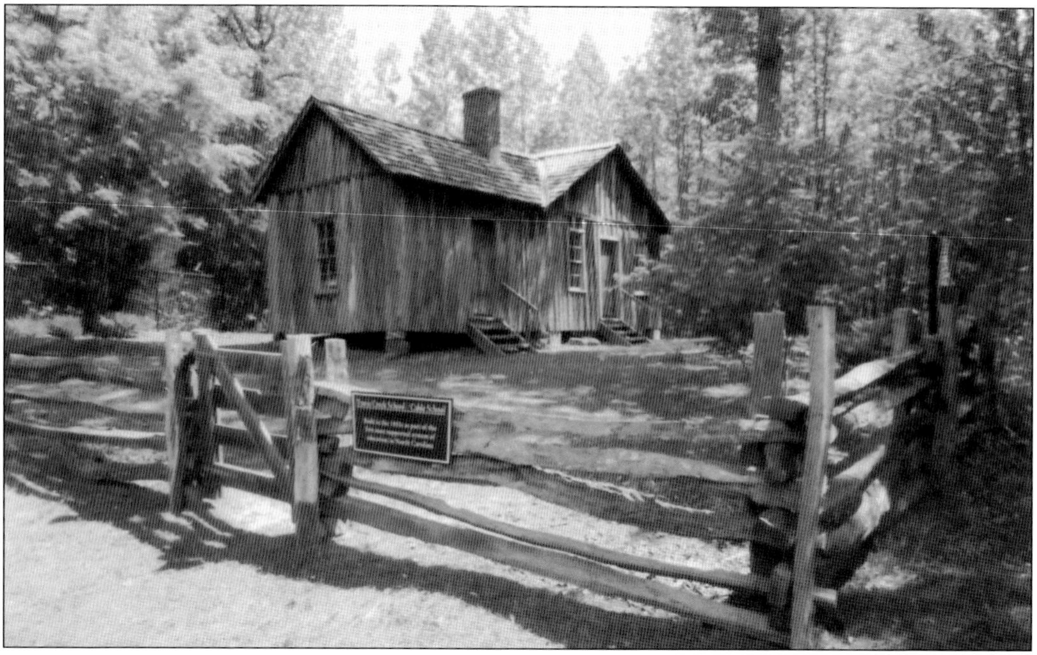

Education was at work on the Elon campus long before the college began in 1889. This little school was built in the 1850s on a site next to the present field house at Rhodes Stadium. Cable School was a part of the first state-supported system of education in North Carolina, and the university has restored it to its original status.

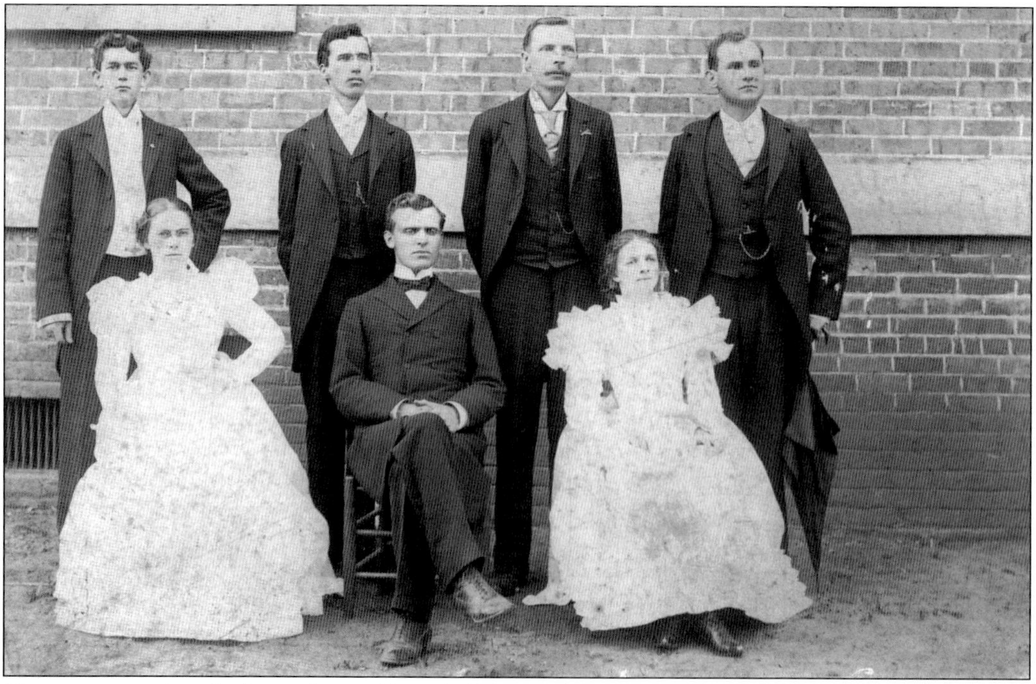

This group is identified as a class at Elon College in the 1890s. The students may be a graduating class, as there were very small numbers of graduates in the first years of the school's history. The largest number in that first decade came in 1899, when 12 students were awarded degrees.

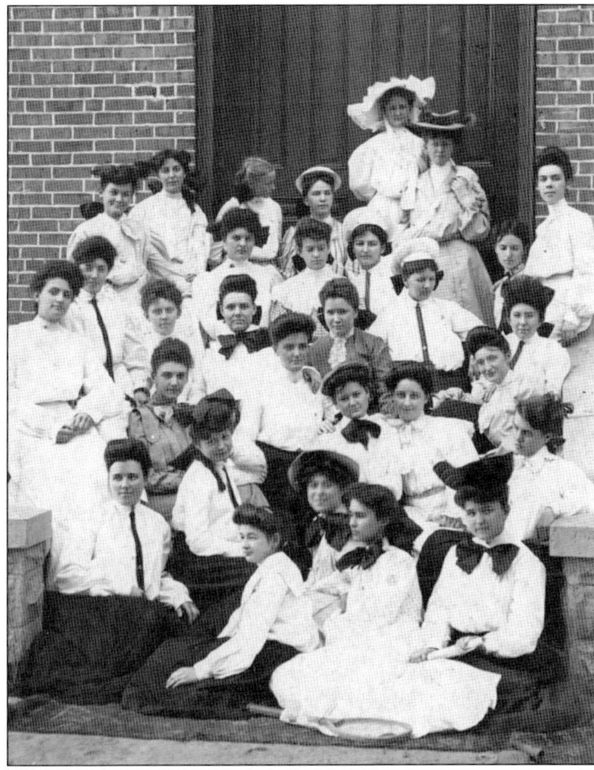

This is a group of women students from the 1890s, most of whom are wearing almost identical outfits of clothing. When Elon's doors opened for the first time, all students came from North Carolina or Virginia. Those two states would be the leading source of students for many decades, but in 2018 Elon University has become an international community.

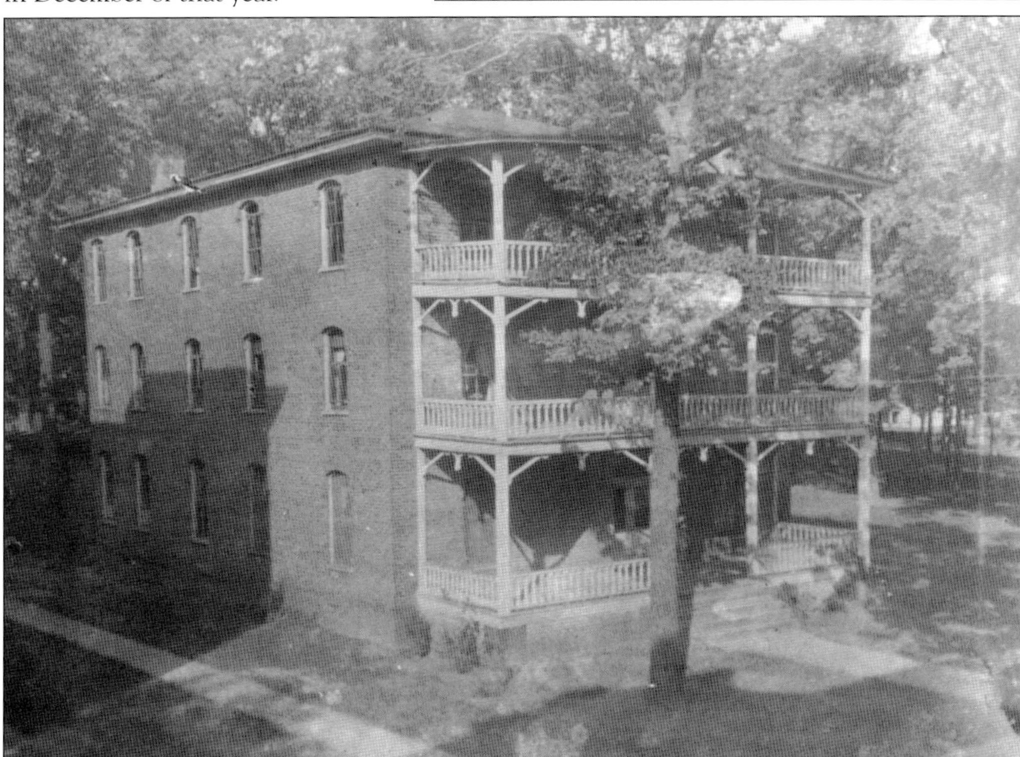

East Dormitory was under construction in September 1890 when Elon College began its first term. It was not ready for students when classes began. Women students had to move into the Williamson House on Trollinger Avenue and live there—four to a room—until East Dormitory finally was ready for occupancy in December of that year.

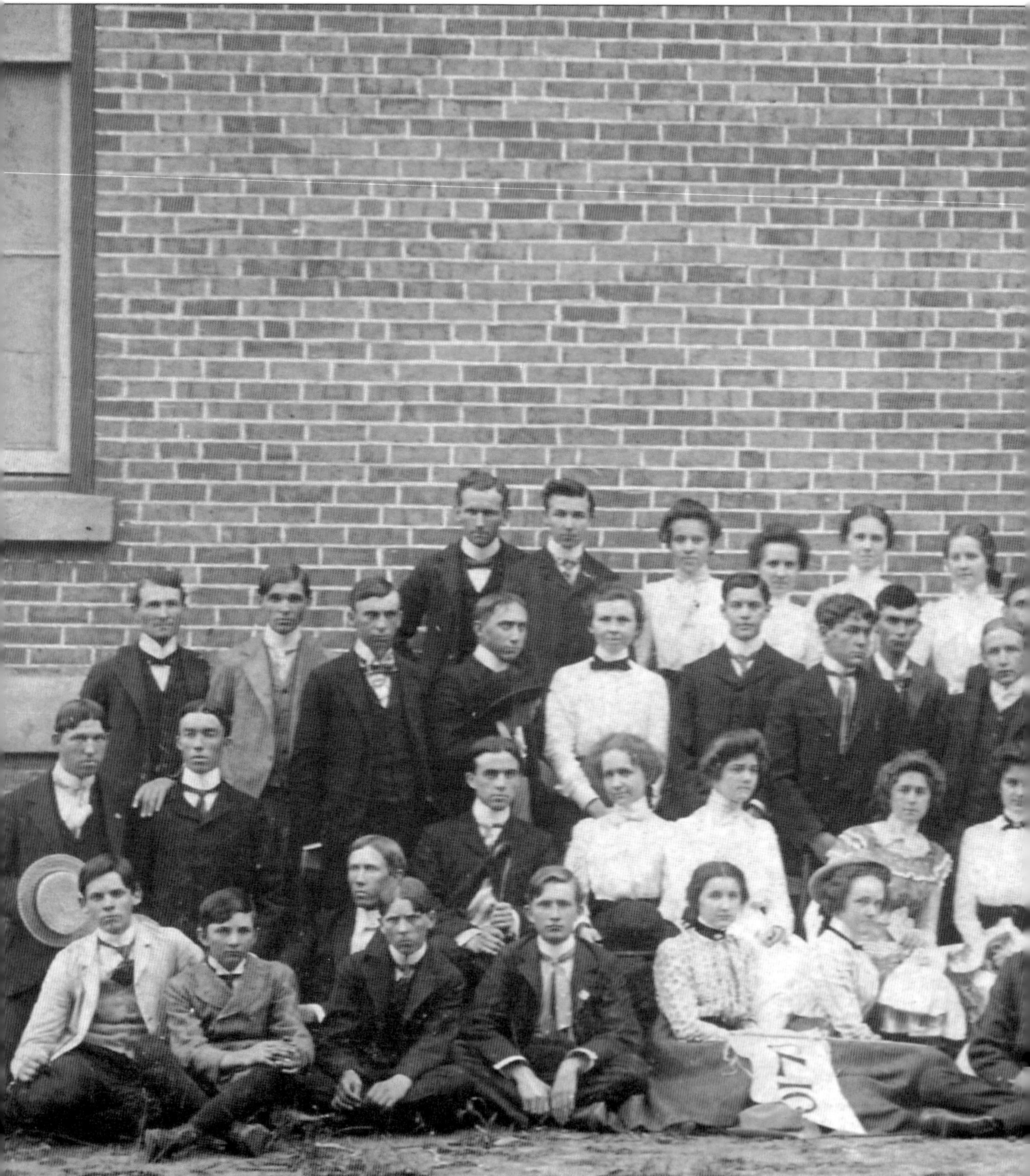

Members of the Elon College student body are pictured in 1901. The college was then more than a decade old, and several classes had already graduated. A large number of female students are seen in the image, as Elon was only the second college in the state to be coeducational, Guilford being the first. The presence of female students at Elon College was a big problem for some in the Christian Church. They believed academic standards would be lower than at all-male schools,

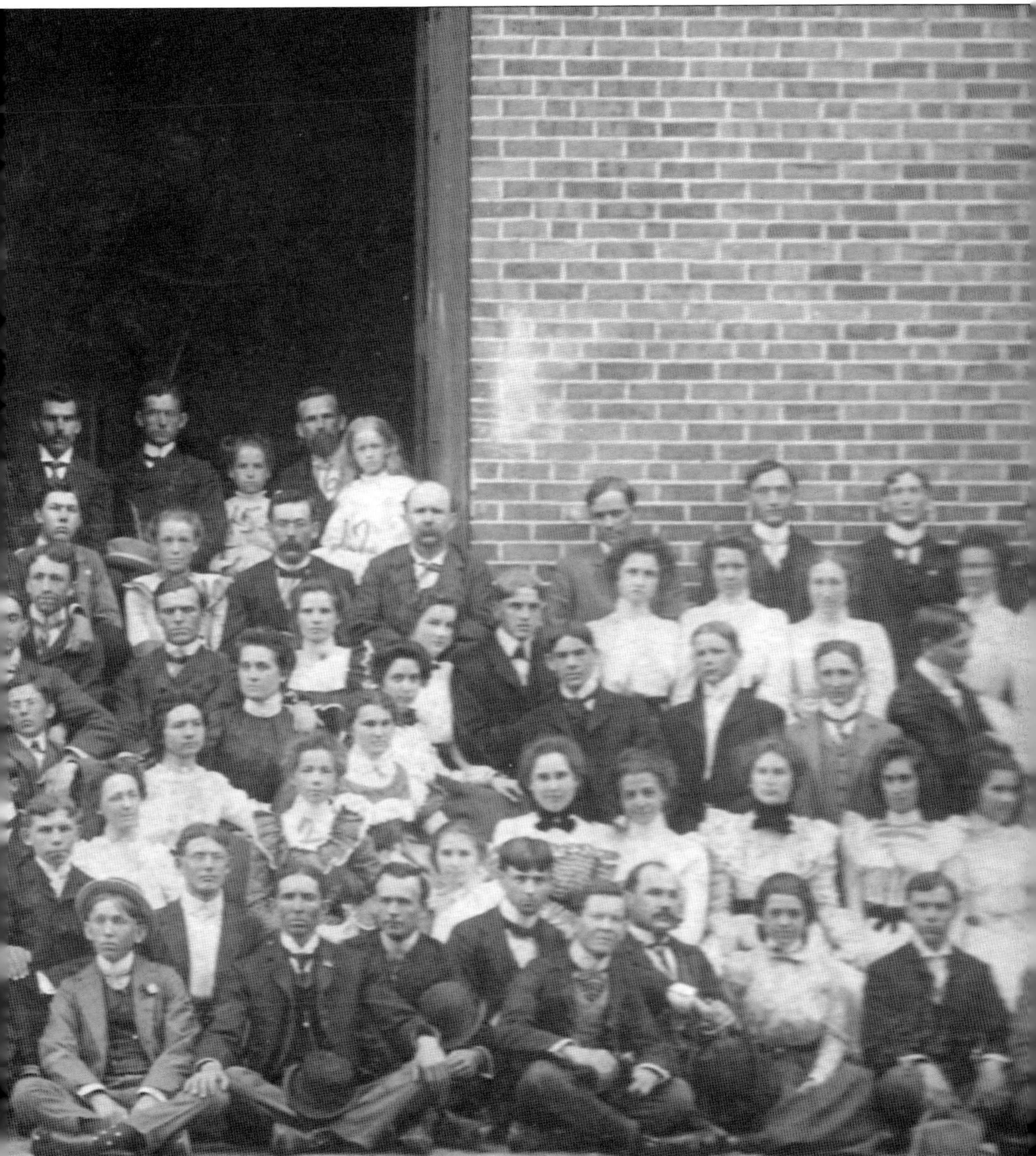

and there were those who had serious problems with moral issues and the teaching of both men and women in the same classroom. A list of expenses shows costs for men ranged from $125 to $145, while for women the cost was $25 higher. While services for both were pretty much the same, the cost for the young women included "servant's attendance." (Elon University.)

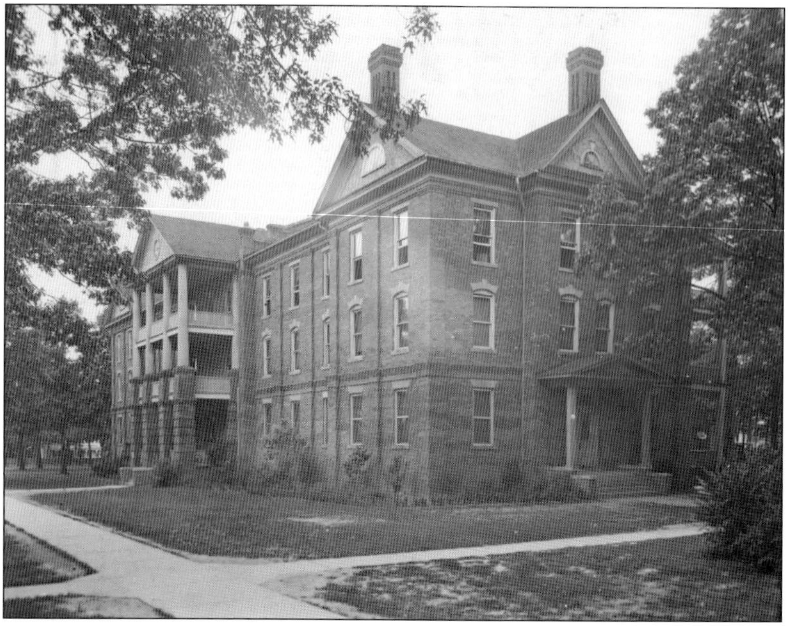

West Dormitory opened in 1906, and it provided accommodations for 100 female students. They lived on the second and third floors. There was an annex to the building with a gymnasium and the college dining room on the first floor. Male students had to enter the dining room using stairs on the outside of the annex. (Elon University.)

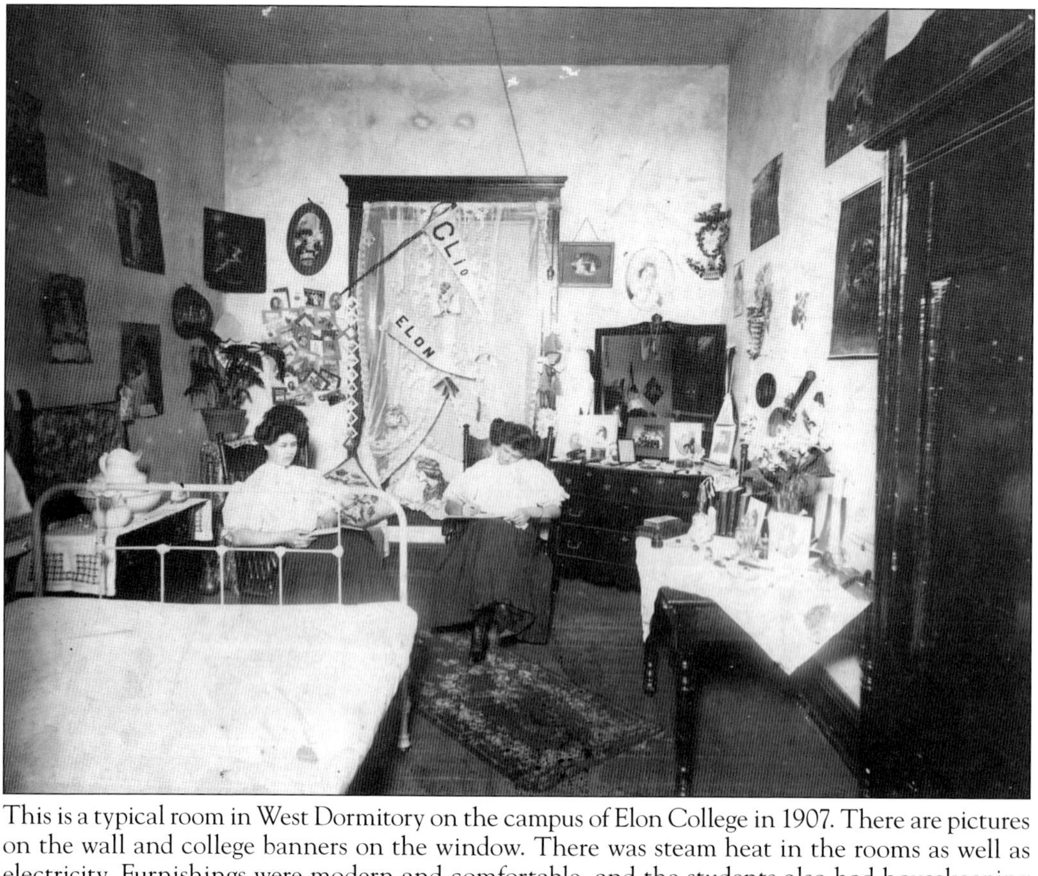

This is a typical room in West Dormitory on the campus of Elon College in 1907. There are pictures on the wall and college banners on the window. There was steam heat in the rooms as well as electricity. Furnishings were modern and comfortable, and the students also had housekeeping services. (Elon University.)

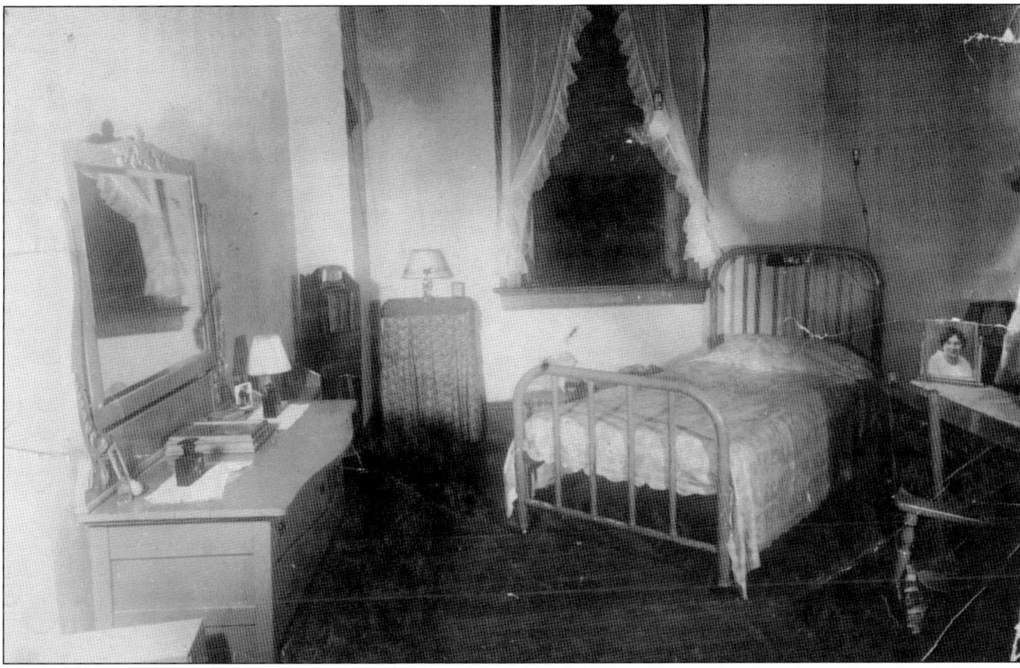

In 1912, Pres. William A. Harper and his wife, Estelle, opened their home as a cooperative boardinghouse for women students. Students did housekeeping and cooking to save on expenses. The idea worked so well that New West Dormitory was built as Young Ladies' Cooperative Hall, where a student could save as much as half on expenses for an academic year. This is a student room in cooperative boarding in 1913. (Elon University.)

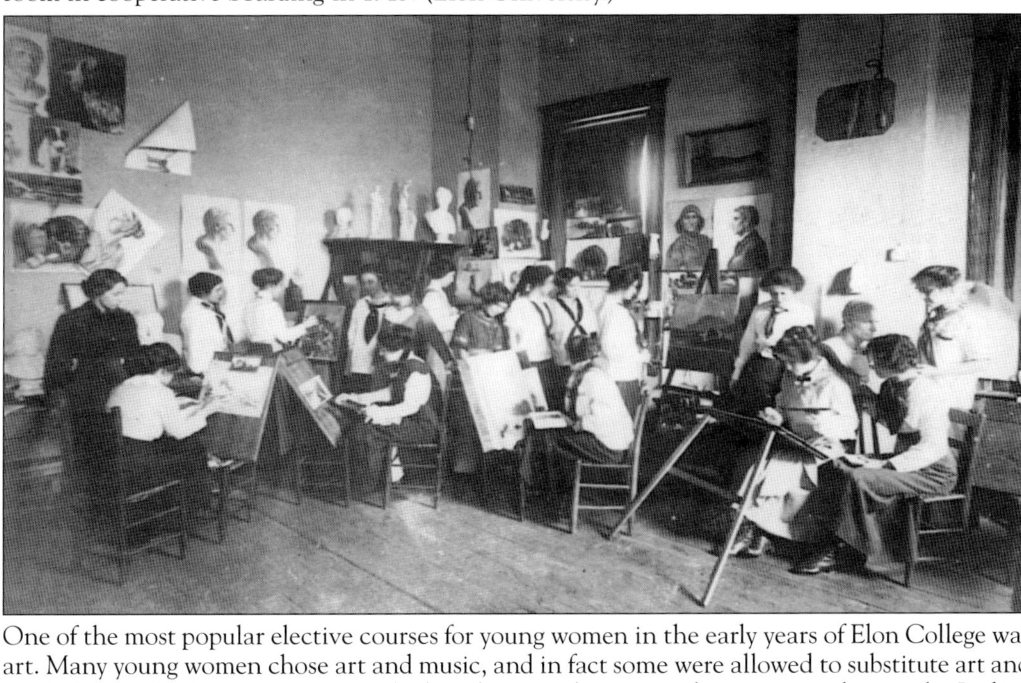

One of the most popular elective courses for young women in the early years of Elon College was art. Many young women chose art and music, and in fact some were allowed to substitute art and music for required courses. Data with this photograph notes it shows an art class in the Ladies' Cooperative Hall after 1913. (Elon University.)

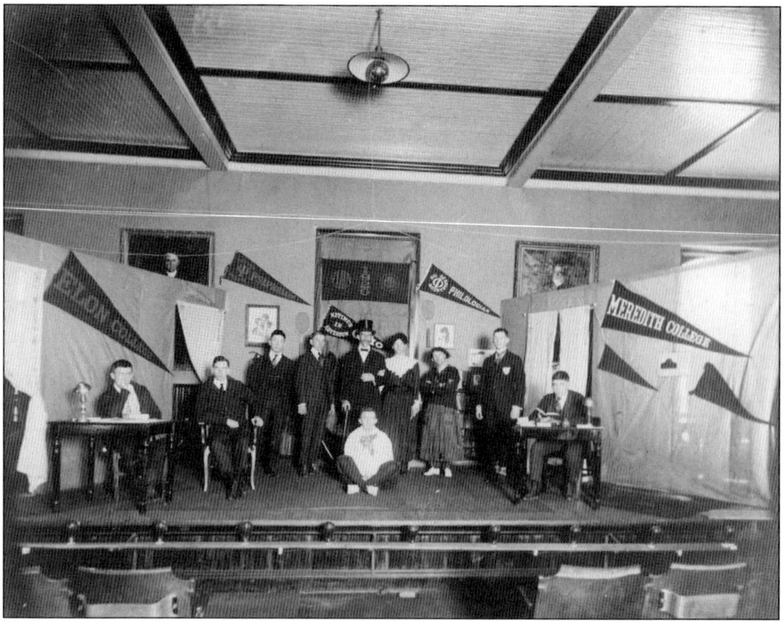

Many students have been attracted to acting throughout the history of Elon University. This photograph shows a group in a performance about 1917. The student seated onstage second from left is Thomas E. Powell Jr., who would join the faculty after graduation and go on to found Carolina Biological Supply Co. near the Elon campus. (Dr. James B. Powell.)

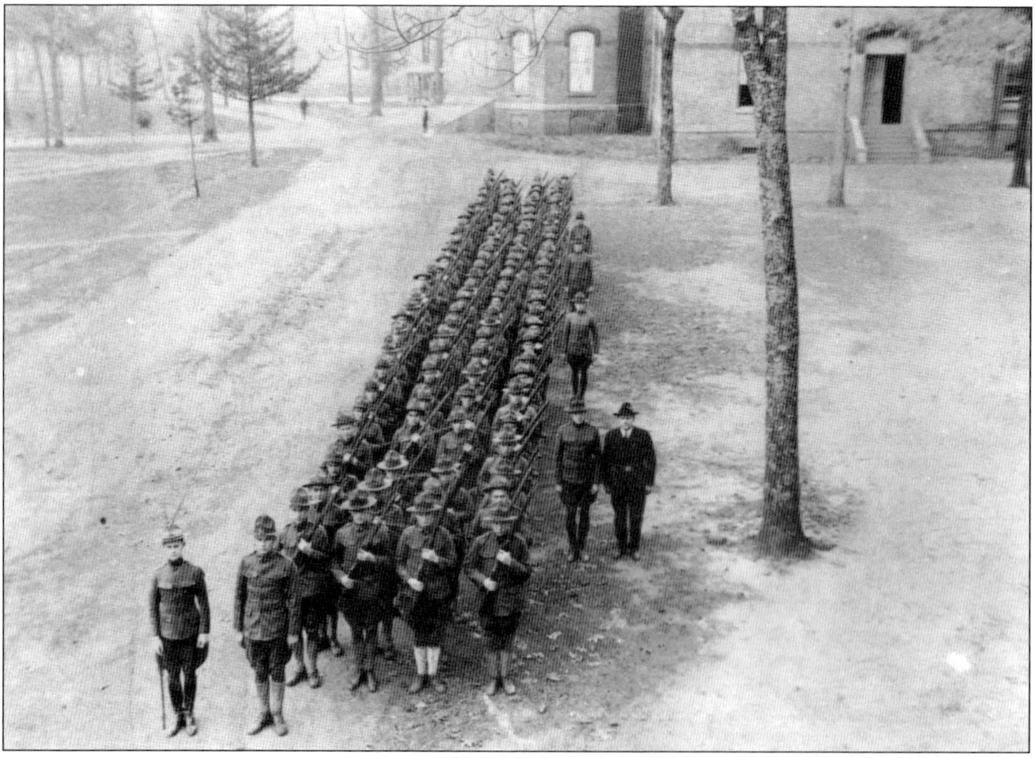

During World War I, the War Department formed the Students' Army Training Corps. Elon College was one of 11 North Carolina colleges to participate, and after training the unit was inducted in October 1918, just weeks before the end of the war in Europe. The unit had 112 men at demobilization in December. (Elon University.)

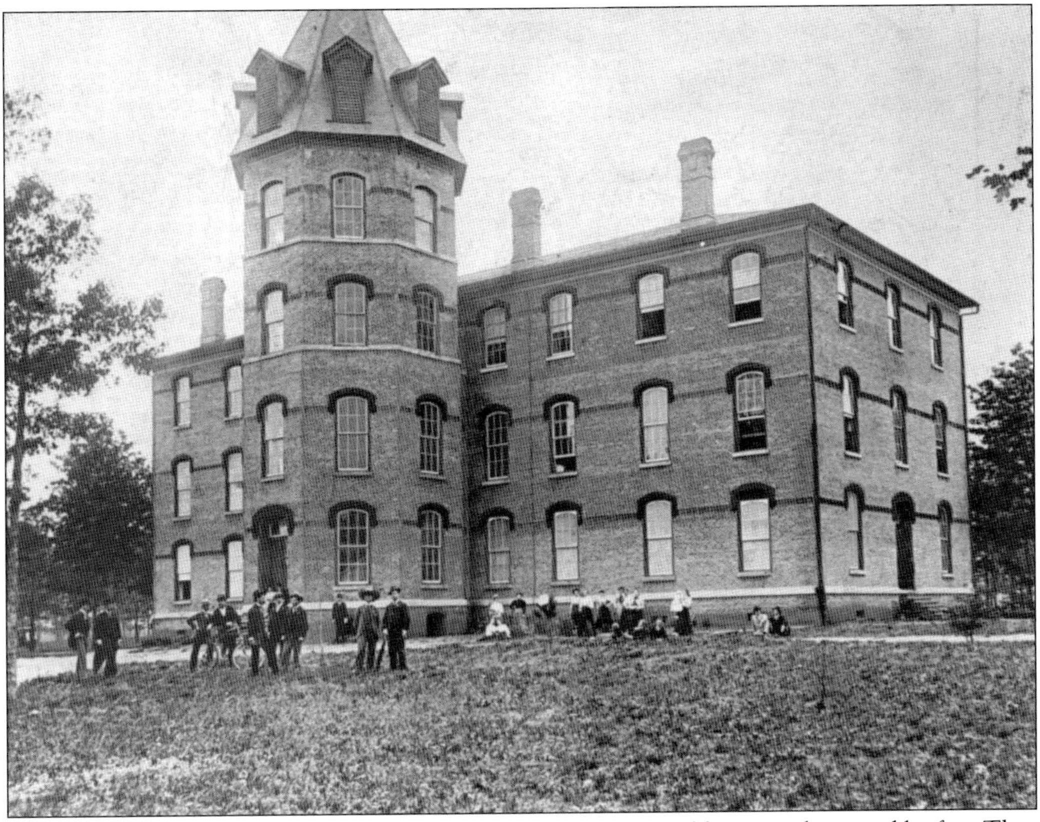

Elon College suffered a devastating loss in 1923 when Main Building was destroyed by fire. That was the administration building with offices, classrooms, and student records, all of which were lost. Before the fire was out, a meeting was called and plans were made to start the recovery, with heavy support from individuals and businesses in the surrounding Alamance County area. Elon College would live on. (Elon University.)

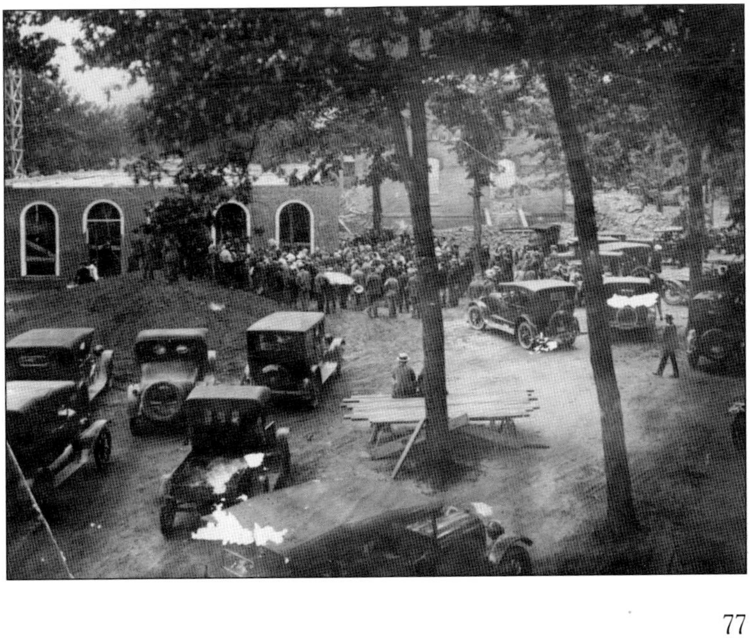

Money to rebuild after the Main Building fire came from many sources, and plans were made quickly and a new building started to rise from the ashes. It would be Alamance Building, in a nod of thanks to all the help that Alamance County had provided. Visitors at an event at the building site here inspect the progress made in construction. (Elon University.)

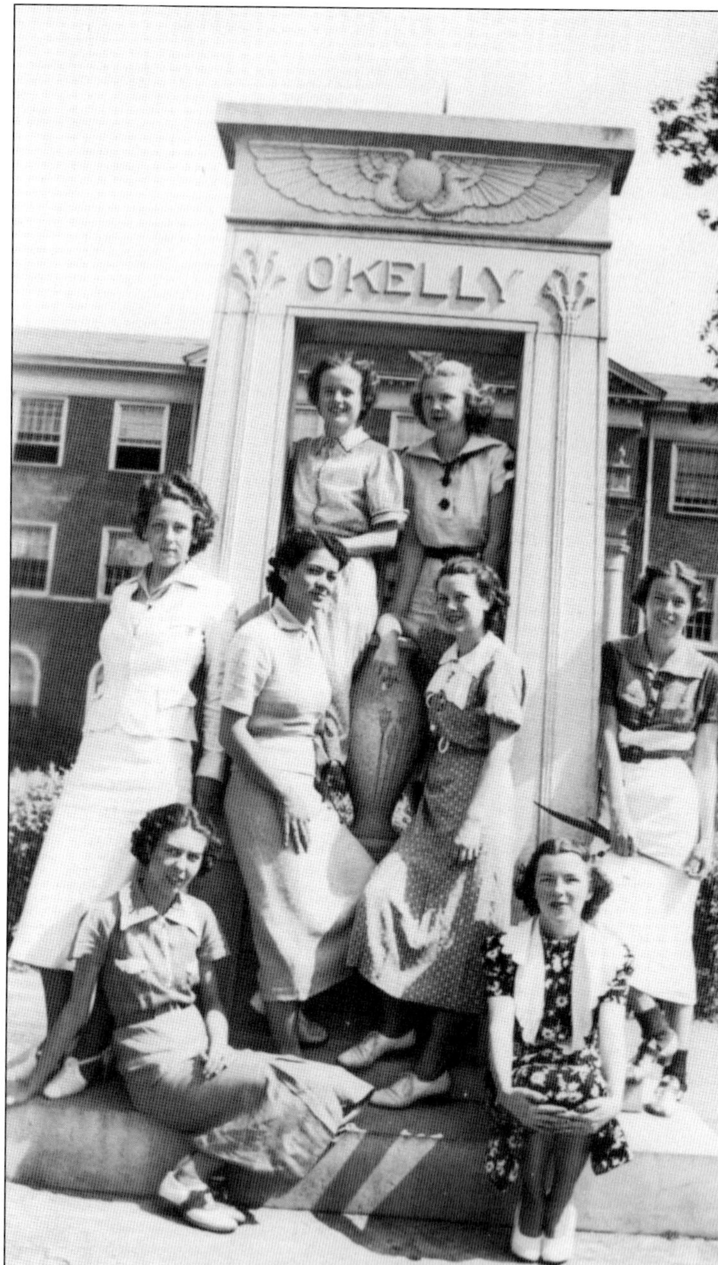

These young ladies pose in the 1930s at a monument on the Elon College campus that honors James O'Kelly, a circuit-riding preacher who moved about Alamance and surrounding counties. After the Revolutionary War, some Methodist ministers had problems with the idea of an American bishop and his authority. O'Kelly led a group of ministers that left that Methodist leadership and formed what became the Christian Church, the body that founded the college. The monument was erected in 1929 in the center of a circular drive that for many years brought traffic through the main entrance to the campus from Lebanon Avenue to the front of Alamance Building. That entrance was later closed, and the entrance was moved to the north side of the building, facing Haggard Avenue. (Elon University.)

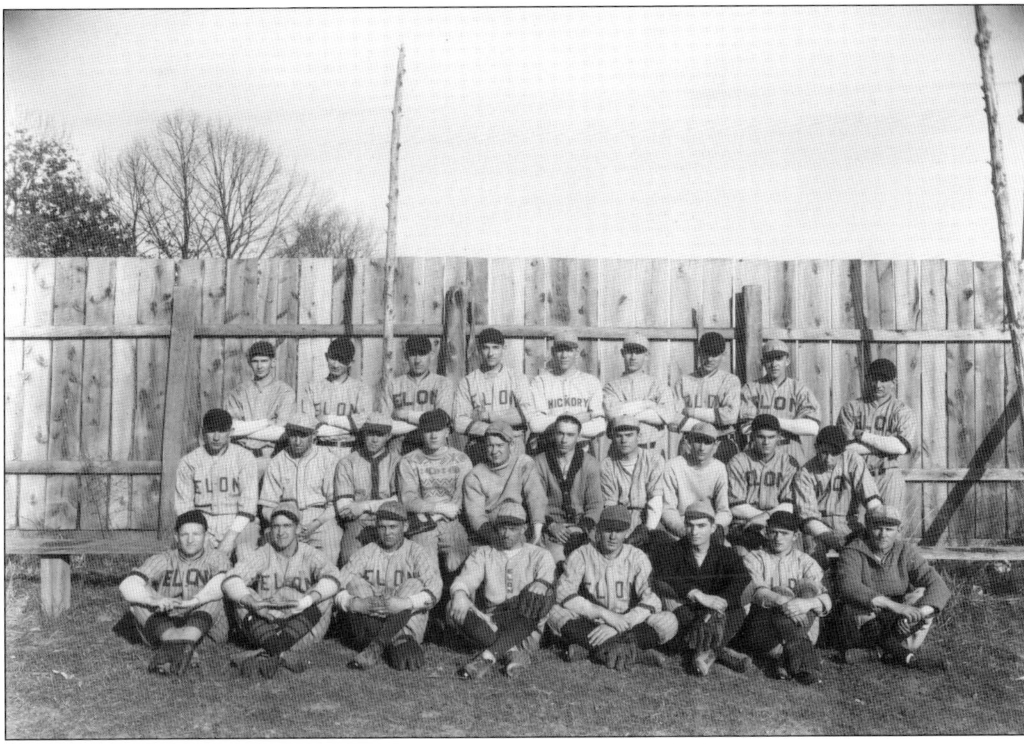

By the 1920s, athletics had become a major part of the Elon College experience and teams were being fielded in a number of sports. Baseball was one of the favorite sports of the era, and this team represented Elon College in intercollegiate competition in the 1930s. Football, track, tennis, and basketball were also a part of the athletic program. (Elon University.)

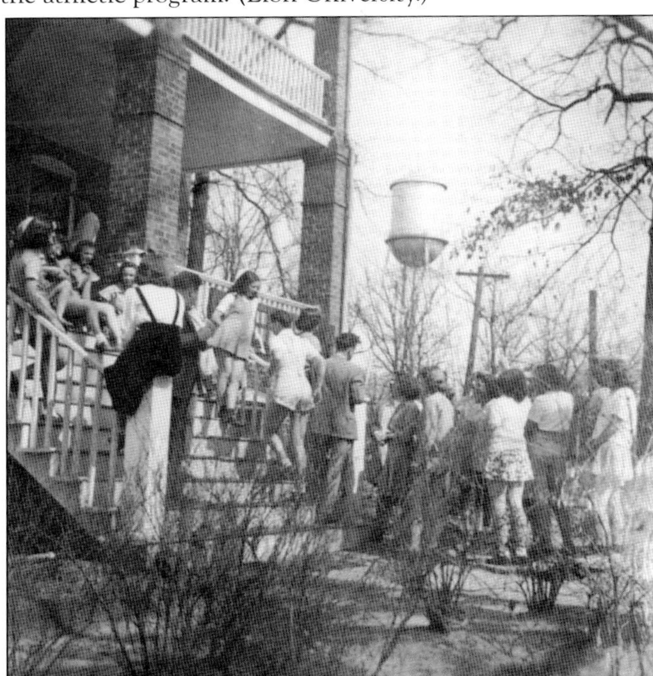

This is another photograph from the Young Ladies' Cooperative Hall program. A group of the students has gathered on the steps of the dormitory in the 1930s. This program began in 1912 and continued for many years, but in 1960 the ladies' building was torn down to make way for new dormitory construction. (Elon University.)

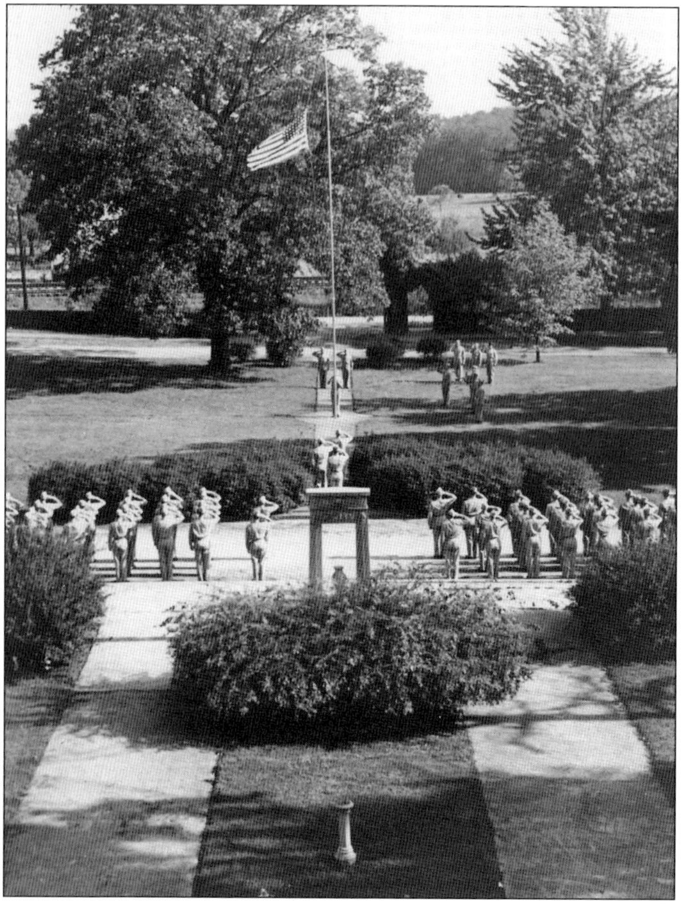

In 1943, in the middle of World War II, Elon College joined the war effort by becoming home to the 325th College Training Detachment of the US Army Air Corps. Cadets came to Elon College, 350 at a time, for five months of preflight training. Then they would move on to other locations for flight training as pilots or other crew members on American war planes. (Elon University.)

By 1913, the gymnasium in use by the college had become totally inadequate. There was not room even for a standard-sized basketball court. With that in mind, approval was given by trustees for a new dormitory-gymnasium combination that would solve that problem. It was named North Dormitory, as it was located on the north side of the Administration Building. (Elon University.)

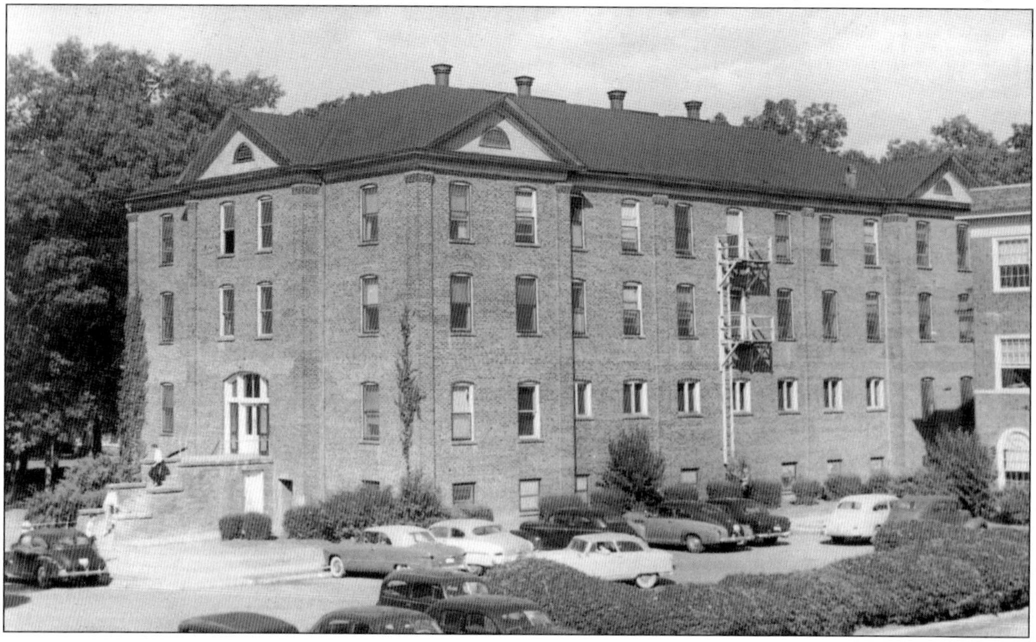

The first floor of North Dormitory featured a gymnasium that was large enough to provide a full-sized basketball court. There were also 44 dormitory rooms on the second and third floors. The rooms on both floors opened onto balconies that overlooked the basketball court. Occupants of the upstairs rooms could stand on the balconies and look down on the basketball games. (Elon University.)

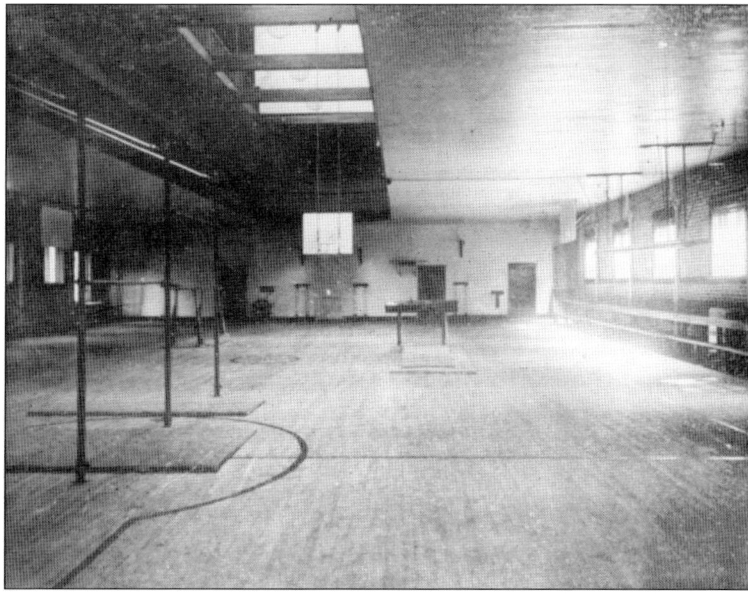

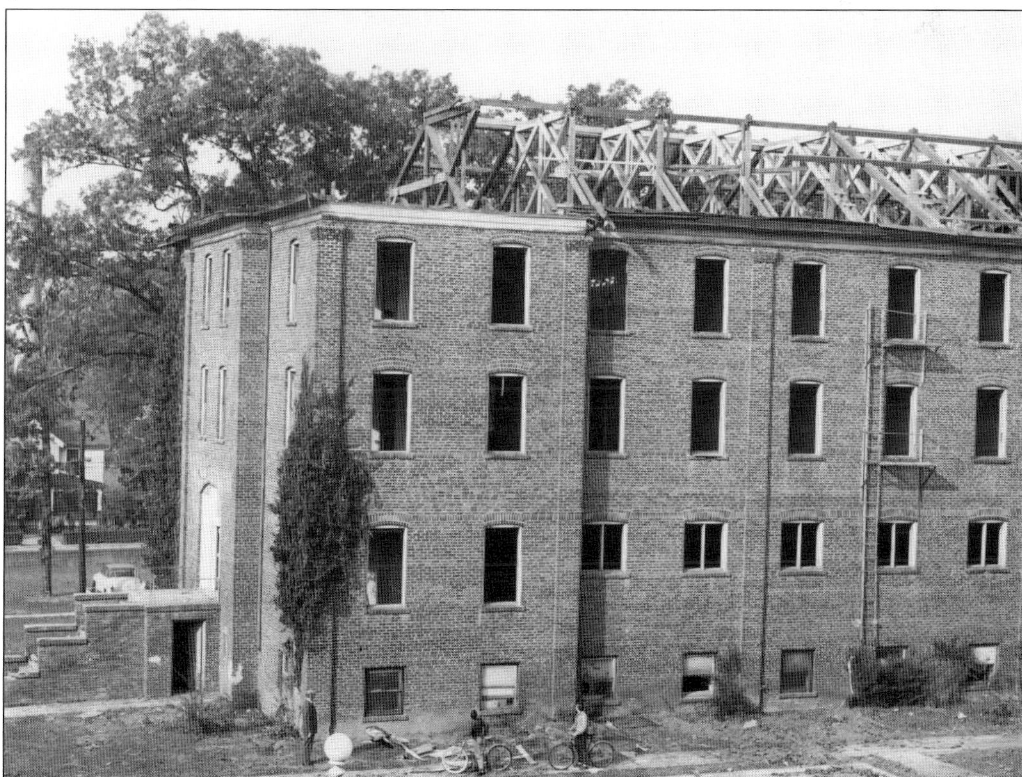

In 1950, Alumni Gymnasium had replaced the gym in North Dormitory and there was new dormitory space for men on campus. So it was decided in 1959 that old North Dormitory would be demolished. This photograph shows that process in its early stages. Dr. J. Earl Danieley, president at the time, is pictured at left, near the bottom of the picture, checking progress. (Elon University.)

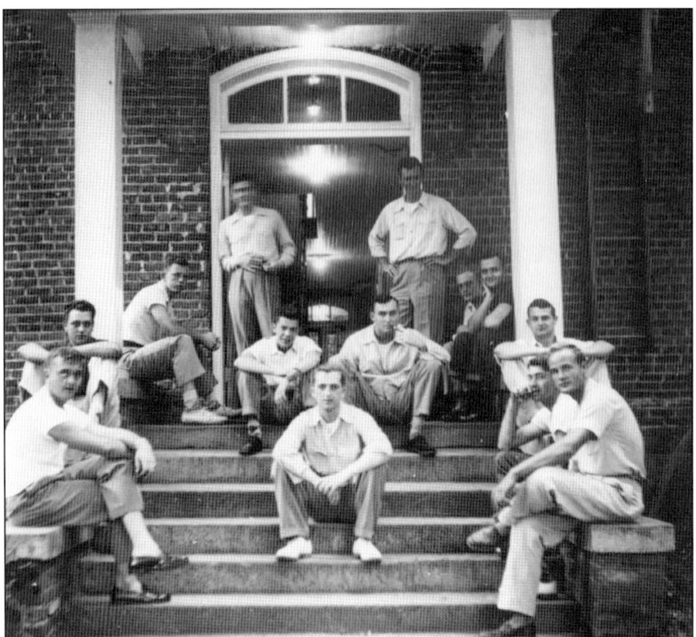

In 1952, these Elon College students gathered on the steps of their dormitory as their day drew to an end. There was another war on at the time, this one in Korea, and the education of a lot of young men had to be put on hold. Many young students like these lived with uncertainty, as the draft was still calling many into service. (Elon University.)

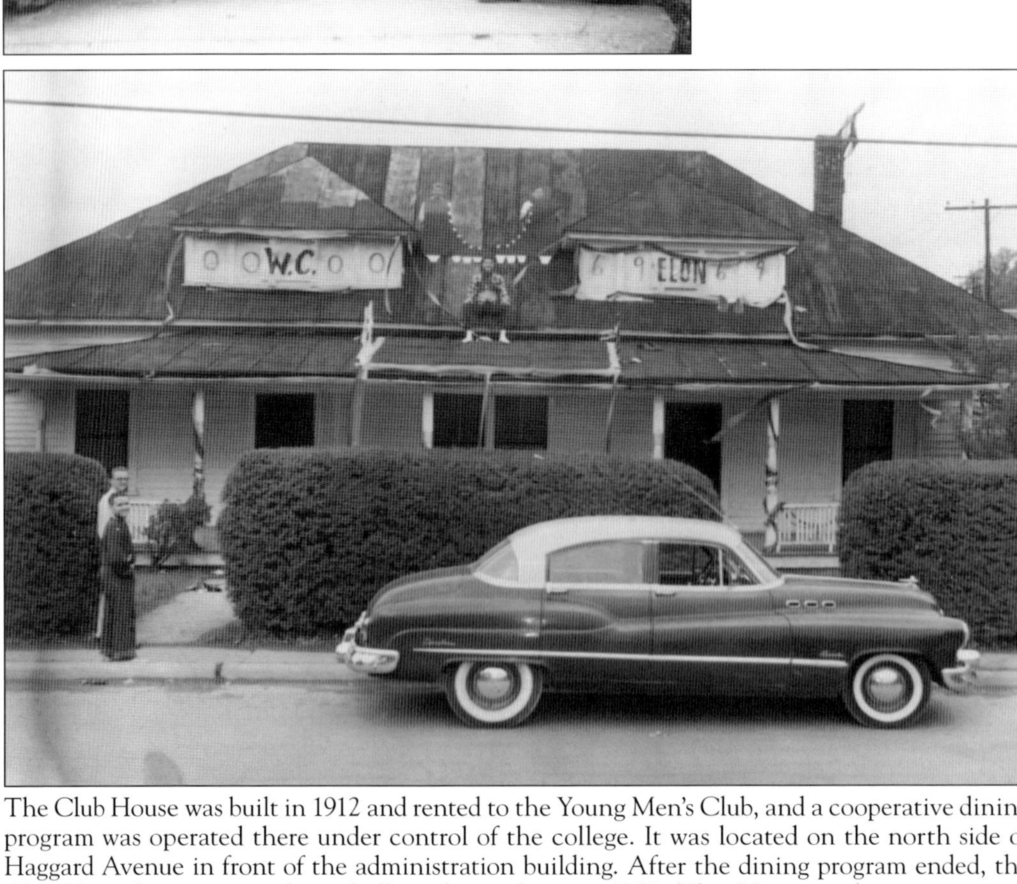

The Club House was built in 1912 and rented to the Young Men's Club, and a cooperative dining program was operated there under control of the college. It was located on the north side of Haggard Avenue in front of the administration building. After the dining program ended, the Club House became a residence hall until torn down in 1958. (Elon University.)

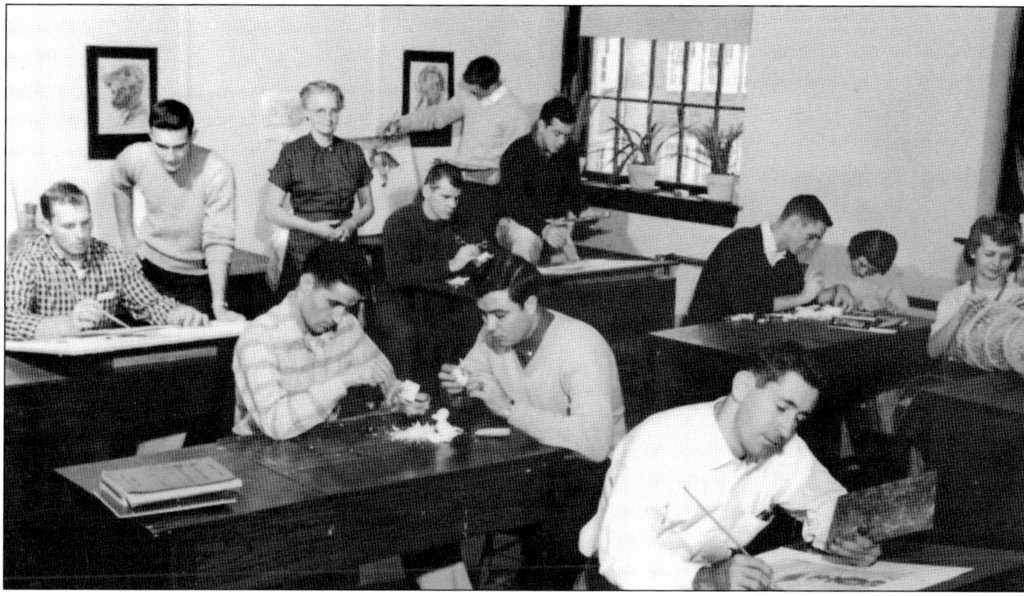

Lila Clair Newman was a popular art professor at Elon College for 41 years, retiring in 1965. She was born to Elon professor Dr. John U. Newman and his wife, Pattie, in 1892. Lila Clair and three of her siblings were deaf, but that had no effect on her teaching, as her mother had taught her lip reading. Lila Clair Newman is shown here with her art class in the 1950s. (Elon University.)

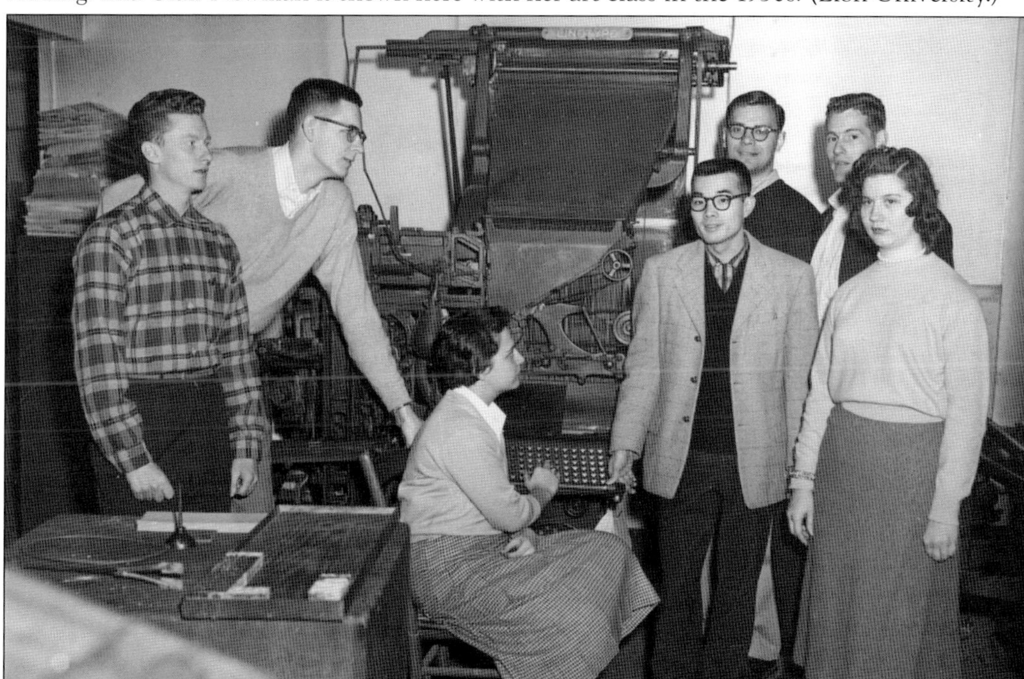

This is the 1957 staff of the *Maroon and Gold*, the Elon College student newspaper at that time. Students wrote and published the newspaper under the direction of faculty members. Students here are in front of an old Linotype machine, which set hot type long before computers were even imagined in the news industry. (Elon University.)

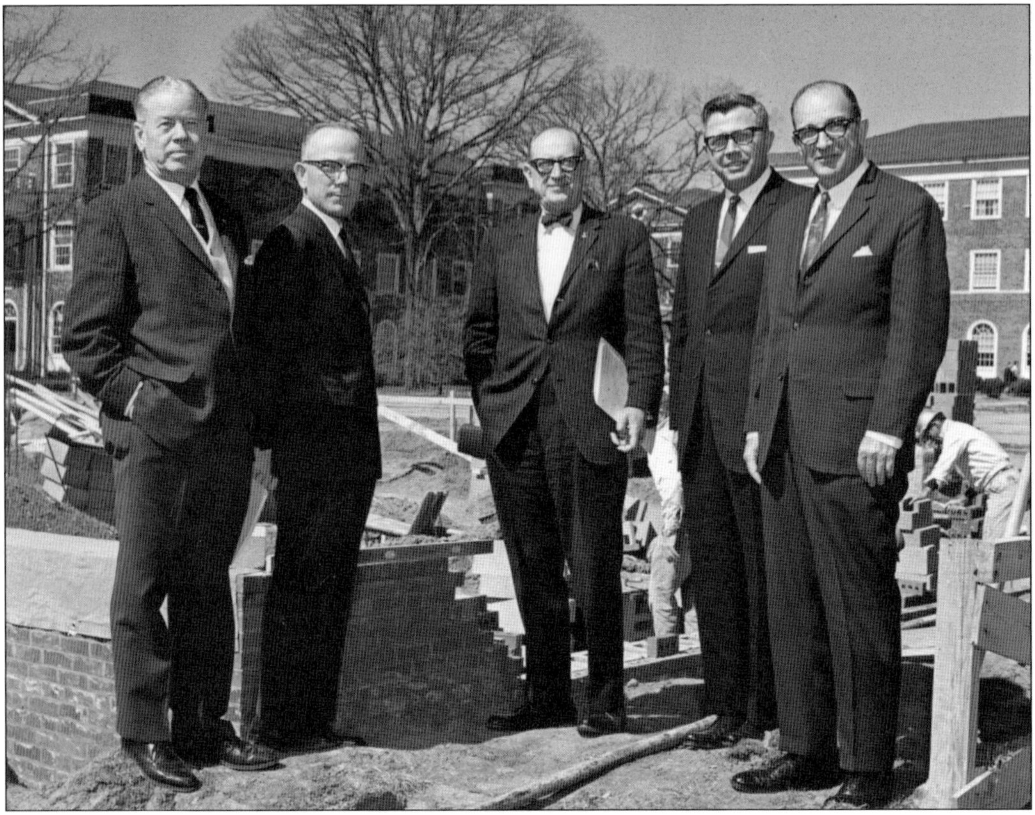

Several trustees participated in the ground-breaking for the William S. Long Student Center in 1965. From left to right are George D. Colclough, Thomas S. Earp, chairman of the board of trustees Thad Eure, Dr. W.D. Rippy, and J. Hinton Rountree. The building was dedicated on November 5, 1966, as was the Brannock, Hook, and Barney dorm complex, honoring three longtime professors. (Elon University.)

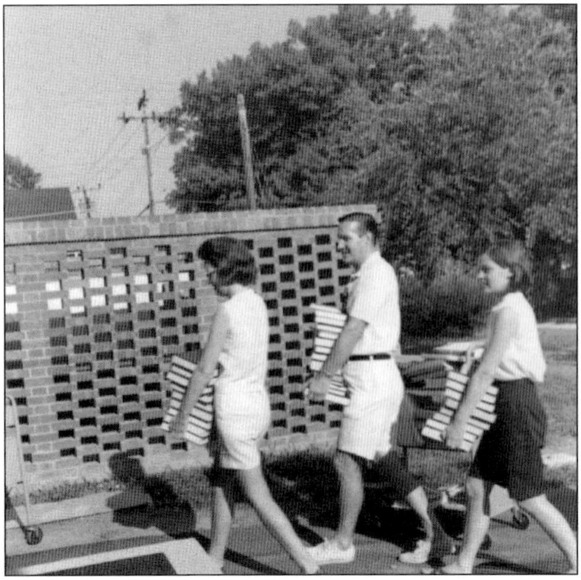

On that same November day in 1966, ground was broken for a new library. On July 15, 1968, the Iris Holt McEwen Library was ready, and scores of students, faculty, staff, and friends of the college turned out to hand carry every volume from the old Carlton Library to the new one. McEwen Dining Hall built in 1956 honored Holt's husband. (Elon University.)

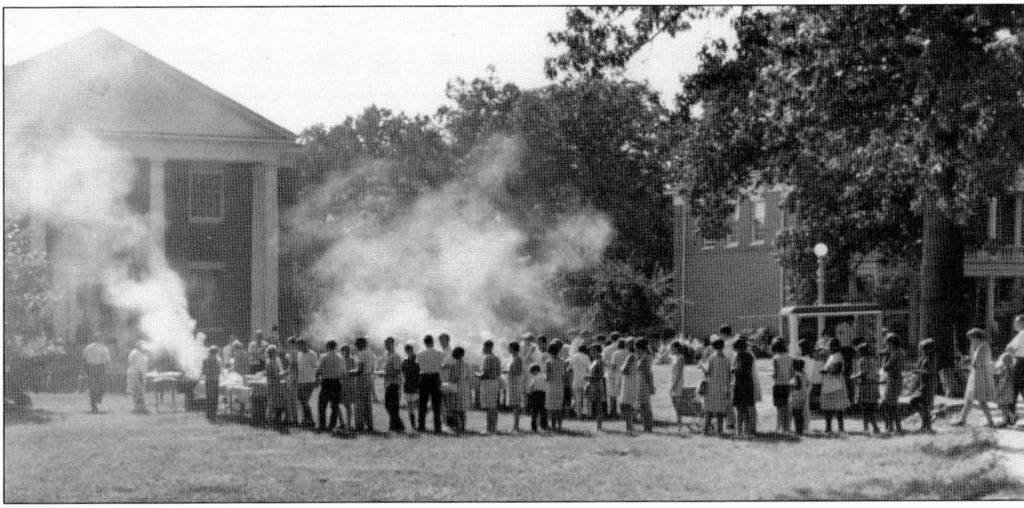

Everyone who made 10 trips carrying books to the new library was treated to a steak dinner on the lawn in front of the building. The Iris Holt McEwen Library is at left and McEwen Dining Hall is at right. The library would continue in this site until the Belk Library was completed in 2000. The School of Communications then occupied this location. (Elon University.)

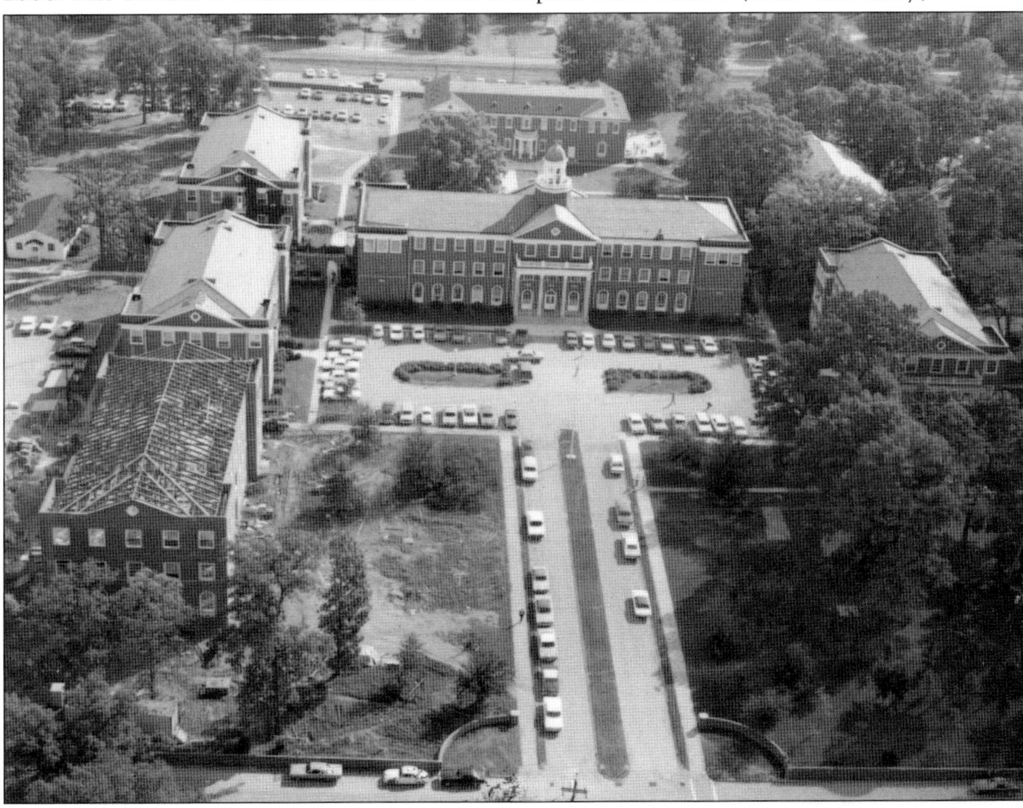

This aerial view shows the Alamance Building and its surroundings on the main campus of Elon College in 1969. The Duke Building at lower left was still under construction, and it was opened in 1970. The entrance to Alamance at this time was from Haggard Avenue. The Lebanon Avenue entrance was closed in 1965 when the Long Building was erected. (Elon University.)

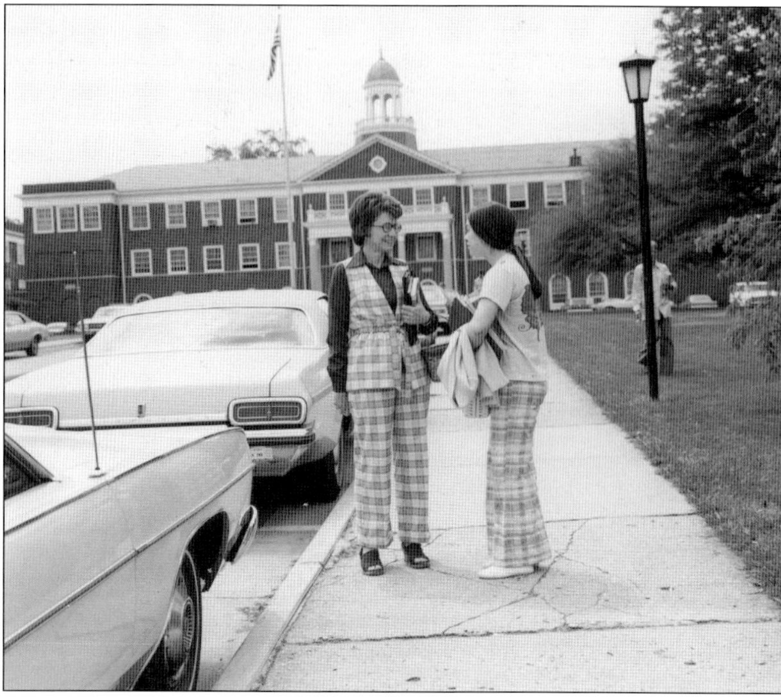

Alamance Building looks much the same in this photograph as it does today, but the fashion styles are certainly different. This image from about 1970 was made in the parking area in front of Alamance. The driveway from Haggard Avenue and a large parking lot covered the area where Scott Plaza and Fonville Fountain are today. (Elon University.)

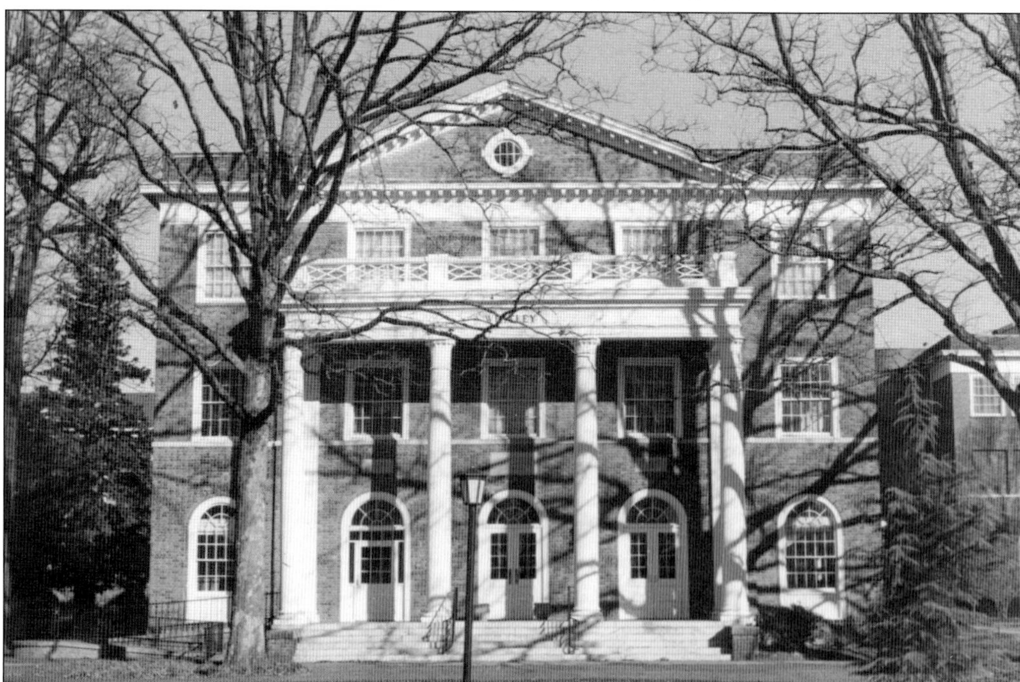

The cornerstone was laid for Whitley Auditorium May 23, 1923, as part of Elon College's recovery from the destruction of the administration building in the January fire that year. Whitley provided a large auditorium that would permit concerts, dramatic presentations, and church services in years to come. The facility had a total renovation in the late 1990s. It is named for Rev. Leonard Whitley of Virginia. (Elon University.)

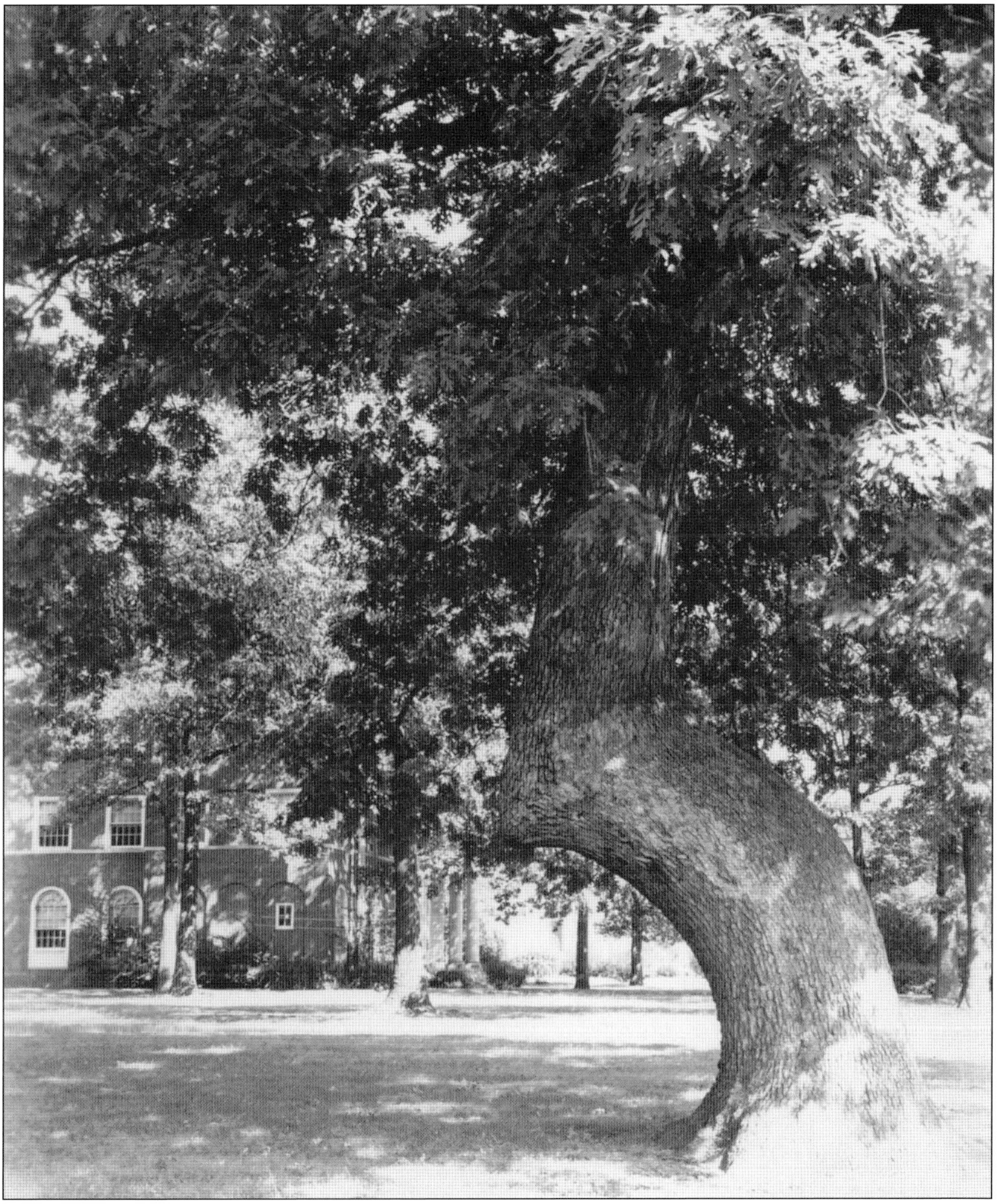

The oak tree has been a part of the Elon College history from its beginning. The oak gave the college its name, as *elon* is the Hebrew word for oak and the site chosen for the college was covered in beautiful oak trees. This oddly shaped oak tree was on campus when the college was founded. While most poorly shaped trees were removed for construction, workers left this one because it was so different. In 1913, seniors planted ivy around it as a class gift. At that time, it became known as the Senior Oak, even though the ivy did not live. Damaged by lightning in 1980, the tree was removed in 1981. For many years, Elon graduations were held "under the oaks" in front of West Dormitory, and it is now tradition that graduating seniors receive along with their diplomas a small potted oak seedling that they can plant at a location of their choice, taking a bit of Elon University with them. (Elon University.)

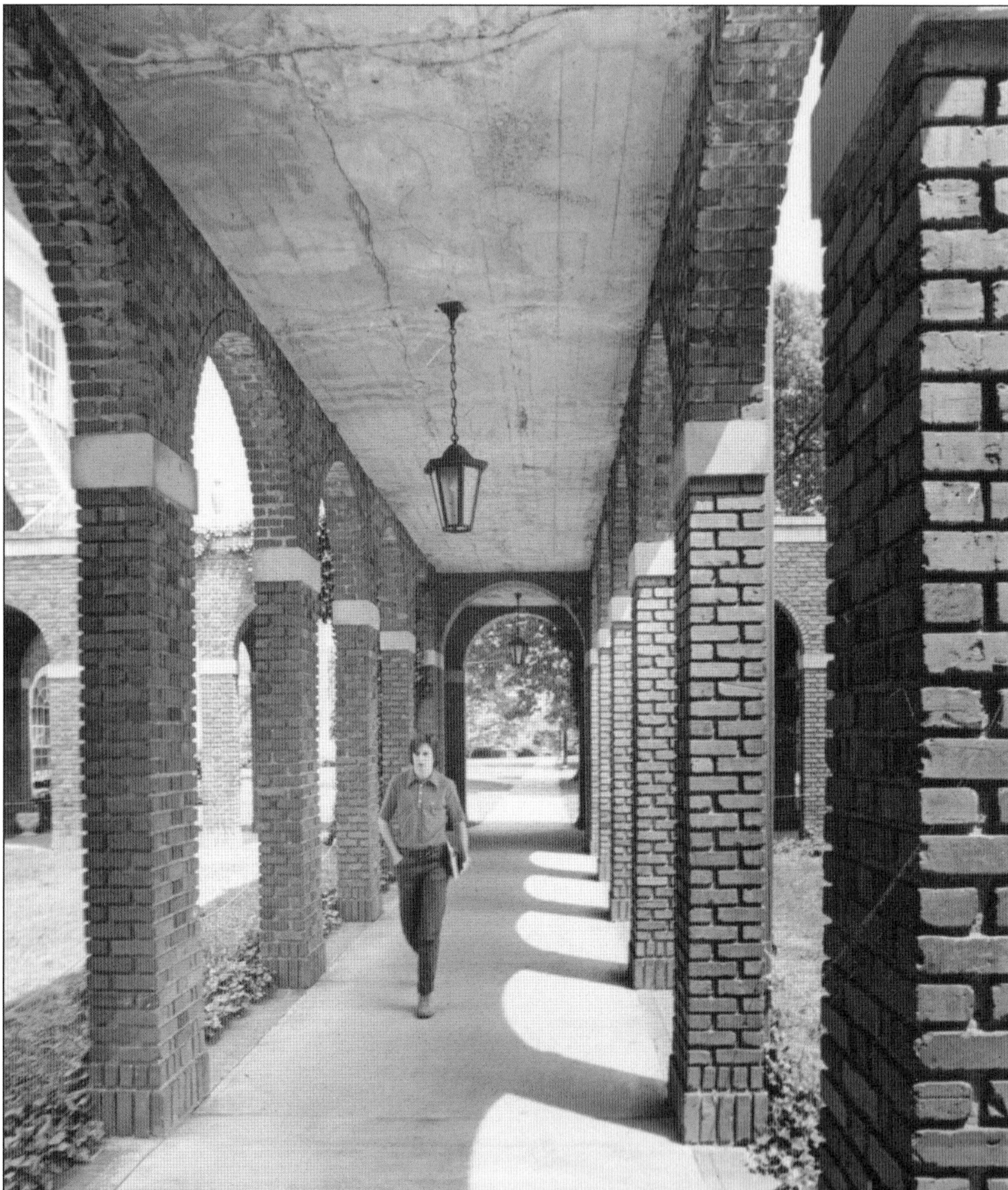

Colonnades seem to be a traditional part of college campuses, and that certainly has been true on the Elon University campus over the years. Colonnades are covered walkways lined with support columns, or, as the dictionary explains, "a roof supported by a row of columns." This photograph shows the older campus adjacent to Alamance Building, dating back to the early years of the school. The passing years brought new buildings, but they were erected to reflect the style of earlier buildings, and there are many areas in which colonnades are used. There is an entire dorm complex named Colonnades with the Colonnades Dining Hall. Belk Library has a beautiful covered walkway, as does the Ernest A. Koury Business Center. There are colonnades on each end of the new Inman Admissions Center and along the side of Alumni Gym. Colonnades also has had another meaning in the history of the school, as the word is the title of the university literary magazine first published in 1937. (Elon University.)

George Wooten was a star for the Elon College football team and is in the school's athletic Hall of Fame. In 1960, playing Catawba College with time for one play left, Elon trailed by two points and Catawba had the ball. Rather than killing time, Catawba tried a field goal. It was wide, and Wooten caught the failed kick and took the ball 108 yards to win the game as time ran out. (Elon University.)

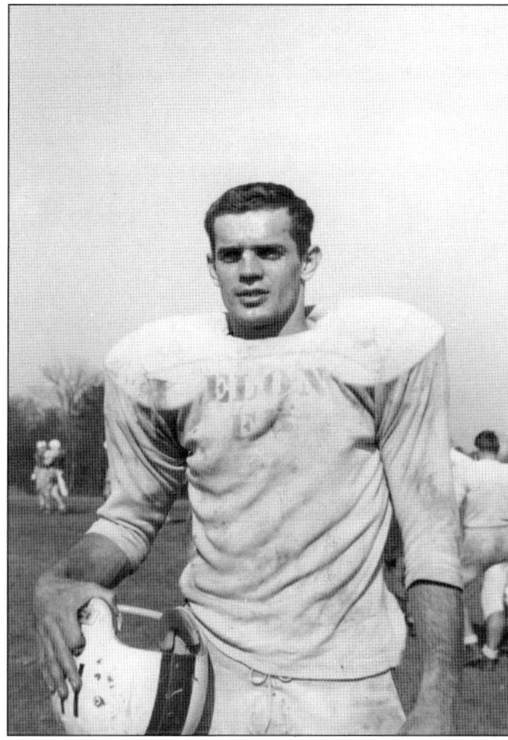

Virginia Hall was completed in 1956, as was Carolina Hall, adding badly needed residence locations to the campus. This is a room in Virginia Hall in the 1960s and, in contrast to many dorm rooms, there are no banners, no pictures, and in fact quite sparse decorations. In years that followed, more housing was added as facilities were converted to meet the growing enrollment in that period. (Elon University.)

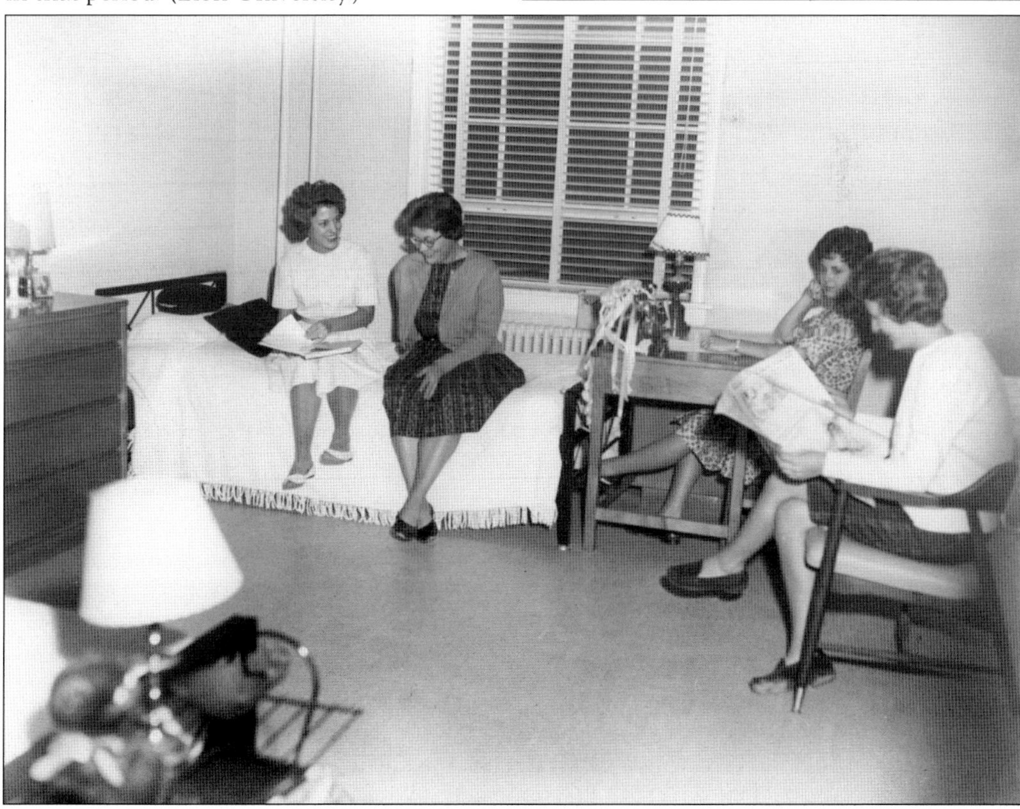

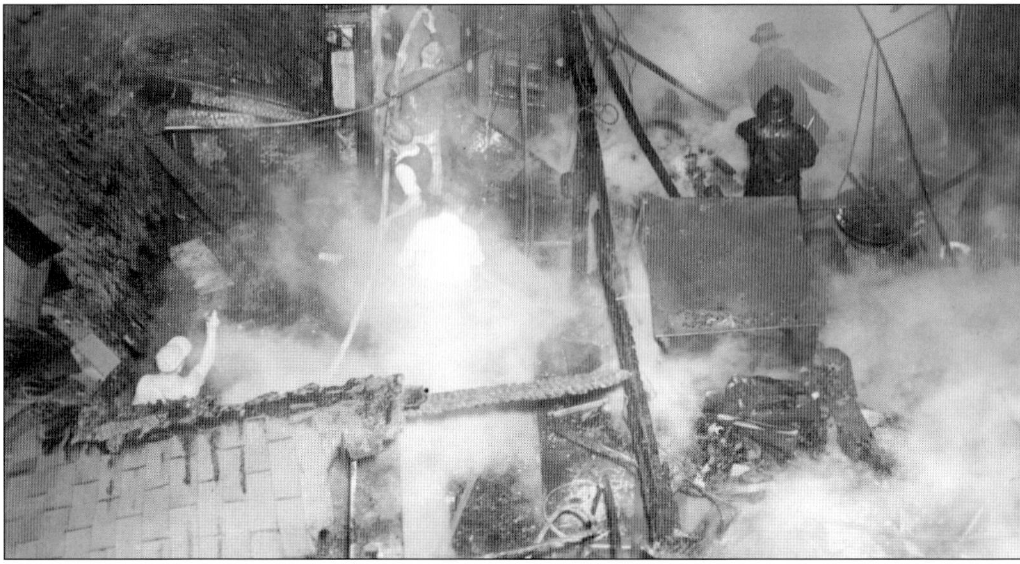

East Dormitory was opened in December 1890 and continued to house students for almost seven decades. On the night of July 4, 1966, fire swept through the building and left it in such shape that it could not be restored. It was demolished, closing one of the longest chapters in the history of the school. (Elon University.)

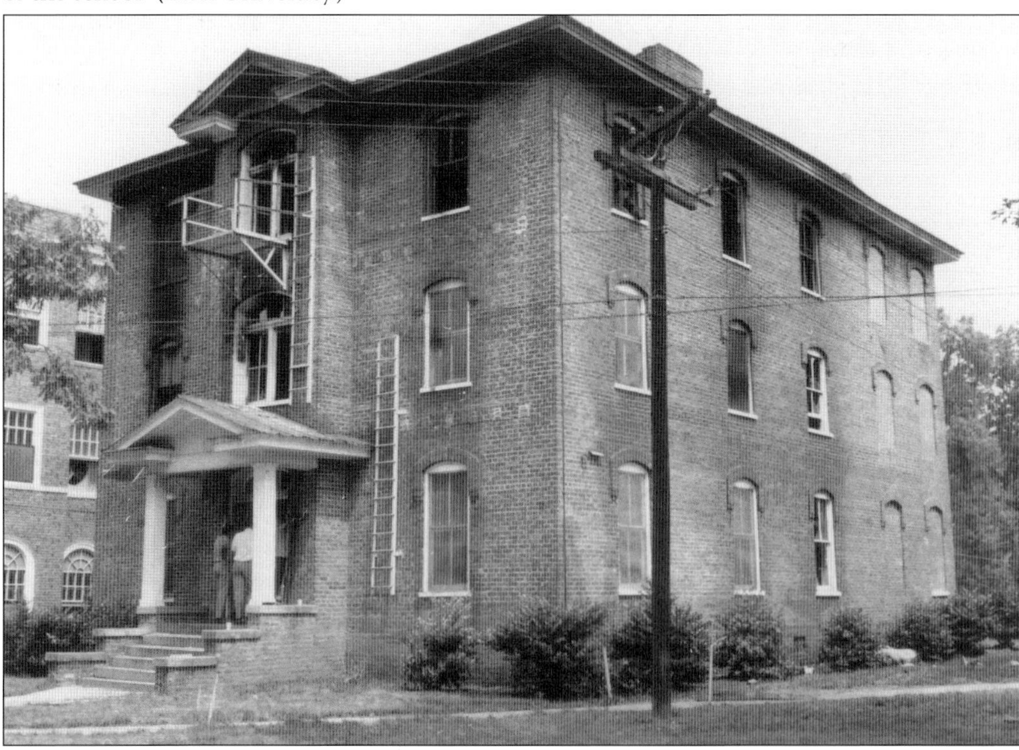

After the 1966 fire, East Dormitory was nothing more than a shell. While the walls were still intact and it looked as if it could be restored, inspectors found that the interior damage was so bad that the building could never be used again. This was one of several fires that occurred at Elon College, the worst being in 1923 when the administration building was destroyed. (Elon University.)

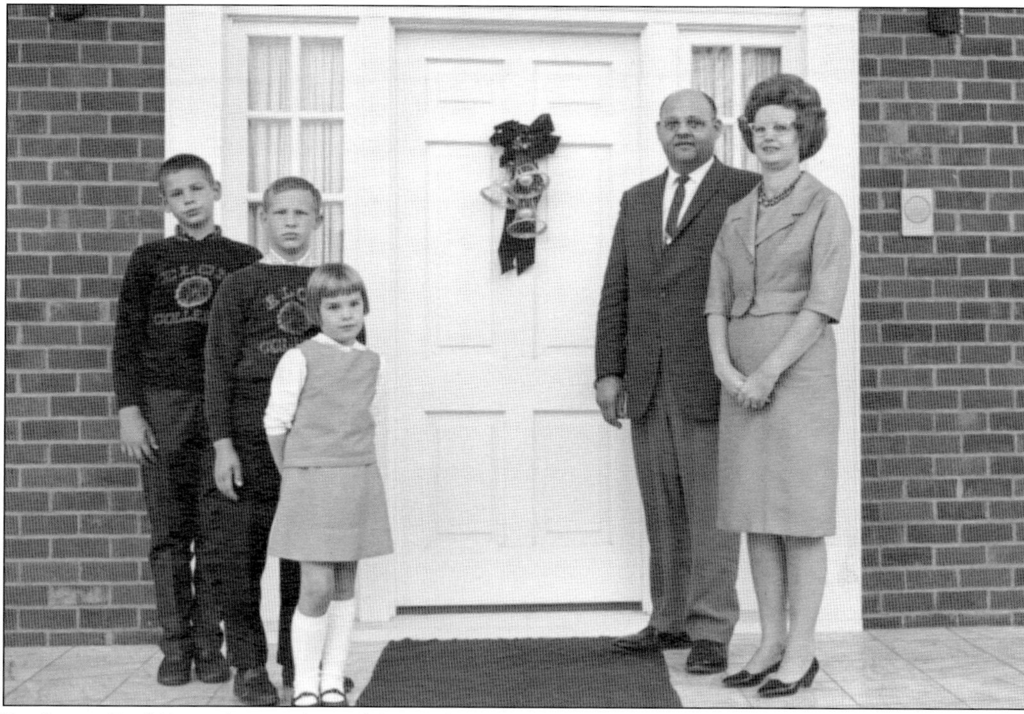

Dr. James Earl Danieley graduated from Elon College in 1946 just a few miles from his Alamance County home and began teaching at the college that year. He later became dean and in 1957 became president. Here, his family is on the porch of Holland House, the new home for the president that was occupied in 1963. With Dr. and Mrs. Danieley are their children, Ned, Mark, and Jane. (Jane Shutt.)

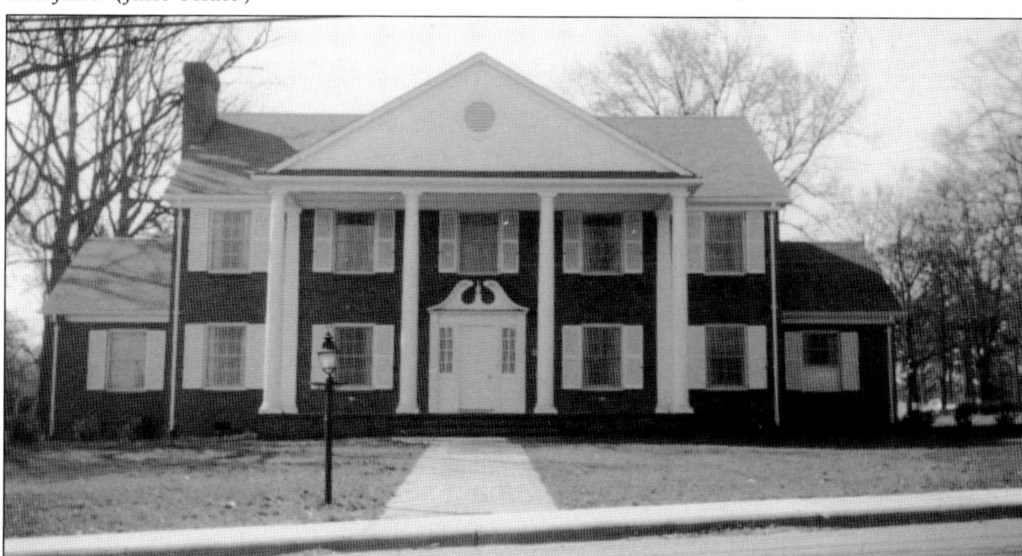

The Holland House was located on Haggard Avenue at the intersection with O'Kelly Avenue. Completed in 1963, it was named in 1985 to honor Shirley T. Holland, an Elon College trustee for 30 years. In 2009, it was moved to the south campus to serve as the Newman Center, home to Catholic Campus Ministries. (Elon University.)

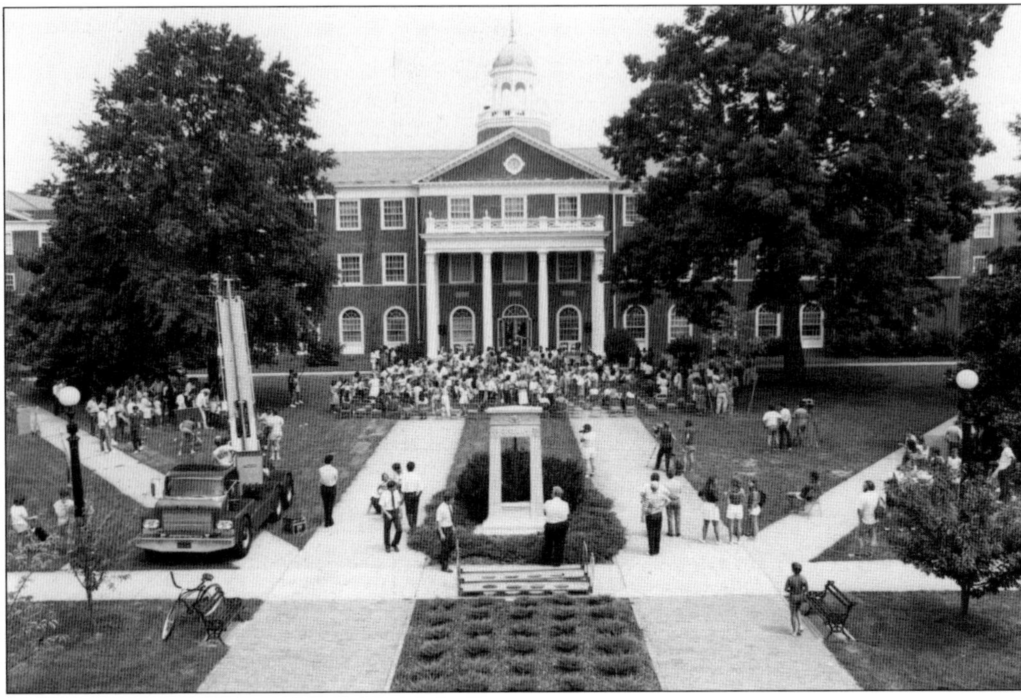

In this image from the 1970s, a large group of people has gathered on the steps of Alamance Building awaiting the appearance of a speaker. The speaker is not identified, but a number of photographers are on hand to record the event. This photograph was made from the Long Building and shows the James O'Kelly monument honoring the founder of the Christian Church and gives a good view of the area. (Elon University.)

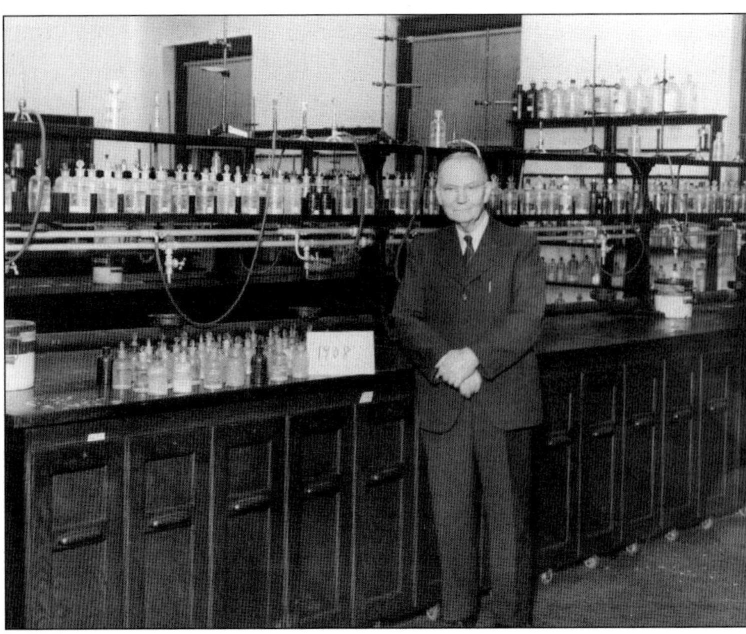

Prof. Ned Brannock graduated from Elon College in 1899 and returned there in 1908 to teach chemistry. He continued to teach until his retirement in 1955. Brannock also studied at Columbia University and Johns Hopkins University. A dormitory was named in his honor some years ago. He was a native of Alamance County, and his daughter Edith also taught at Elon, from 1962 to 1980. (Elon University.)

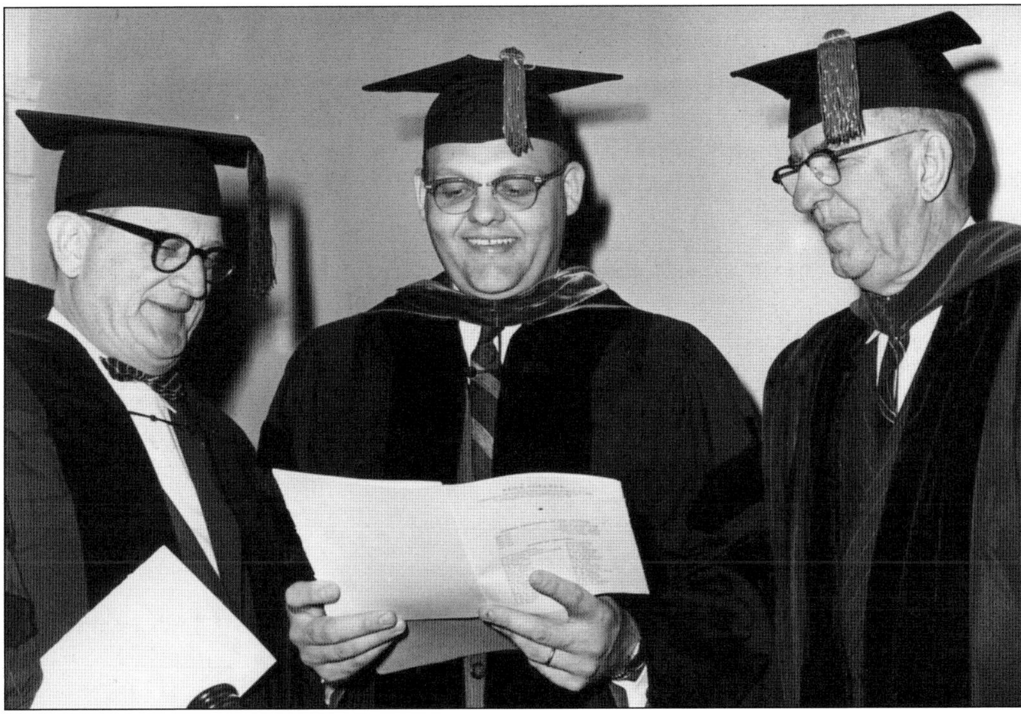

These Elon College leaders gathered for an event in 1958, a year after Dr. Earl Danieley, center, had become president. At left is Thad Eure, longtime chairman of the board of trustees, and at right is Dr. Leon Edgar Smith, who had retired a year earlier as president after having served since 1931 during some of the most critical times in the history of the school. (Elon University.)

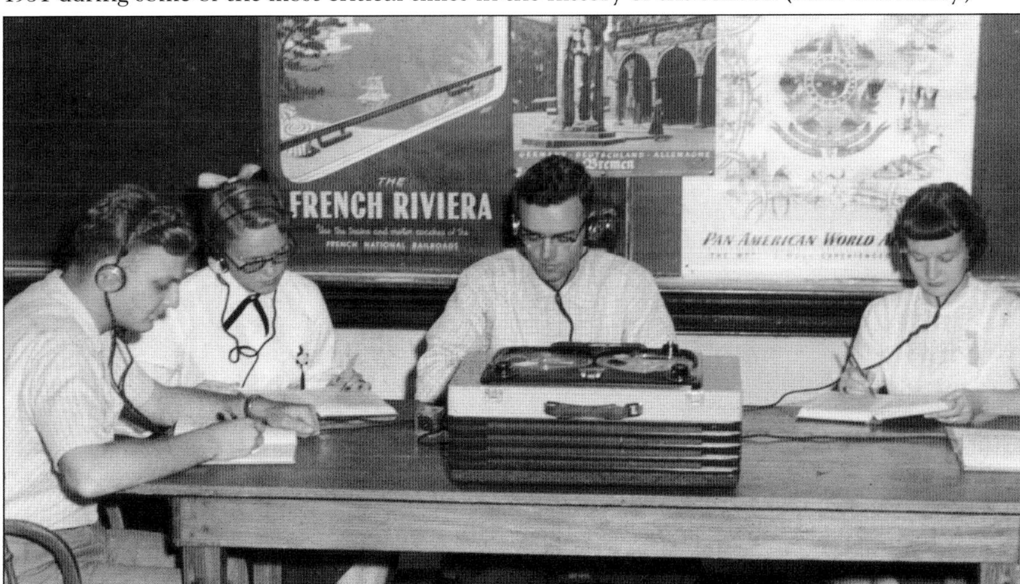

Carlton Hall was built in the 1920s and for many years housed the library. When McEwen Library opened in 1968, the art and music departments were able to use the Carlton space for expansion with art classes, a band room, and faculty offices. This picture from the 1970s shows students working in foreign languages in Carlton, which is adjacent to Alamance Building. (Elon University.)

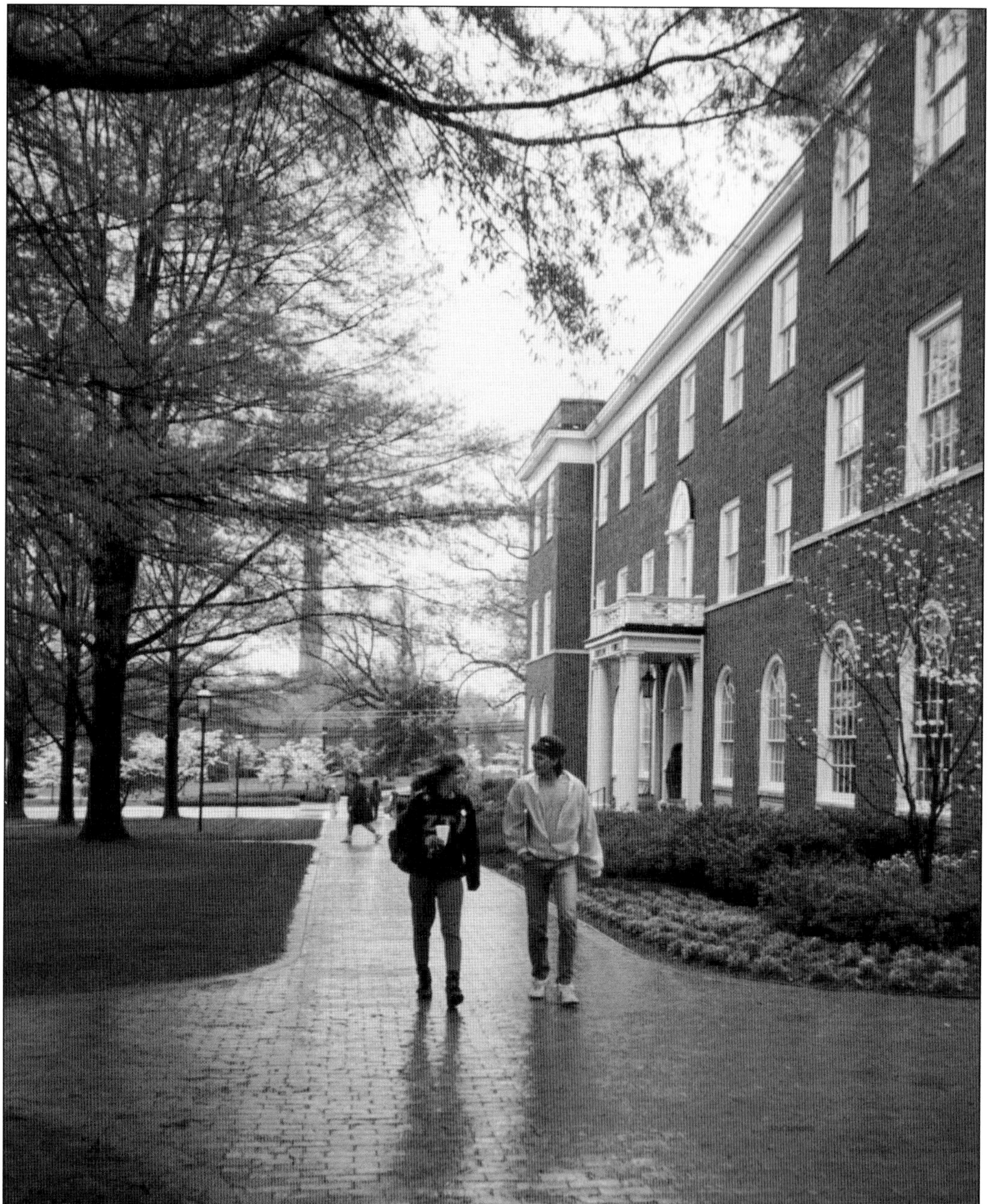

Students are walking in the rain past the Powell Building in the 1970s. The building was originally known as the Classroom Office Building and is located overlooking today's Scott Plaza and Fonville Fountain. In 1978, nephews of Caroline E. Powell, secretary of Carolina Biological Supply Co., made a donation to name the building in her honor to retire the building's debt. Thomas E. Powell III, Joseph E. Powell, Samuel C. Powell, James B. Powell, and John S. Powell joined to make the gift and honor their aunt. Caroline Powell had been a schoolteacher when she came to Burlington to help her brother at the company he had founded in 1927 while he was teaching at the college. The Powell Building continues as a classroom-office building, with the offices of the university president on the first floor. (Elon University.)

This beautiful home sat for many years at the corner of Holt Avenue and West College Avenue. At one time, it was the home of Pearl McDonald, a French teacher at Elon College, and at yet another time it was called the Faculty House, where several faculty members resided. In its last years, it was owned by Andy Meredith.

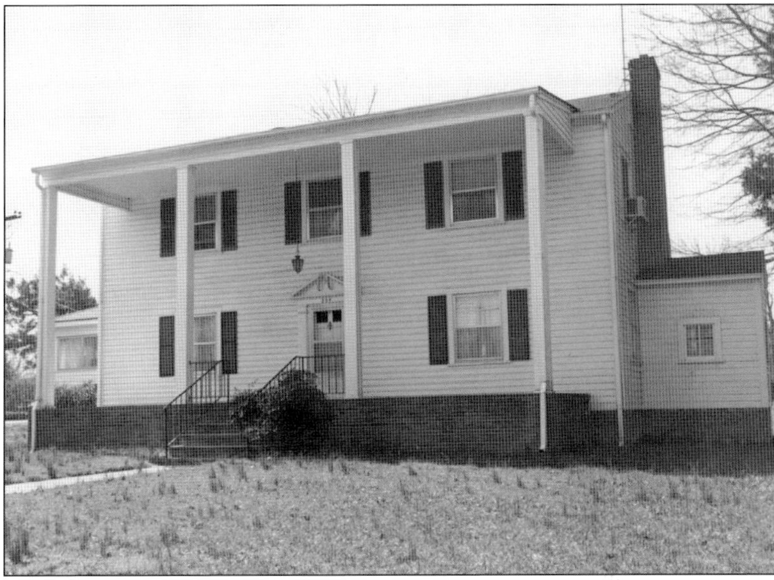

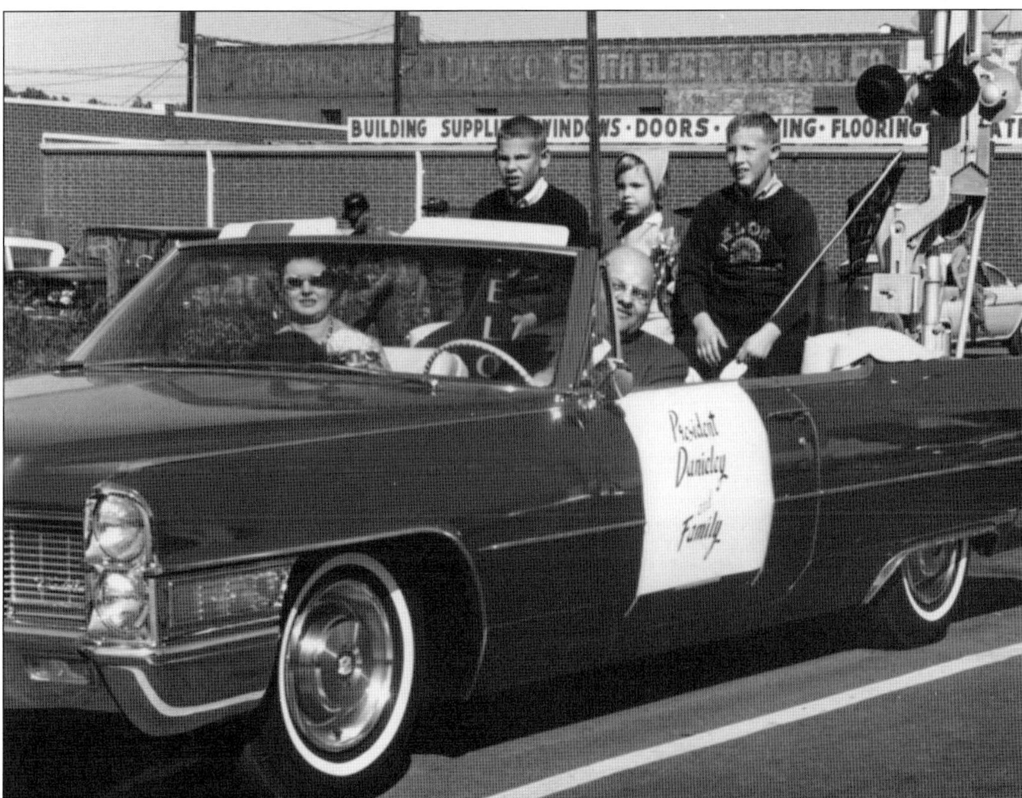

When he became president of Elon College, Dr. J. Earl Danieley did many things to promote the work of the school—including driving his family in the Christmas parade in Burlington. Dr. Danieley, his wife, Verona, and children Ned, Mark, and Jane appeared in the parade in the 1960s to welcome another Christmas season. (Elon University.)

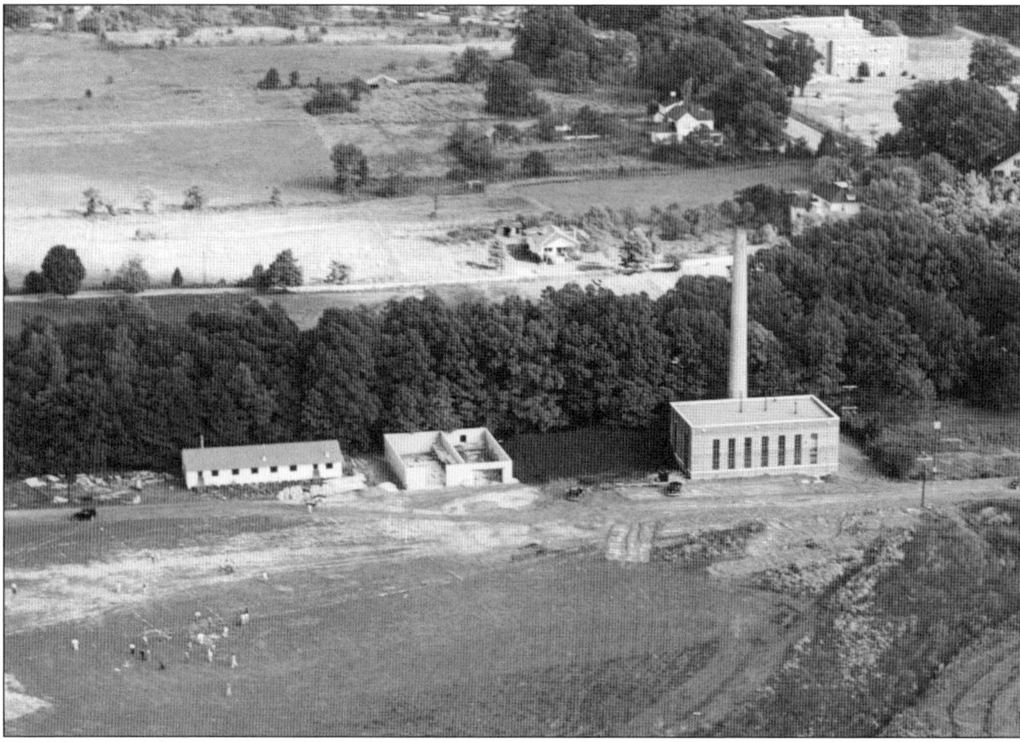

This power plant served the Elon College community for half a century after its construction in 1948. It was the second power plant in use, and it was located where Belk Library is today. East Haggard Avenue runs in the far right side of the photograph, and the Elon College Public School is visible in the upper corner. (Elon University.)

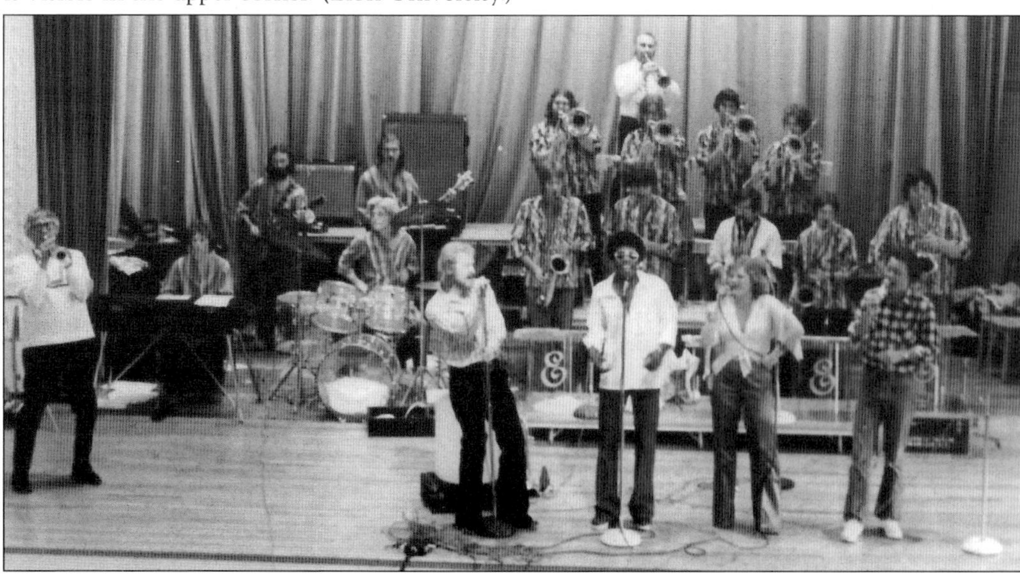

Prof. Jack White was the Elon College band director for a number of years, and in the 1960s he formed a jazz band among students that would perform in many parts of the nation and overseas as well. The ensemble became very popular and played at the New York World's Fair in 1964 and 1965, and every January did a tour in North Carolina and Virginia. (Elon University.)

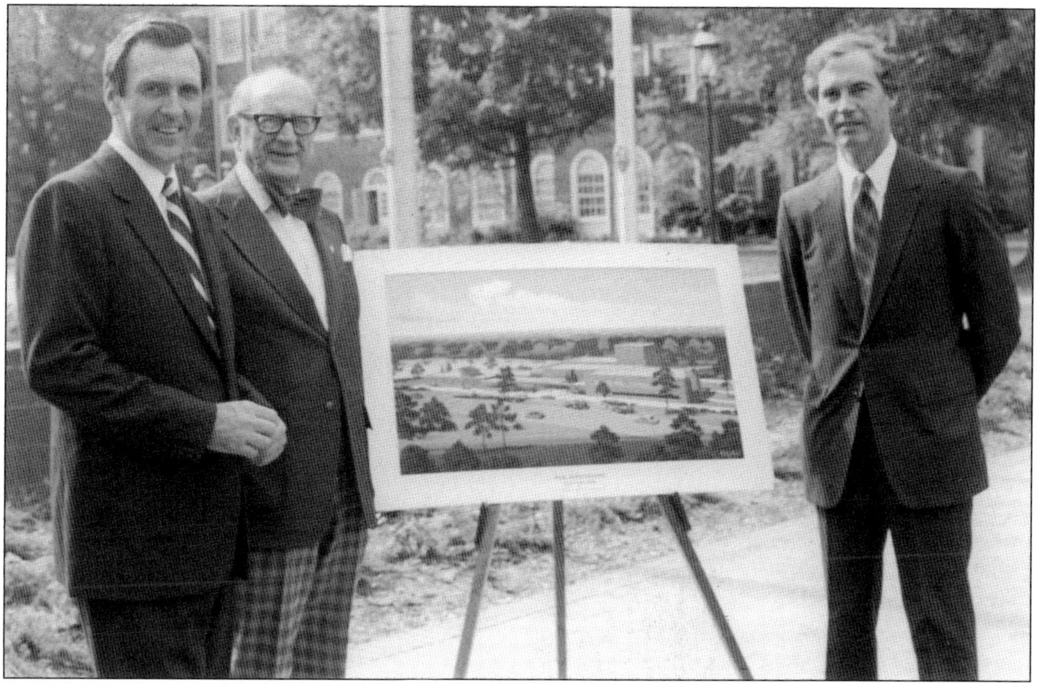

Dr. Fred Young, left, became Elon College president in 1973 and would serve for the next 25 years. Early in his tenure, he is seen here with Thad Eure, center, chairman of the board of trustees, and trustee Dr. James B. Powell, right, as they announce a program to add new facilities to the campus. (Elon University.)

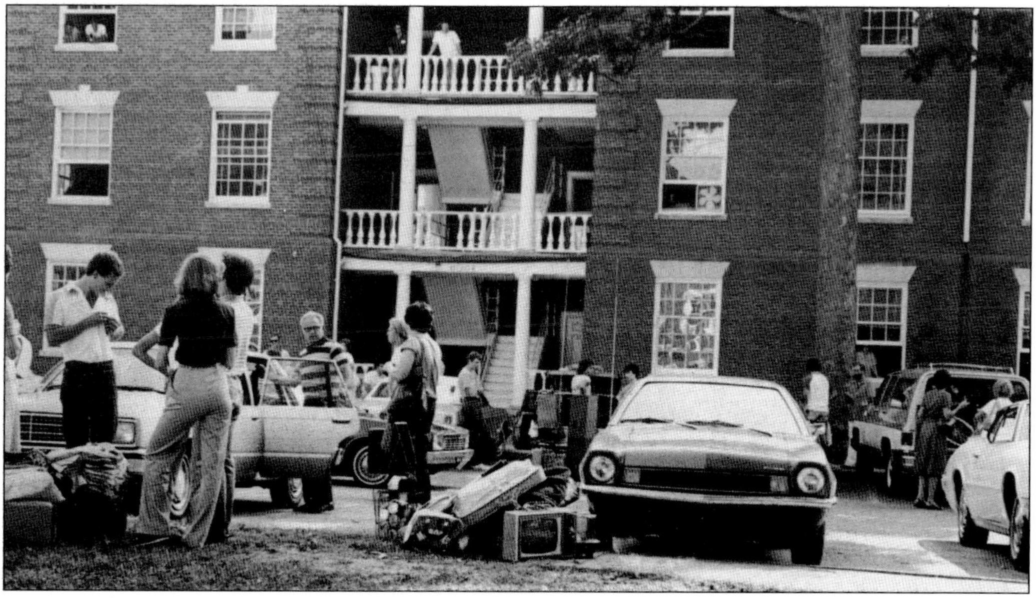

Move-in day is always exciting as a new academic year begins. Pictured in 1980, these students, moms and dads, and other family members are hauling things into the Hook, Brannock, and Barney residence community. The population of Elon grows by several thousand every August when the students return for a new year, and move-in is one of the heaviest traffic days of the year in town. (Elon University.)

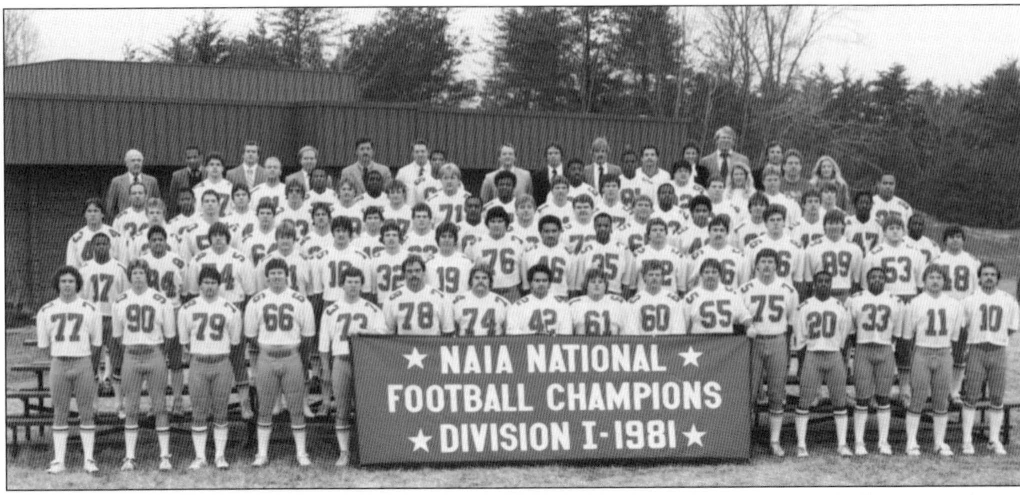

In 1981, the Elon College football team won its second consecutive national championship in the NAIA division of competition. The team finished the 1981 regular season with an 8-1-1 record and then won two playoff games to qualify for the national championship game against Pittsburgh State at Burlington's Memorial Stadium. Elon won 3-0 on a field goal by Phil Renn. (Elon University.)

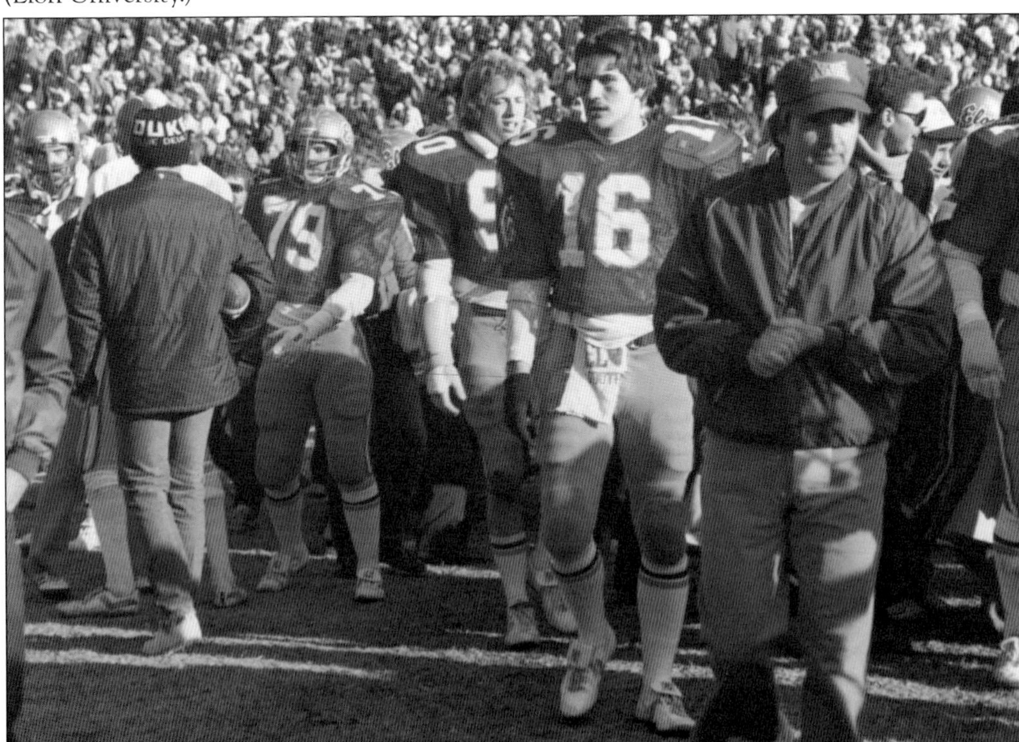

Coach Jerry Tolley is at right in the NAIA national championship game in 1981 where Elon won its second straight title. A year earlier, Elon defeated Northeastern Oklahoma 17-10 after a regular season with a 9-1 record. The team finished with a 13-1 record overall. The football team played in Burlington's stadium until 2001 when Rhodes Stadium was opened on the Elon campus. (Elon University.)

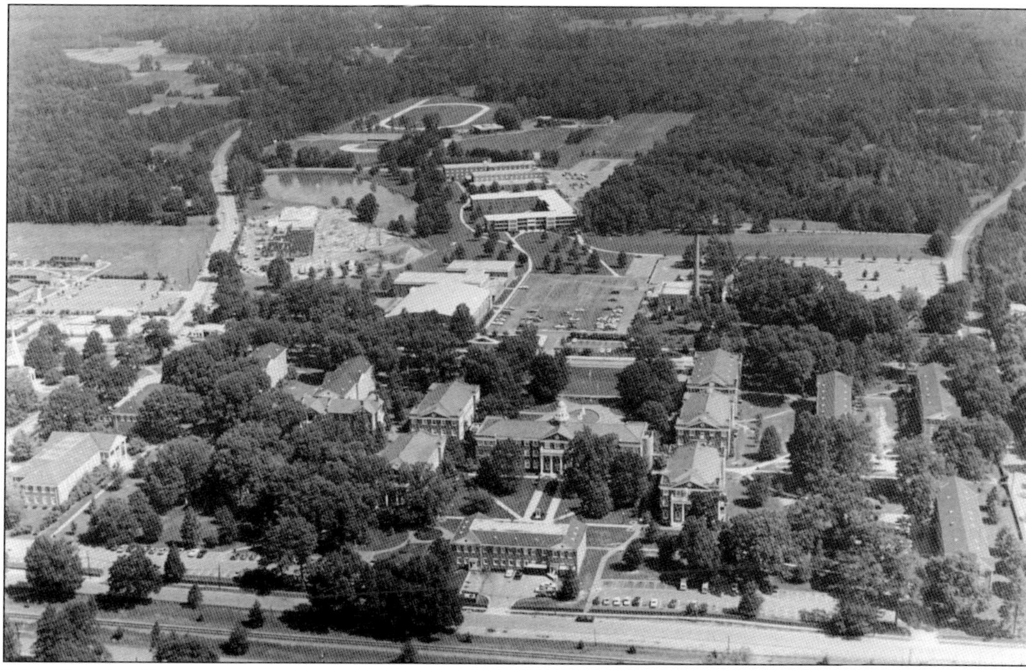

The Elon College campus is pictured in the 1980s. The railroad track is at the bottom of this view looking north. The area between Alumni Gym and the power plant is open, a location later to be filled by Moseley Center, Belk Library, and Young Commons. The area at far north is the site where Rhodes Stadium would be located in 2001. (Elon University.)

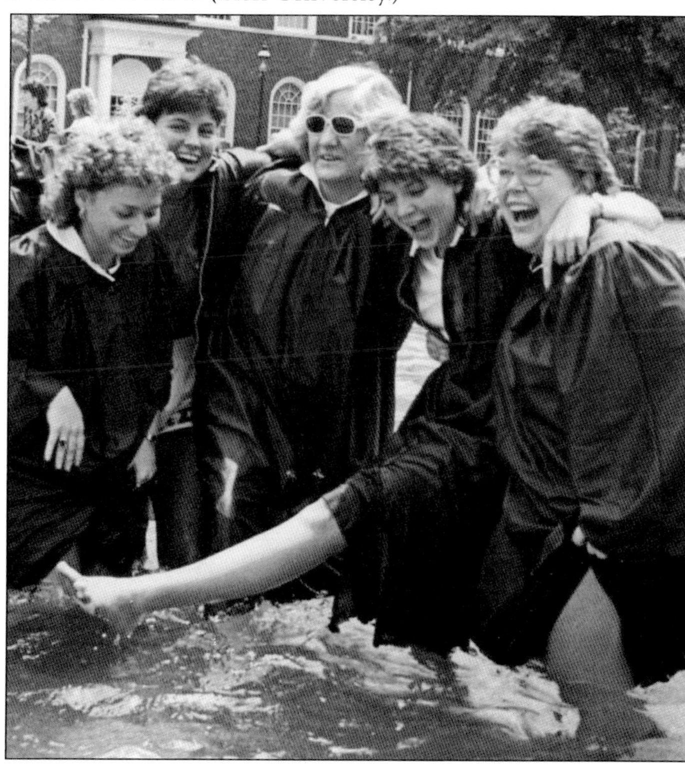

These unidentified girls in the 1980s found Fonville Fountain to be the perfect spot to share some graduation day fun with their friends. The fountain is in front of Alamance Building and is in Scott Plaza. Sen. Ralph Scott of Haw River funded the plaza in memory of his wife, and Rudy and Frances Fonville gave a donation to build the fountain. (*Burlington Times-News*.)

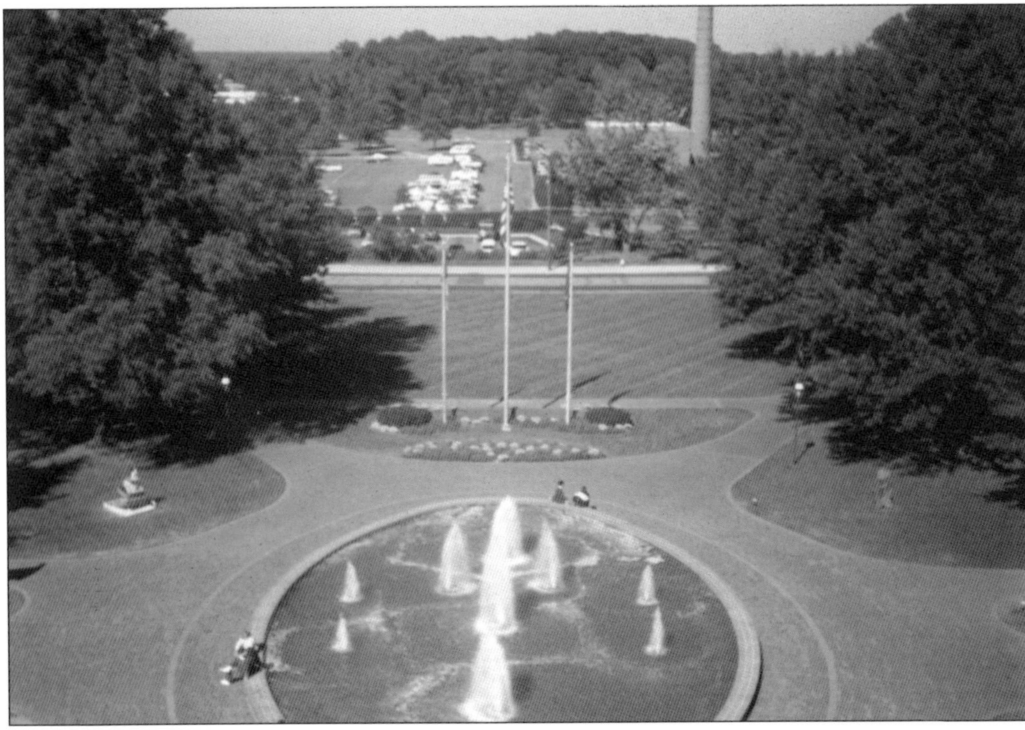

This view shows Fonville Fountain and Scott Plaza after they were finished in the mid-1980s. Note the area across Haggard Avenue. There is a parking lot between Alumni Gym on the left blocked by trees and the old power plant on the right side. In another few years, that would be a beautiful part of the campus including Belk Library and Young Commons with the Moseley Center at the far end. (Elon University.)

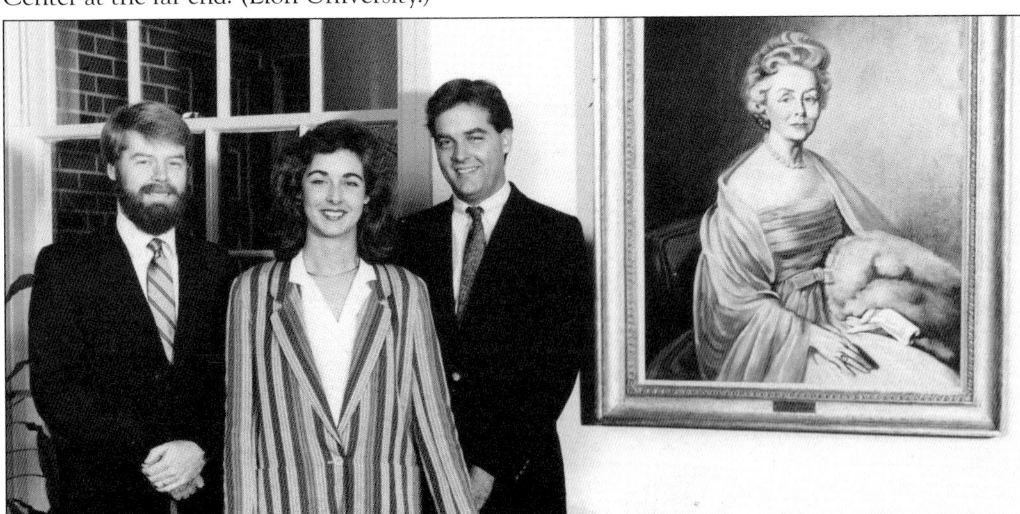

In 1985, three members of the Iris Holt McEwen family—Alex McCrary, Kate McCrary Johnson, and Mac McCrary—established the Iris H. McEwen Community Service Endowment to honor her contributions to the college. She made donations for the McEwen Dining Hall and McEwen Hall, which was built as the library but is now part of the School of Communications. (Dr. Jo Watts Williams.)

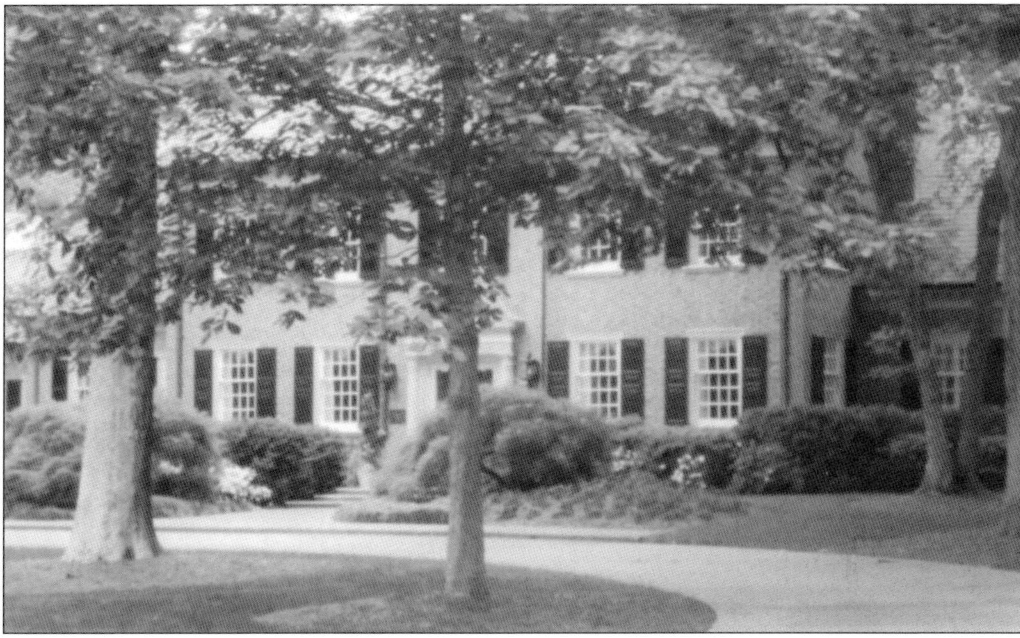

In 1988, Elon College received the home of Reid A. Maynard and Grace Maynard in Grace Maynard's will. It would be used for the Elon president's home. Reid Maynard was a trustee of the college from 1948 to 1983 and was a hosiery manufacturer and community leader in Burlington. Pres. Fred Young and his wife, Phyllis, moved there in 1990, and Holland House was used for alumni and development.

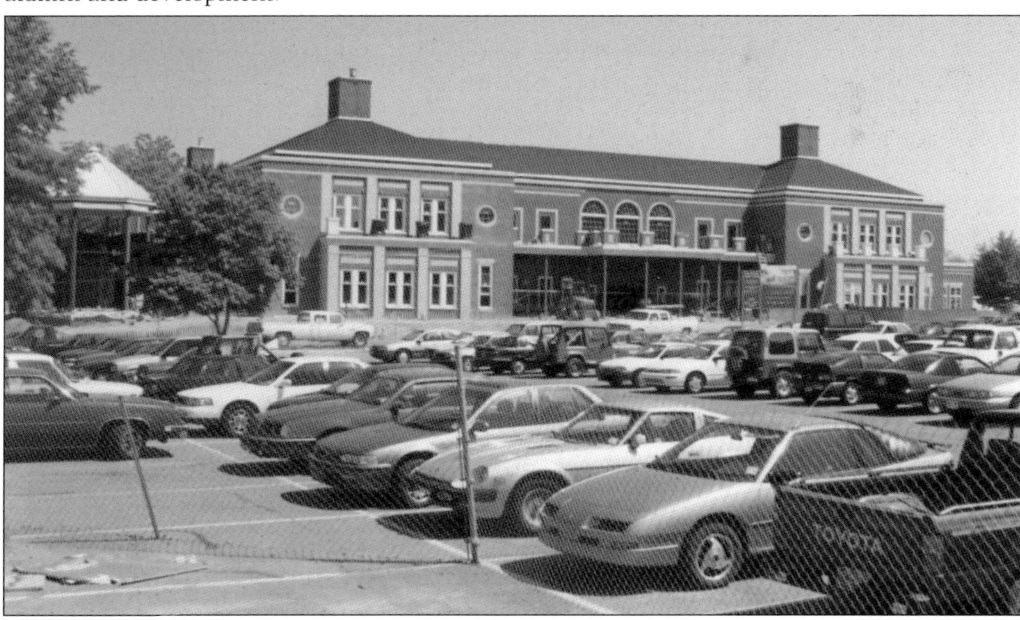

On April 28, 1995, former British prime minister Margaret Thatcher came to Elon College to dedicate the Moseley Center. Named for donors Furman and Susan Moseley, it had opened in December 1994. The building brought most student life operations under one roof. McKinnon Hall, honoring Bob McKinnon, seats 280 for dinners, and there is a full kitchen, a café, a patio, along with several other operations related to student life in the building. (Elon University.)

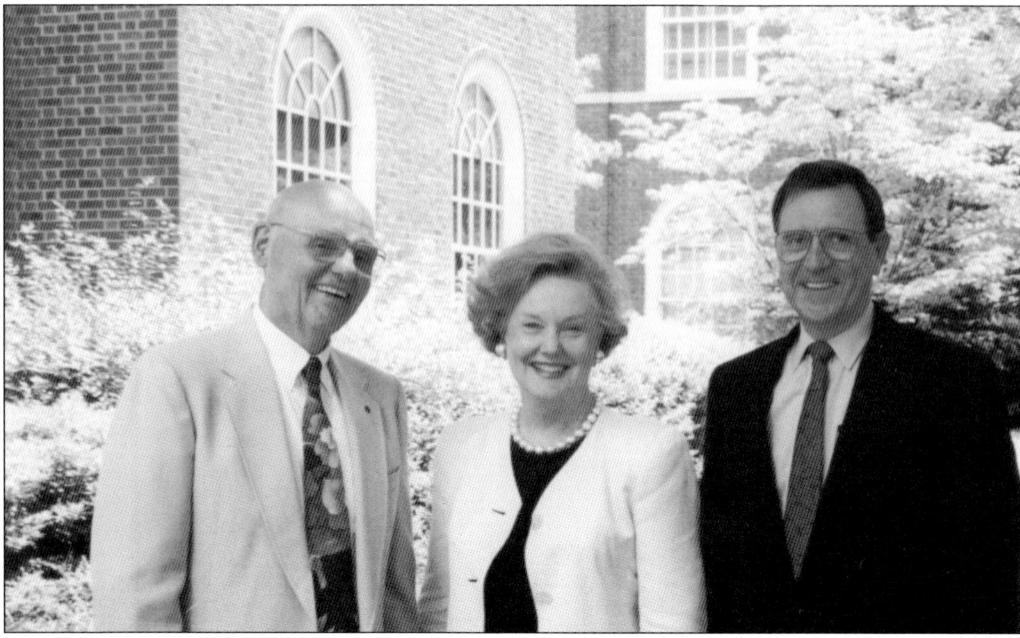

Dr. J. Earl Danieley, and Dr. Fred Young were both presidents of Elon, and Dr. Jo Watts Williams, a 1955 Elon graduate, served in special roles with both. She taught and then became associate dean. Williams later became vice president of development. She retired in 1995 but continued as special assistant to the president. She was named vice president emerita in 2010. (Elon University.)

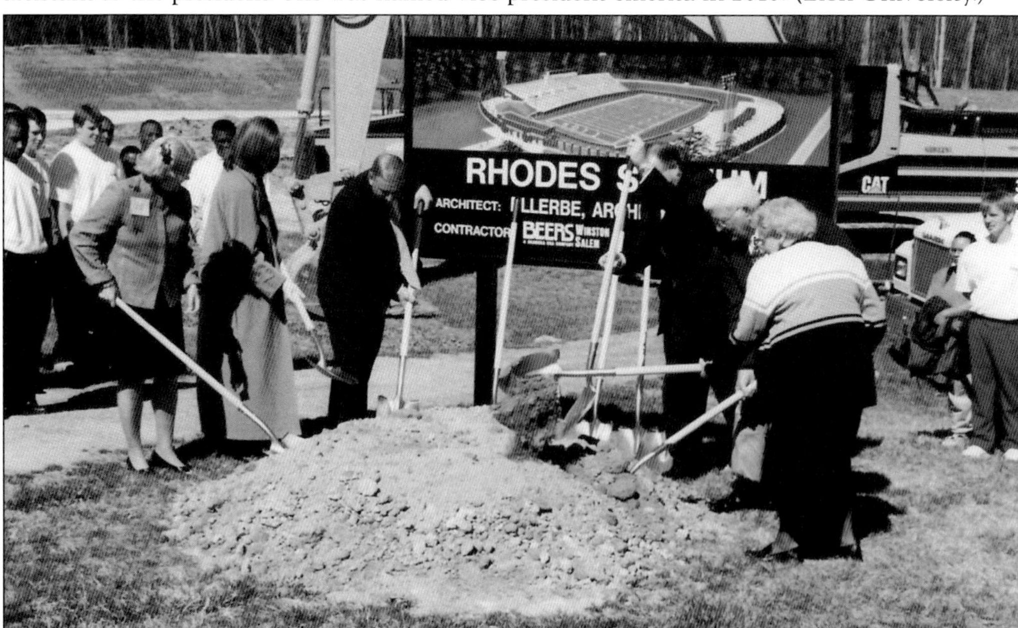

On March 14, 2000, ground was broken for the construction of a football stadium on the Elon campus. A gift from Dusty and Peggy Rhodes made the stadium a reality. Here, they are at right, with shovels, as they join university trustees and staff in beginning the construction process. For many years, Elon had played its home football games in Burlington's Memorial Stadium. (Elon University.)

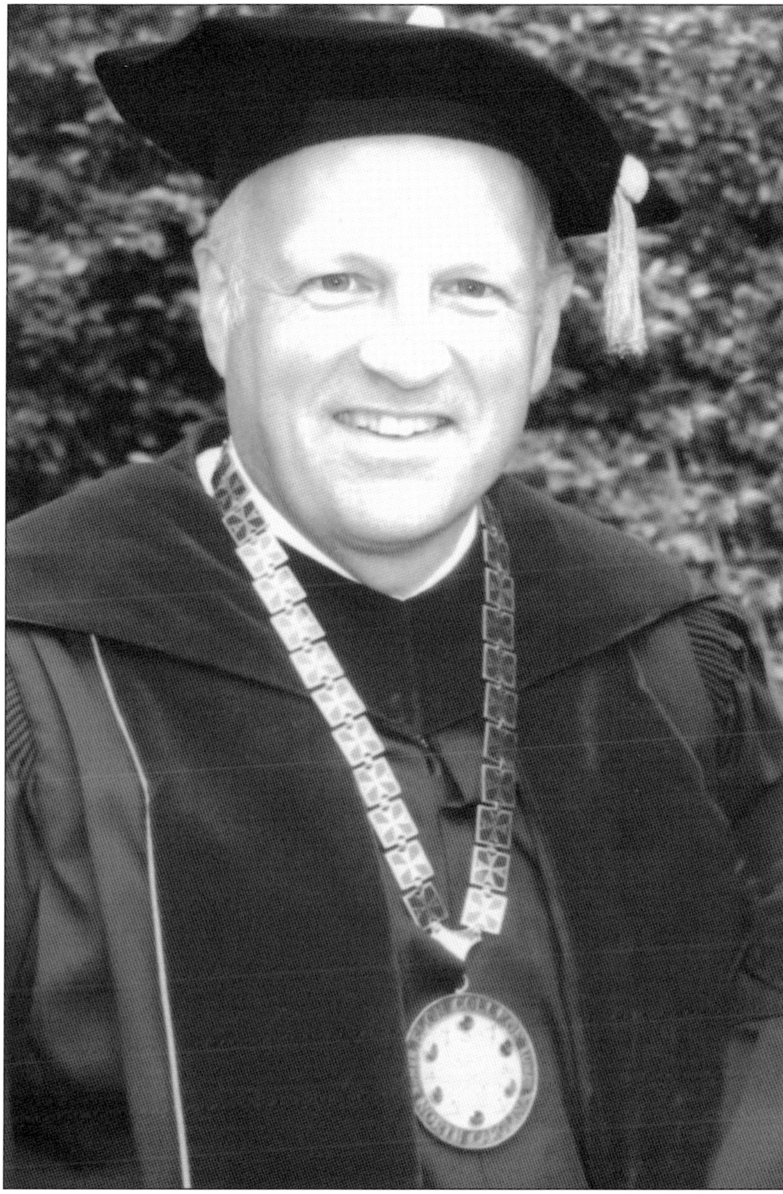

On January 1, 1999, Dr. Leo Lambert became the eighth president of Elon University. He came to Elon from the University of Wisconsin–LaCrosse. Lambert graduated from State University of New York at Genesco and earned his master's degree from the University of Vermont. He earned his doctorate from Syracuse University and then for the next 12 years worked at Syracuse as the associate dean of the graduate program. He was provost and vice chancellor for academic affairs at Wisconsin–LaCrosse. In 2001, Elon became a university, and Dr. Lambert led the school to new achievements in many different areas. Elon University has achieved a national reputation as one of the finest private universities in the United States and now attracts students from across the nation and from many foreign countries. Lambert is married to his high school sweetheart, Laurie Fordham. They have two daughters, Callie Lambert Brown and Mollie Lambert, and two grandchildren, Caleb and Anna Brown. Dr. Lambert announced in 2017 that he would retire in early 2018.

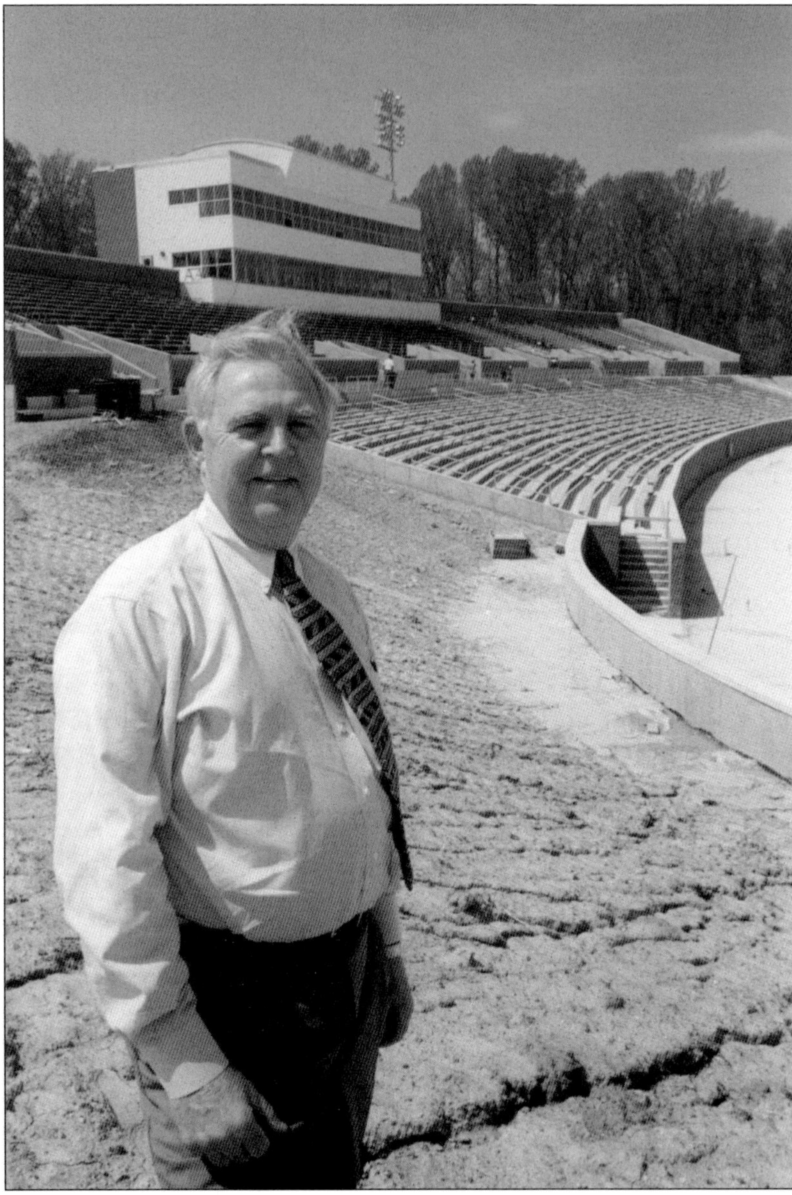

Dr. Alan White was athletic director at Elon College/University for 27 years, making him one of the longest-serving college athletic officials in the nation and one of the most respected. His association with Elon began in 1964 when he came as an assistant football coach. He moved to Mississippi State in 1967 but returned in 1974. White became athletic director in 1979. During his tenure, Elon moved from the NAIA to the NCAA and moved to the Southern Conference. Elon won 53 conference championships, 12 Conference Excellence Awards, and four national championships. White was an All–Atlantic Coast Conference football star at Wake Forest University and is in that school's Hall of Fame as well as the North Carolina Sports Hall of Fame. After retirement, White was honored when the Rhodes Stadium bell tower was named for him through a gift from trustee Jeanne Robertson and husband, Jerry. White and wife, Norma Rose, still live in Burlington. They have one son, Kyle, and two grandsons, Tyler and Bryson. (Elon University.)

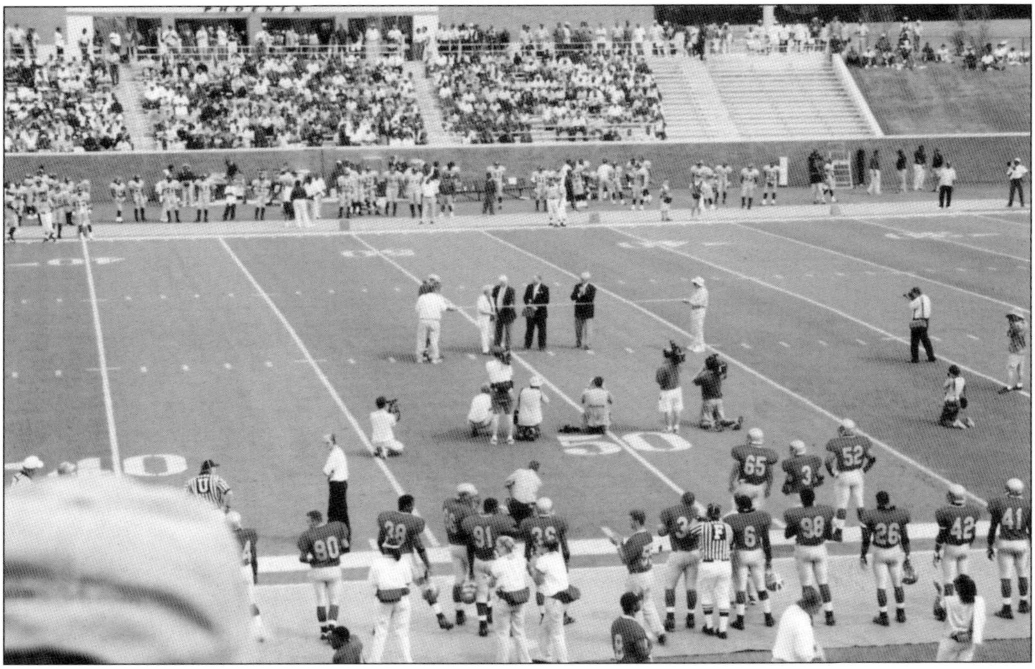

Rhodes Stadium opened on September 22, 2001. Dusty and Peggy Rhodes cut the ribbon with Dr. Leo Lambert and Dr. Alan White. The opening game was set for September 15, but the 9/11 attacks led to a postponement. Eastern Kentucky was en route here to play but turned back after the attack. North Carolina A&T then became the first opponent in the new stadium.

Elon University was in the limelight in a very prominent location on March 9, 2009. Dr. Leo Lambert and a number of Elon friends were invited to the New York Stock Exchange, and Lambert had the honor of ringing the bell closing stock trading for that day. Elon has a large group of alumni and friends in the New York City area. (Elon University.)

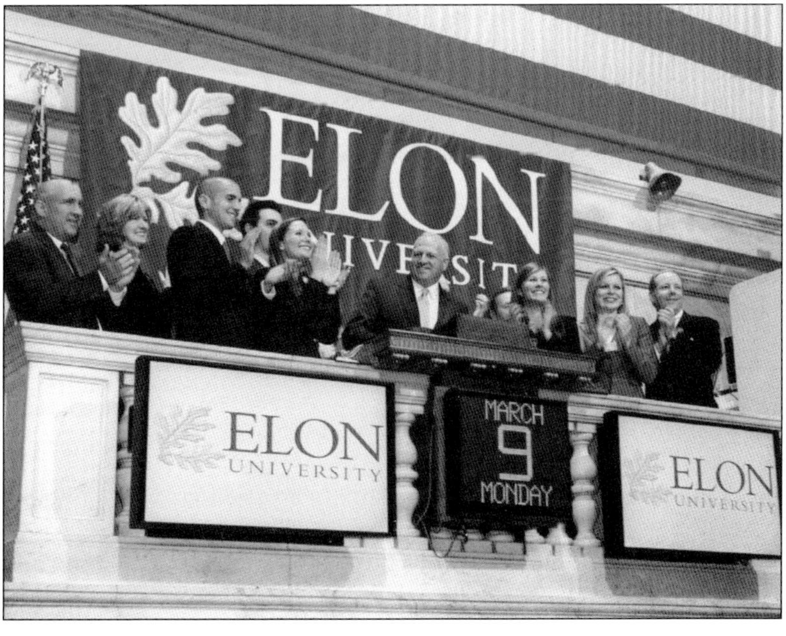

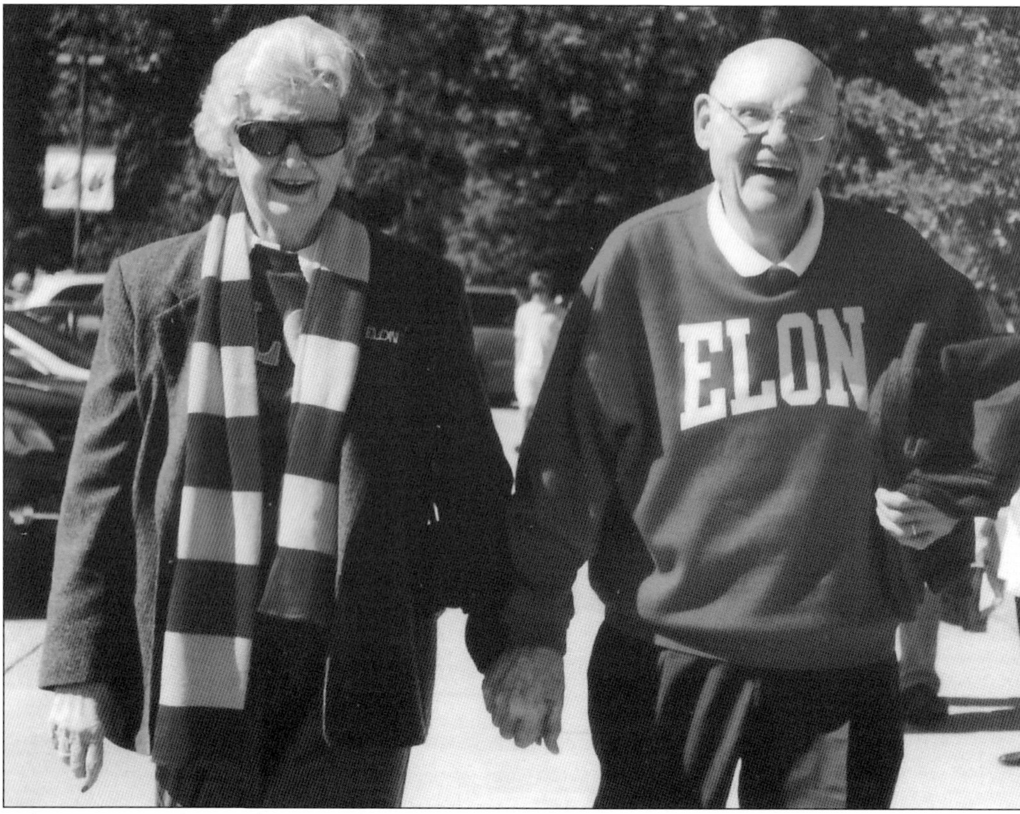

When Dr. J. Earl Danieley retired in 1973, he went back to teaching, but he also took the title president emeritus. In that role, he supported the school in every way possible, especially in athletics. Danieley's was a most familiar face at sporting events of every type as long as his health allowed. Here, he and his wife, Verona, arrive for a football game at Rhodes Stadium in 2010. (Elon University.)

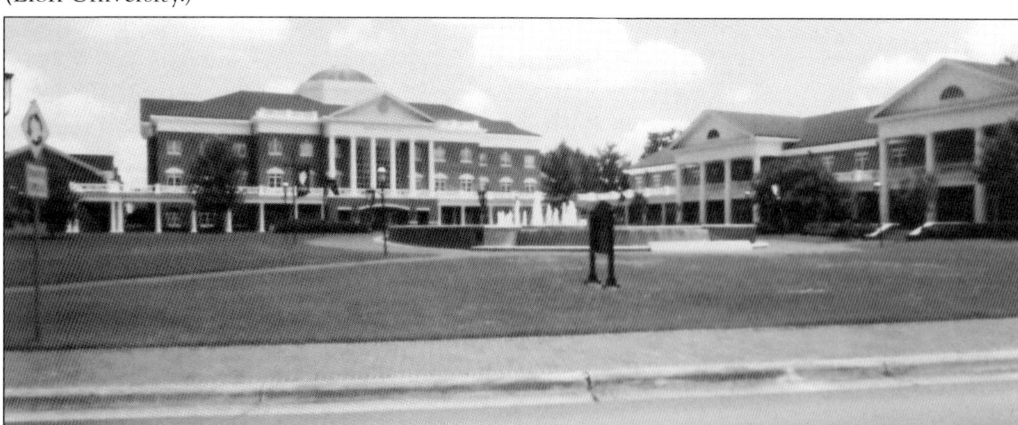

Year after year, the Elon University campus is named one of the most beautiful campuses in the nation. A look at the Ernest A. Koury Business Center and the Wallace Chandler Fountain and Plaza and surrounding complex provides a reason why that recognition is given. The beauty of a campus is not the only reason to choose it for an education, but many feel it is a good starting place.

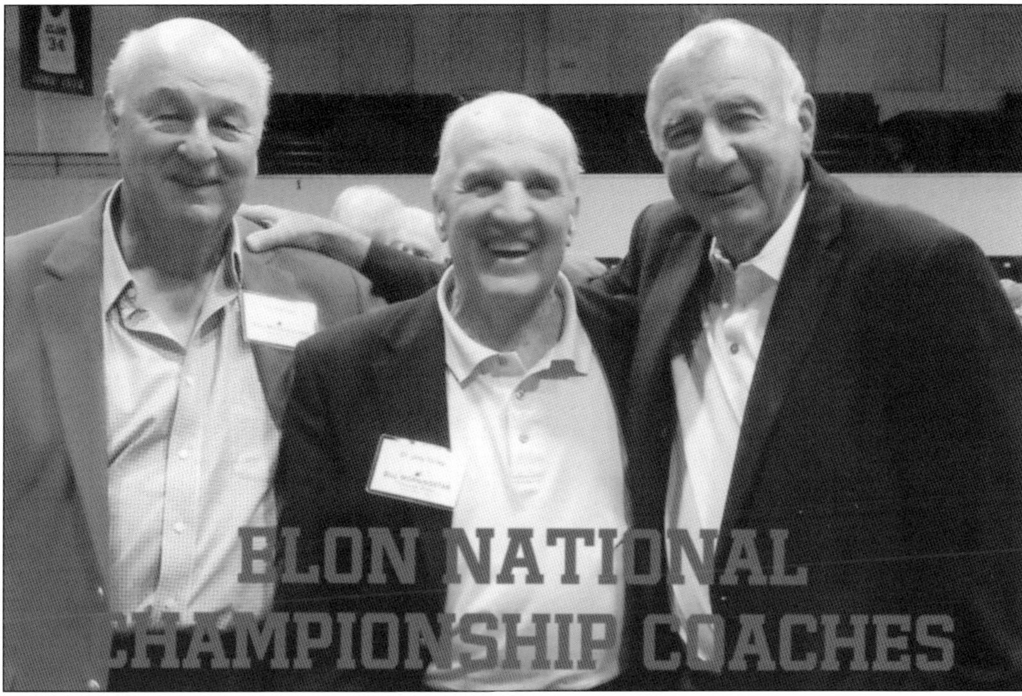

Elon University athletic teams have won four national championships since 1980. These three coaches directed the teams that won those titles. Tom Parham (left) coached the tennis team, NAIA national champions in 1990. Jerry Tolley (center) coached football, NAIA national champions in 1980–1981. Bill Morningstar coached golf, NAIA national champions in 1982. This photograph was taken in 2013. (Elon University.)

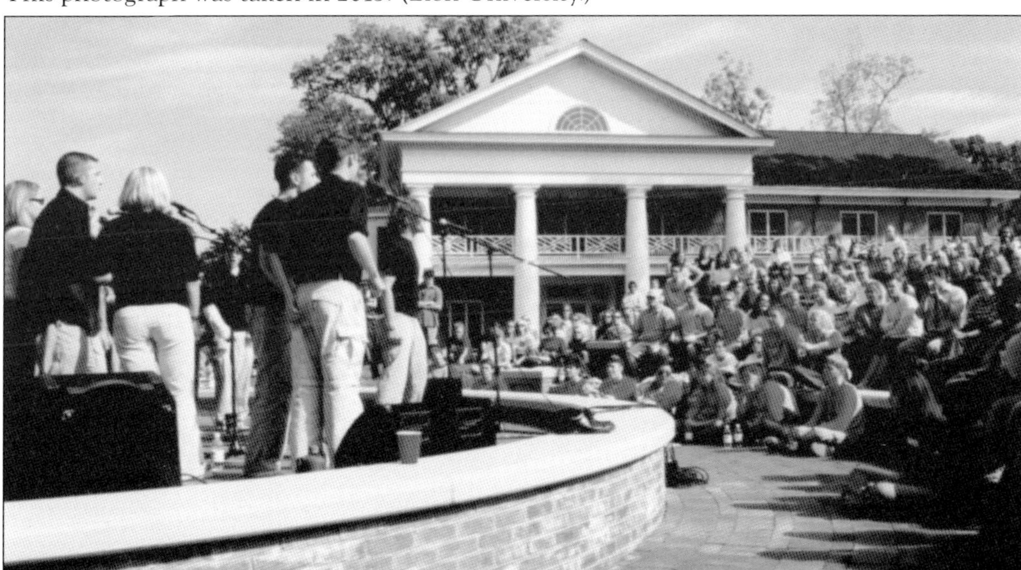

The first units of the Academic Village opened in 2002 to accommodate various parts of Elon College, the College of Arts and Sciences. The pavilions have classrooms on the first floor, and on the second floor are student rooms and a faculty apartment. The village extends from Lebanon Avenue to Haggard, where the new Phi Beta Kappa Commons is located. (Elon University.)

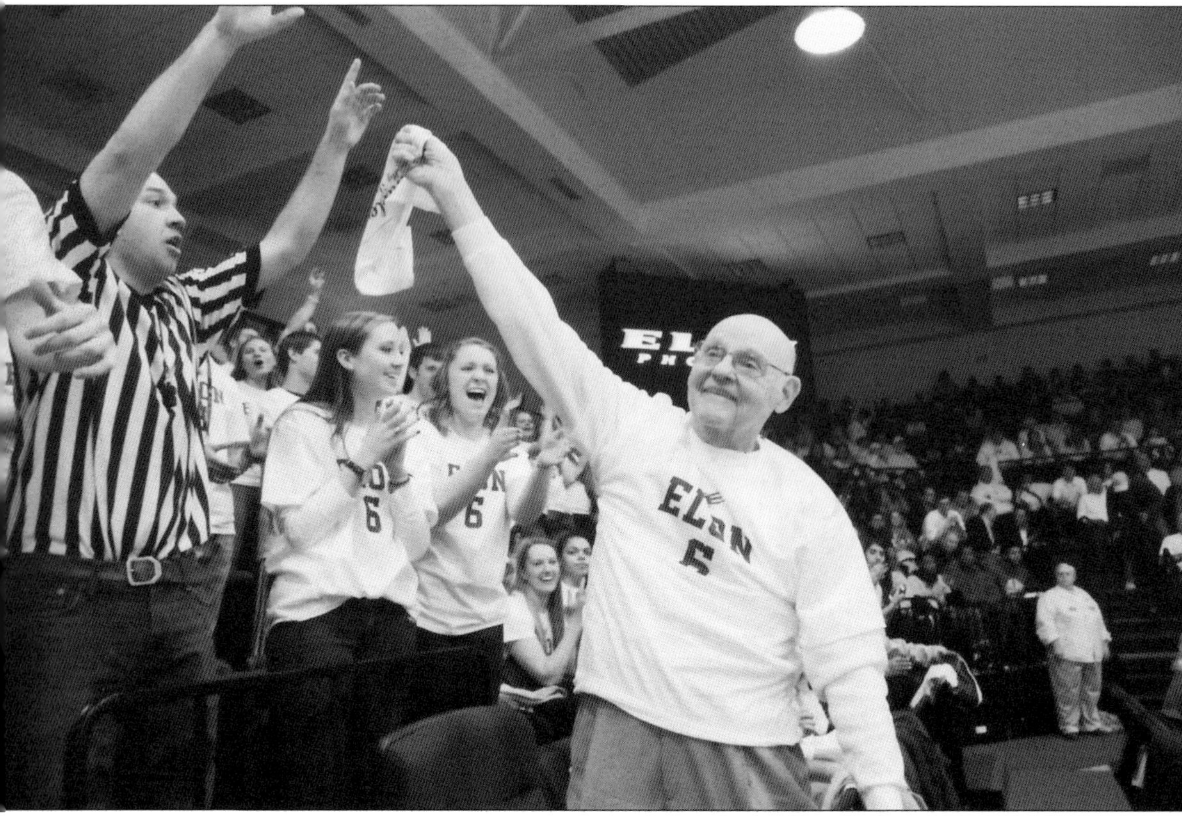

For many years, Dr. Earl Danieley attended almost every basketball game at Alumni Gym. He had a special seat on the west side of the gym facing the teams seated on the opposite side. At every game, for both the men's team and the women's, there was a special thing that happened at the third time-out in the second half. The student section, on the same side where Danieley was seated, would begin a chant—"DOC-tor DAN-lee. DOC-tor DAN-lee." In response, Danieley would rise from his chair and wave his white rally flag. The applause rocked the gym. Then at the end of the game, Danieley would go to courtside and greet every player and coach on the team, win or lose. He wanted them to know that he was there for them. Danieley died in 2016 at the age of 92. After his death, his chair was still there, with the white rally towel lying in it. (Elon University.)

Five

Famous Elon Visitors

The town of Elon is not a big place. With a population of less than 10,000, it is not the place one might expect to find former presidents of the United States, a former prime minister of Great Britain, or perhaps the former queen of an important country in the Middle East. But such visitors come to Elon every year as part of the cultural calendar of Elon University. Of course, the visitors are brought to enhance the educational experience for the young men and women who make up the university.

Though primarily for the university community, those events are open to the general public, and residents of the communities surrounding Elon are able to share sometimes once-in-a-lifetime opportunities to meet those who have been world leaders. Jimmy Carter, George W. Bush, Bill Clinton, and Lyndon B. Johnson are among the names of those who have been at Elon in years past. Margaret Thatcher came in 1995, and Queen Noor of Jordan visited in 2000.

Such speakers are the norm at the annual convocations in fall and spring. Also each year there is the Baird Pulitzer Lecture, a program that brings some of the leading individuals in journalism and literature to the campus. Dr. James H. Baird and his late wife, Jane, have made this series possible over a long period of years.

While on campus, speakers in both of the series interact with students. Students in the School of Communications, for instance, have had the opportunity to sit in class with Walter Cronkite, famed CBS anchor; Ben Bradlee, editor of the *Washington Post* in the era of the Watergate scandal; and Bob Woodward, one of the two reporters who broke the stories that led to the resignation of Pres. Richard M. Nixon.

These visitors allow Elon University students the opportunity to hear stories of important times in American and world history from the people who were there and helped shape those events and reshape the world.

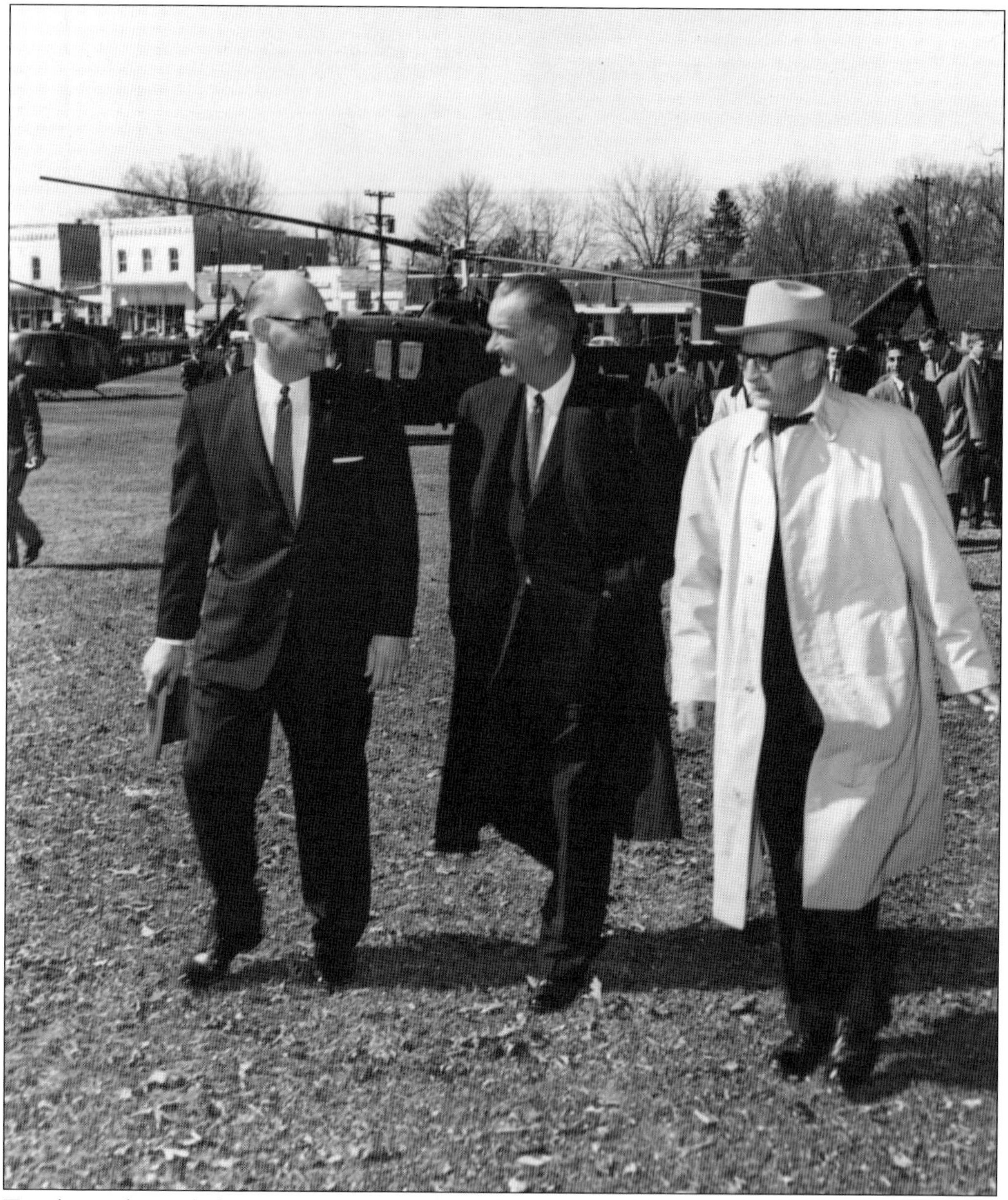

Two big military helicopters came from the west and settled down on the edge of the Elon College campus just off North Williamson Avenue. Out stepped the vice president of the United States, Lyndon B. Johnson. He was greeted by Elon College president J. Earl Danieley, left, and chairman of the board of trustees Thad Eure. It was March 1962, and the vice president came to Elon College as speaker for the annual college Founders Day observance. He had flown into the Greensboro Airport and then made the trip to Elon College by helicopter. The arrival of the military helicopters was something not seen in the town before. The vice president spoke to an overflow crowd in Alumni Gymnasium, where he received an honorary degree from the college. He also spent time with officials of the college and met many of the students. He later told reporters, "The occasion was one I shall long remember." It was one Alamance County residents would long remember as well. (Elon University.)

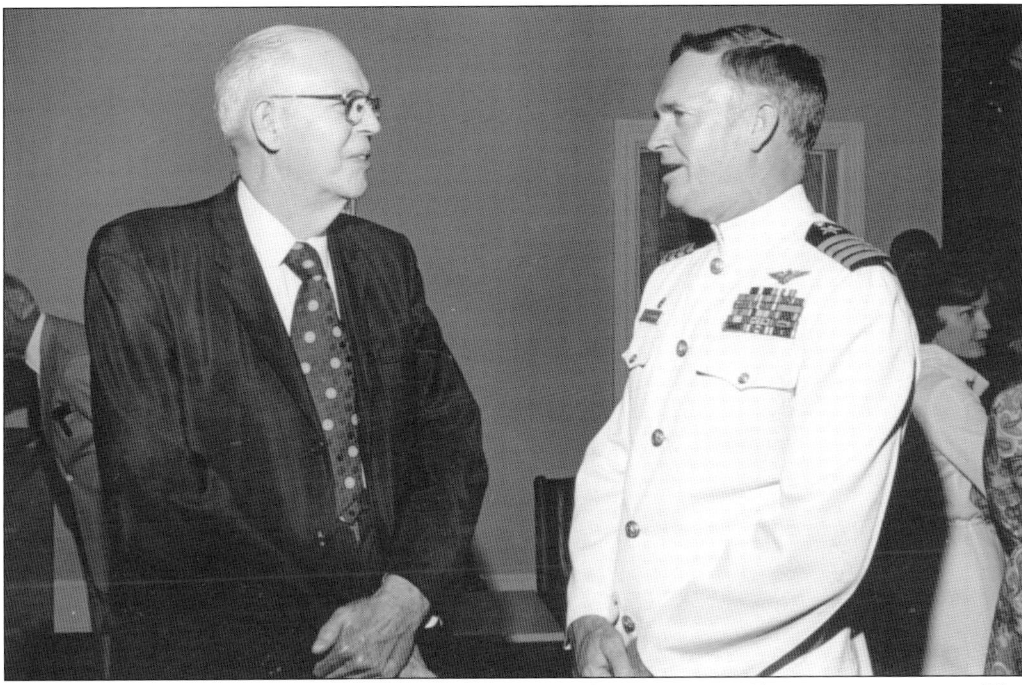

Capt. Eugene "Red" McDaniel, right, talks with Dr. Thomas E. Powell Jr. at a reception in Elon College in 1978. Capt. McDaniel, an Elon graduate, was a prisoner in Vietnam for several years. Just weeks after his release in 1973, he and two others were on campus and for the first time were allowed to talk in a national news conference about the horrors they experienced while imprisoned. (Elon University.)

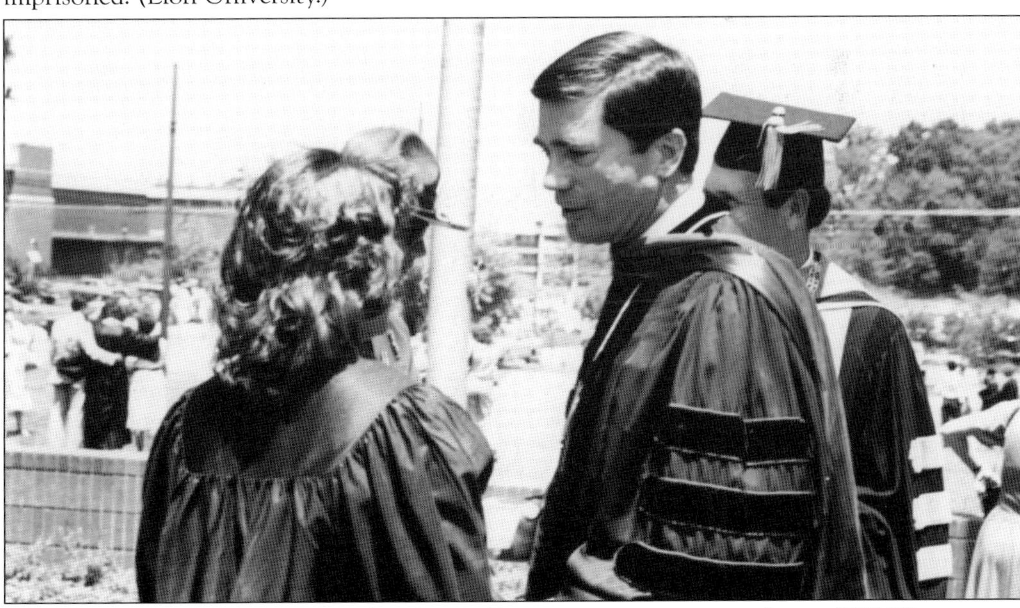

Gov. Chuck Robb of Virginia was the Elon College commencement speaker in 1985. The governor was the son-in-law of former president Lyndon Johnson, married to Johnson's daughter Lynda Bird. Virginia governors were often speakers on campus, as there has always been a strong historical connection between Virginia and Elon College. (Elon University.)

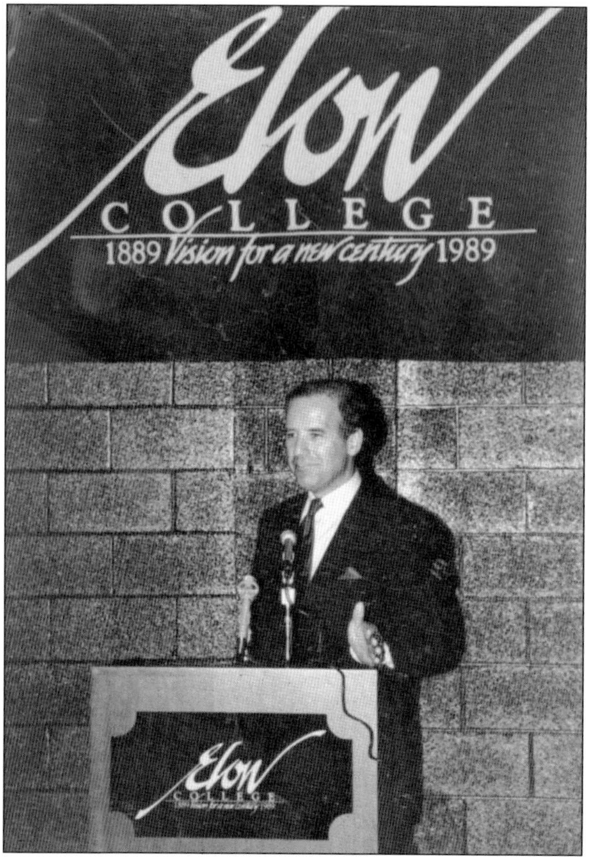

In 1988, Sen. Joe Biden came to Elon College to speak. The Delaware senator was one in a long line of political figures who have visited the Elon campus over the years. Former presidents, secretaries of state, governors, and congressmen have visited. Senator Biden in 2008 would become vice president with Pres. Barack Obama. (Elon University.)

Former president Jimmy Carter came to Elon College in 1989 to offer support to students involved in the Habitat for Humanity program, an organization he continues to support and work with even now that he is in his 90s. President Carter's predecessor, Gerald Ford, came to speak at Elon College in the late 1960s while he was still in the House of Representatives. (Elon University.)

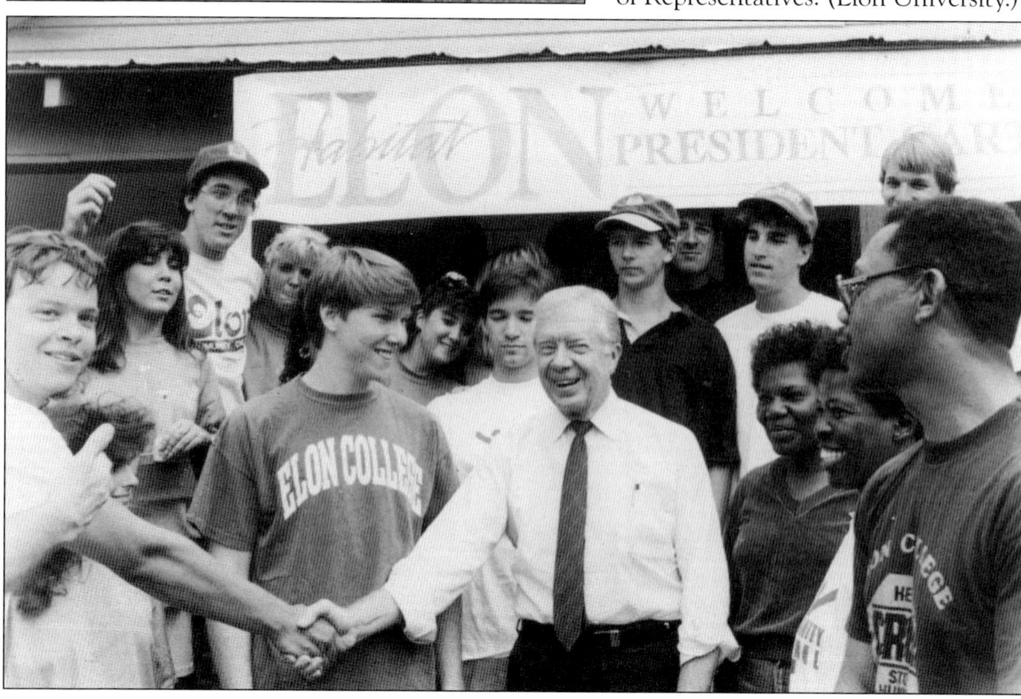

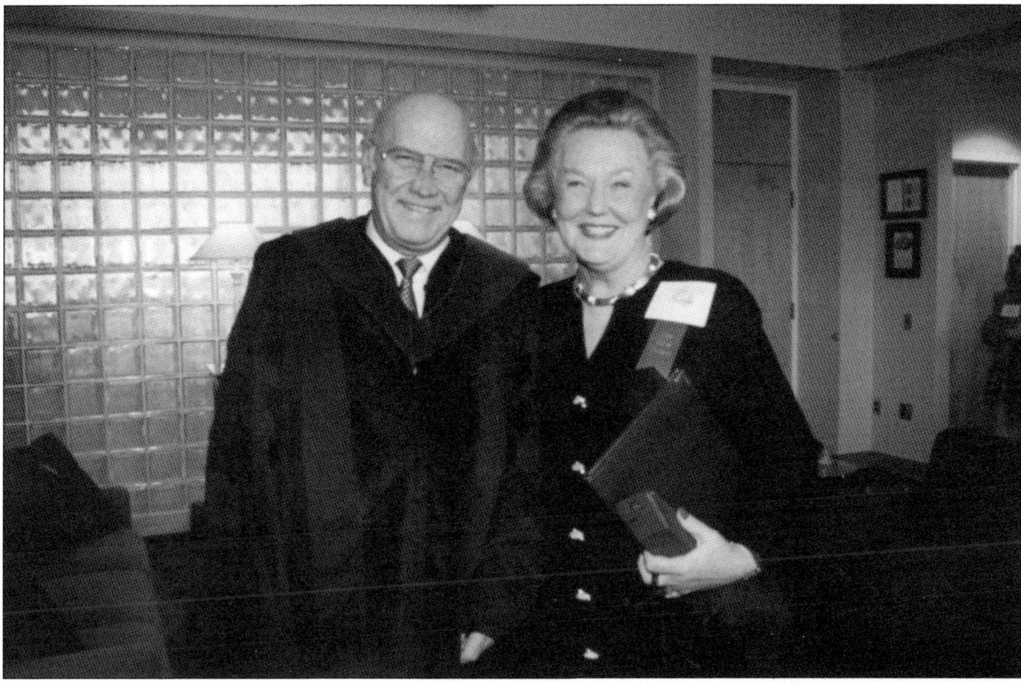

F.W. de Klerk, former president of South Africa, spoke to Elon College at convocation in 1997. Shown here with Dr. Jo Watts Williams, special assistant to the president, de Klerk was the seventh and last president of South Africa under apartheid. He worked to end apartheid, and he and later president Nelson Mandela won the Nobel Peace Prize in 1993 for that effort. (Elon University.)

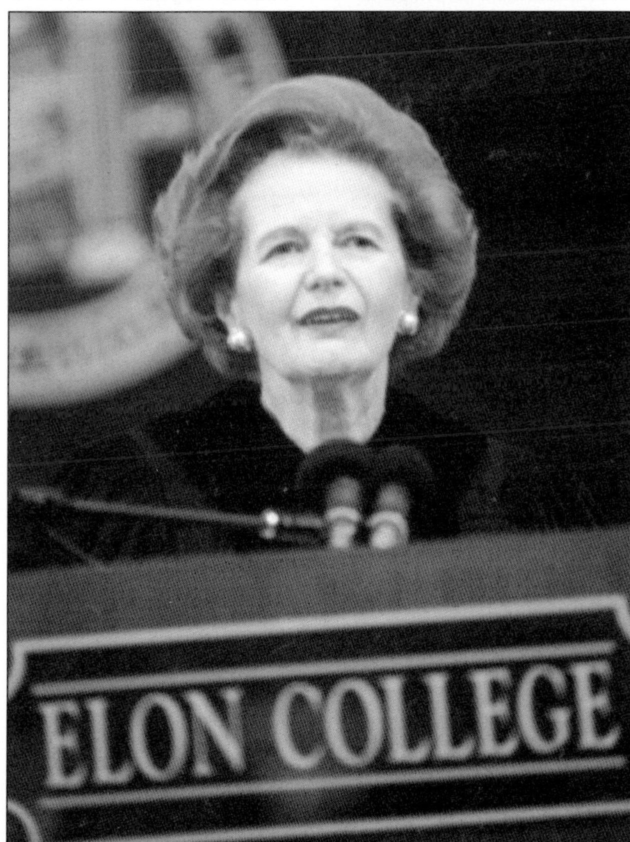

Former British prime minister Margaret Thatcher came to Elon College in 1995 to speak and dedicate the new Moseley Center on the north campus. Thatcher had been prime minister of Great Britain from 1979 to 1990 and was the first woman to be elected to that position. In her third term in 1990, she resigned her post due to struggles within her Conservative party and opposition to some of her policies. (Elon University.)

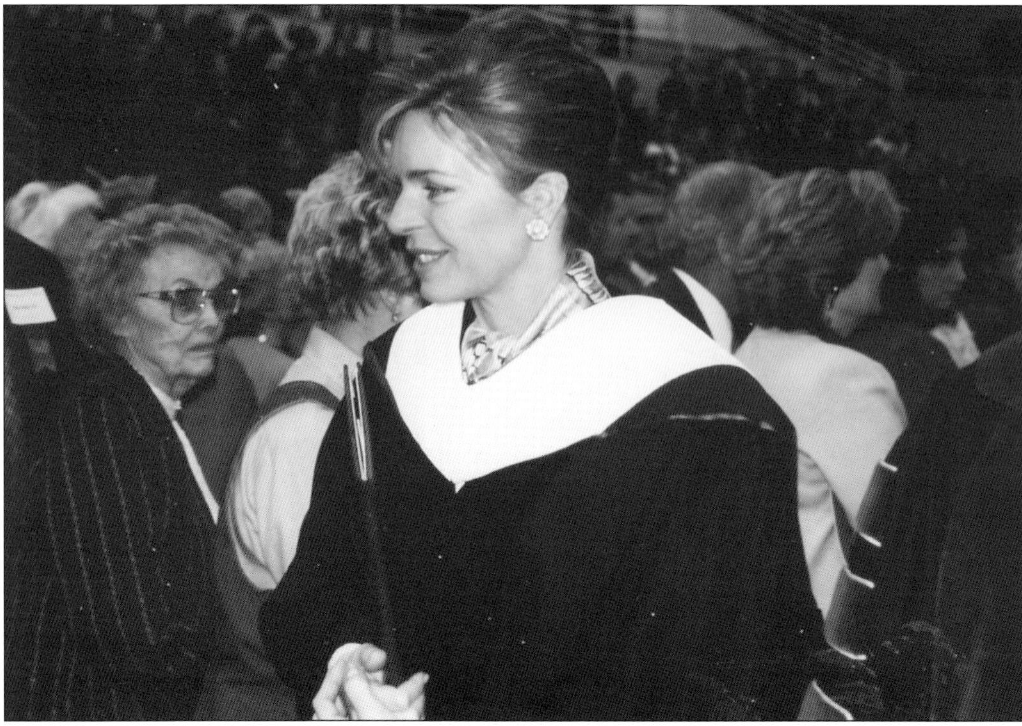

Queen Noor of Jordan visited the Elon College campus in October 2000. The queen is an American by birth and in 2000 was the widow of the late king and stepmother of the current king. On her visit, she received an honorary degree and established a scholarship at the school to be used by students from Jordan.

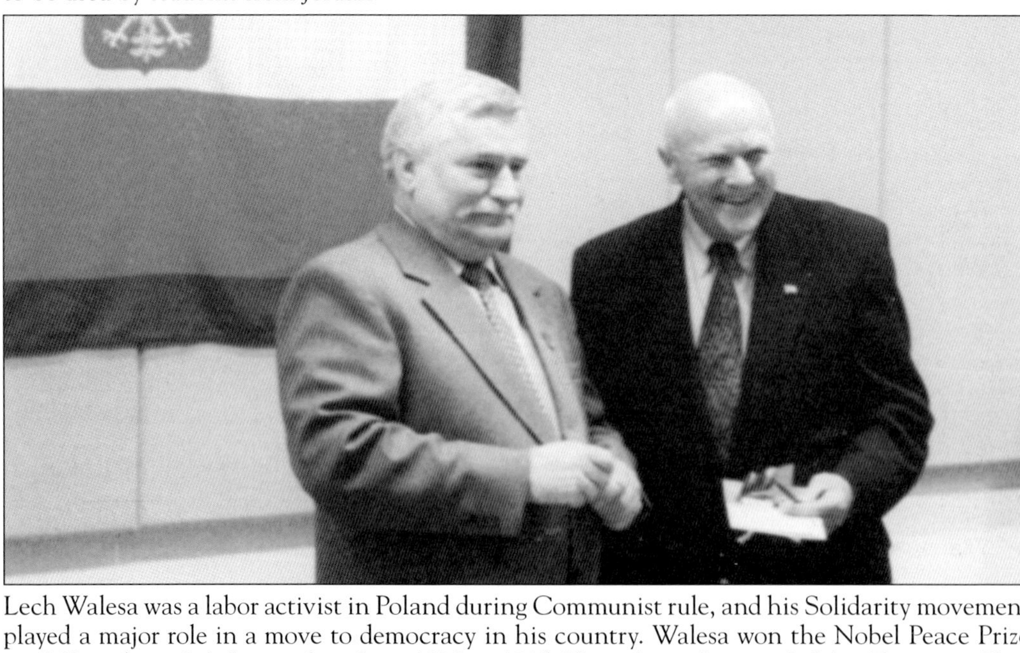

Lech Walesa was a labor activist in Poland during Communist rule, and his Solidarity movement played a major role in a move to democracy in his country. Walesa won the Nobel Peace Prize in 1983 and was Polish president from 1990 to 1995. He is shown here with John Truitt, an Elon College resident and graduate at the 2001 convocation.

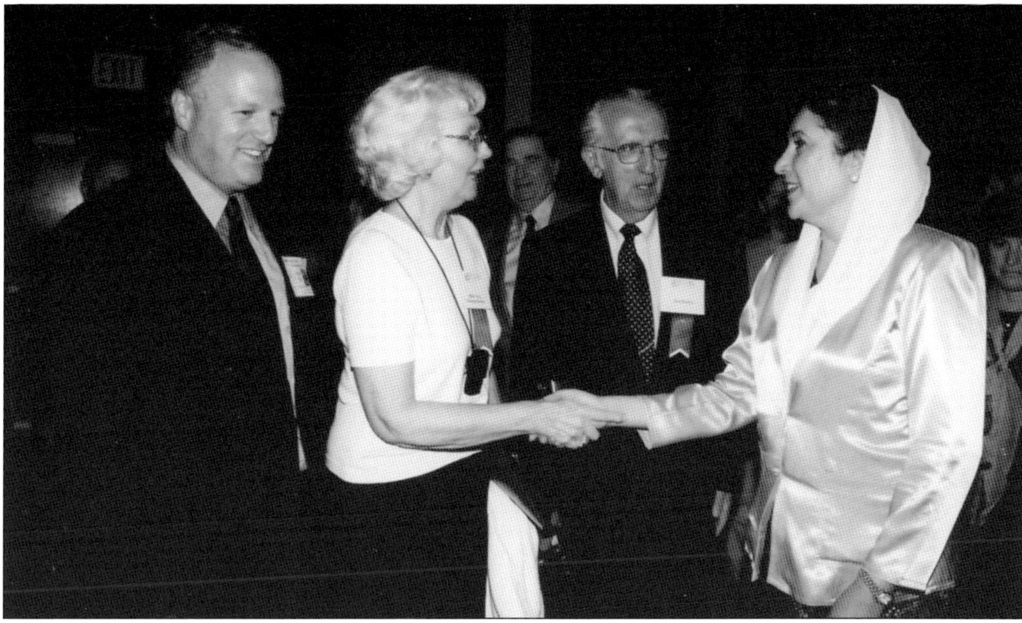

Benazir Bhutto visited Elon College in 2002 for convocation. She was prime minister of Pakistan twice—from 1988 to 1990 and from 1993 to 1996. She returned to politics in 2007 and was assassinated in December of that year. Here, Bhutto greets Billie Faye Bolden. Bolden's husband, Don, is between the two, and Dr. Leo Lambert, Elon College president, looks on at left.

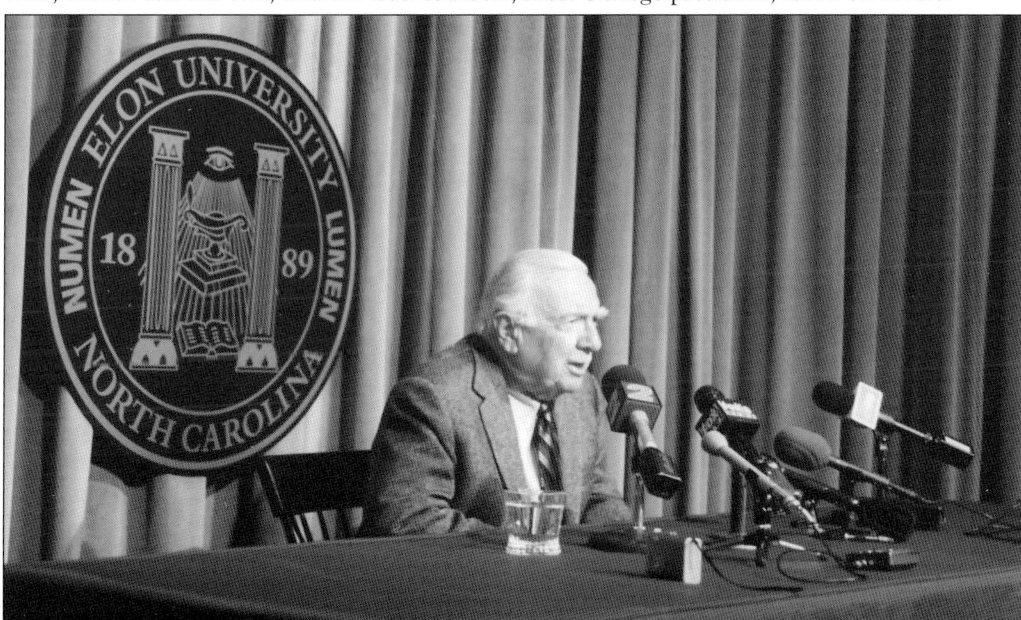

Famed CBS newscaster Walter Cronkite appeared at Elon University in 2003, speaking to convocation and spending time with School of Communications students. They were excited about being able to sit down with the legendary television journalist face-to-face and hear him tell the story of his career in television news reporting. Cronkite reported on the assassination of Pres. John Kennedy in one of the first major television news stories in history.

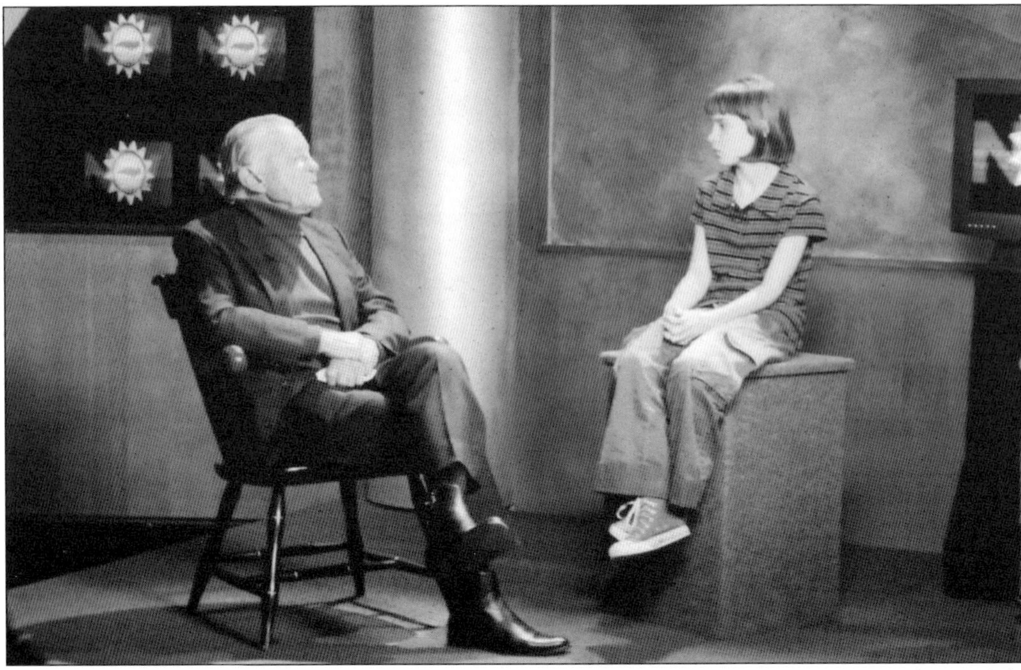

Ben Bradlee visited the School of Communications in 2006. He was executive editor of the *Washington Post* during the Watergate scandal. Interviewing Bradlee is Kacie Anderson, one of several fifth graders at Elon Elementary invited to talk with him. Bradlee and Kacie are in the School of Communications studio. Kacie, in 2017 a senior in computer science at the University of Southern California, is the daughter of Dan and Janna Anderson.

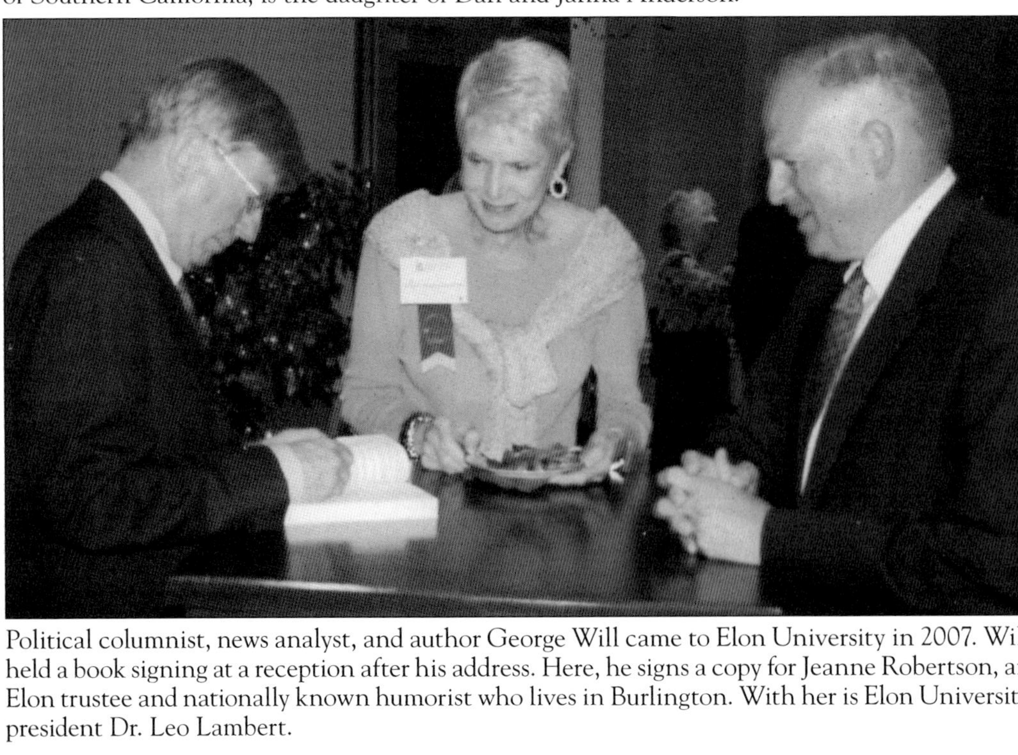

Political columnist, news analyst, and author George Will came to Elon University in 2007. Will held a book signing at a reception after his address. Here, he signs a copy for Jeanne Robertson, an Elon trustee and nationally known humorist who lives in Burlington. With her is Elon University president Dr. Leo Lambert.

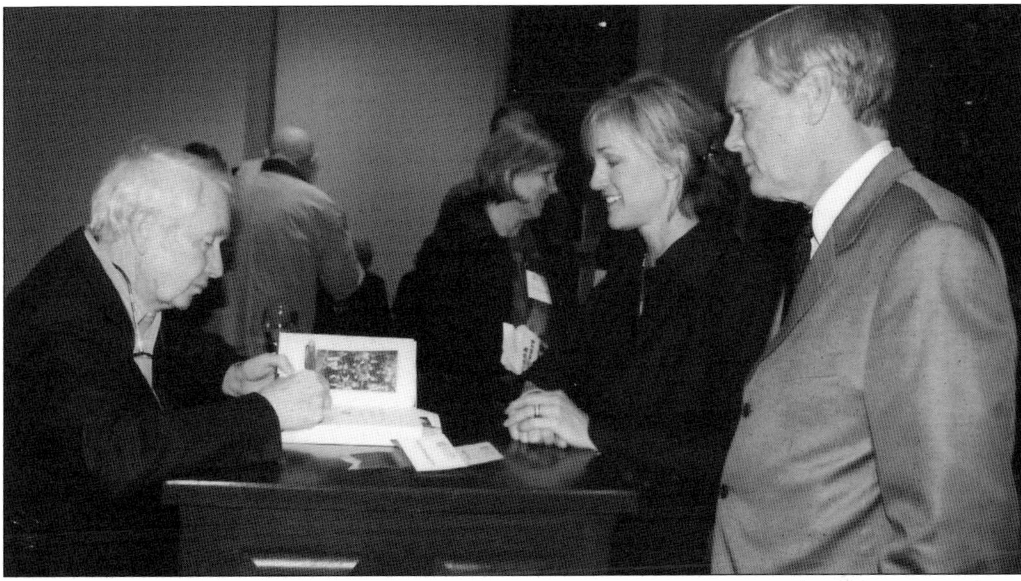

One of the Baird Pulitzer lecturers to visit Elon College in 2007 was Frank McCourt. McCourt won the Pulitzer Prize in 1997 for *Angela's Ashes.* That book is the story of his growing up years in Brooklyn and in Limerick, Ireland. Dr. Gerry Francis, right, and his wife, Laine, center, talk here with McCourt as he signs a book for them. Dr. Francis retired in 2015 as executive vice president of Elon University.

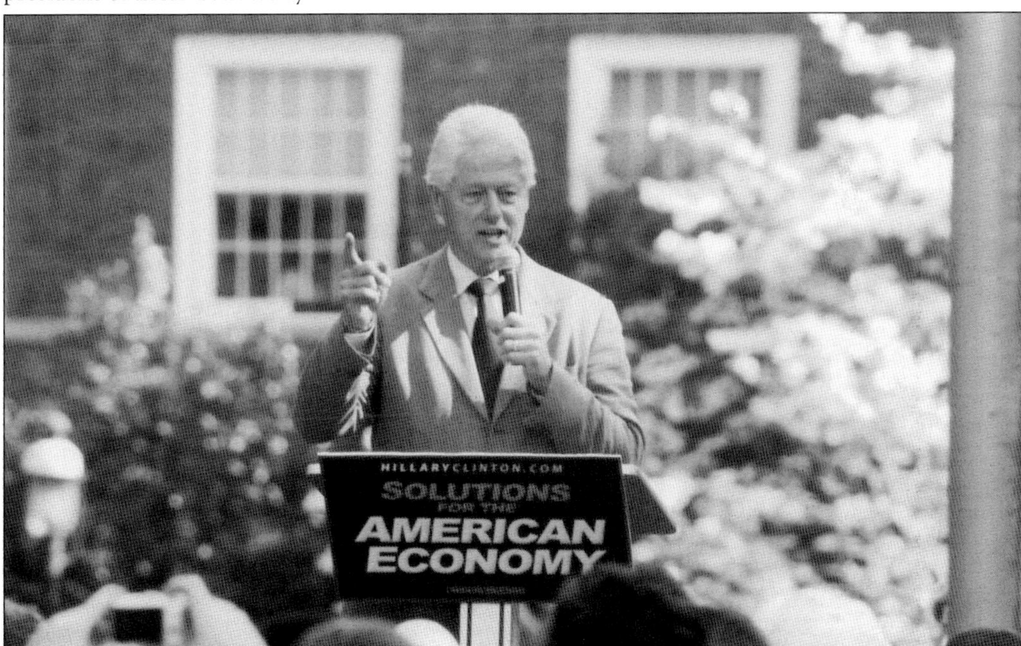

In 2008, former president Bill Clinton came to Elon University, not as a convocation speaker but as a political supporter. He was campaigning for his wife, Hillary, as she sought the Democratic nomination for president of the United States. In 1992, the Clintons as well as vice presidential candidate Al Gore and his wife, Tipper, campaigned on campus in Bill Clinton's presidential race against George H.W. Bush.

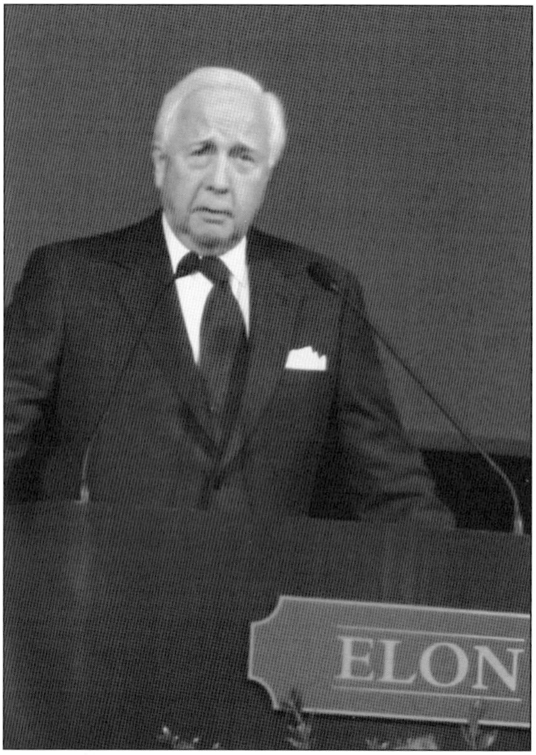

Famed historian and author David McCulloch has appeared at Elon University on two occasions. He spoke here in 2001 and 2008. His 2001 visit came just days after the 9/11 terrorist attacks. McCulloch put his planned speech away and talked about the attack and what it might mean to the United States in the coming months and years. He is a two-time Pulitzer Prize winner. (Elon University.)

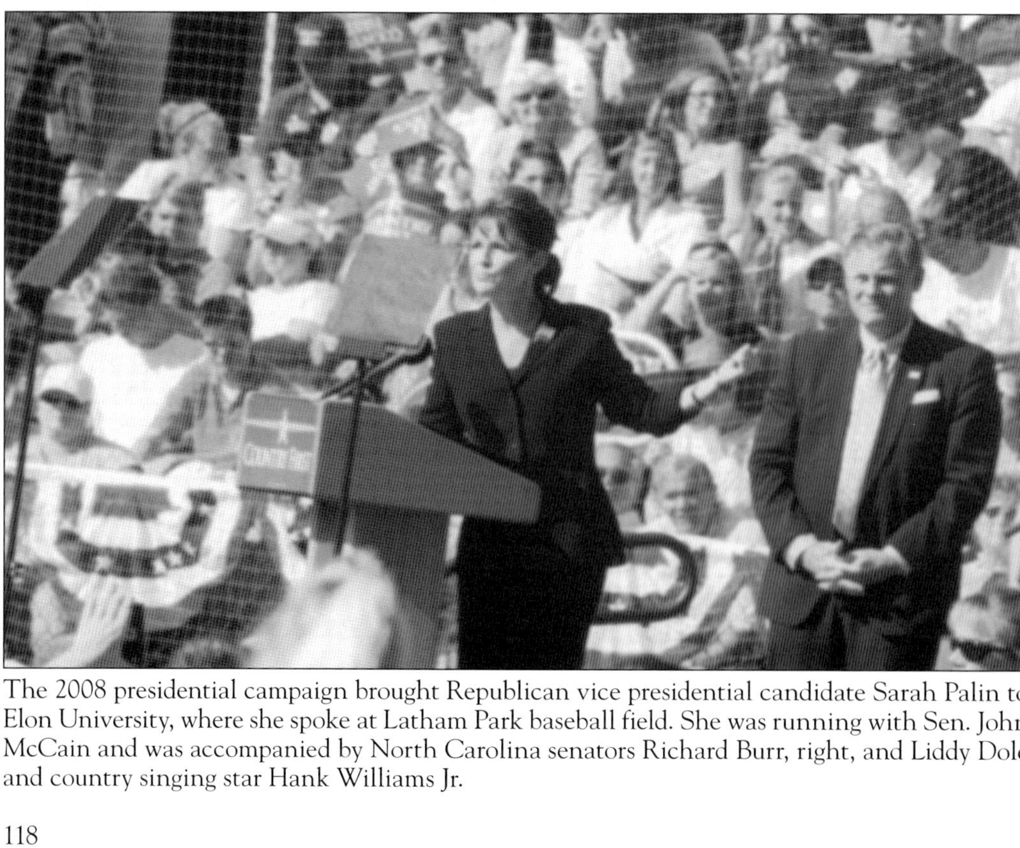

The 2008 presidential campaign brought Republican vice presidential candidate Sarah Palin to Elon University, where she spoke at Latham Park baseball field. She was running with Sen. John McCain and was accompanied by North Carolina senators Richard Burr, right, and Liddy Dole and country singing star Hank Williams Jr.

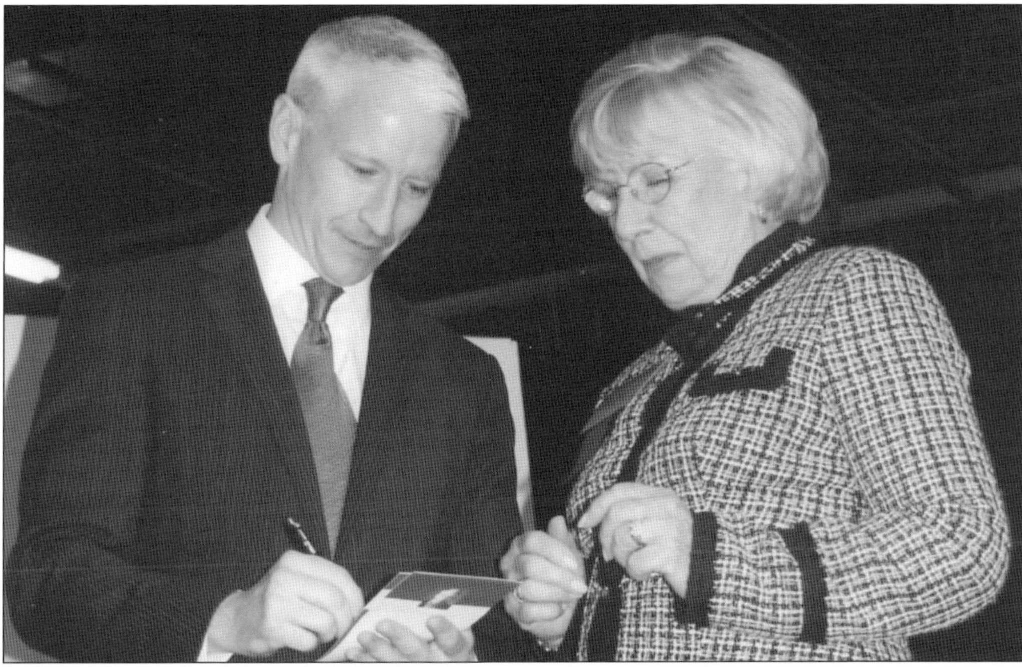

Journalist Anderson Cooper signs a copy of his book for Dolores Truitt, an Elon alum and resident of the town of Elon. Cooper visited the campus in 2009 and spent considerable time with students, meeting with them personally in the classroom and then sitting down in a question and answer program in Whitley Auditorium. He also spoke to 2,400 people in Alumni Gymnasium.

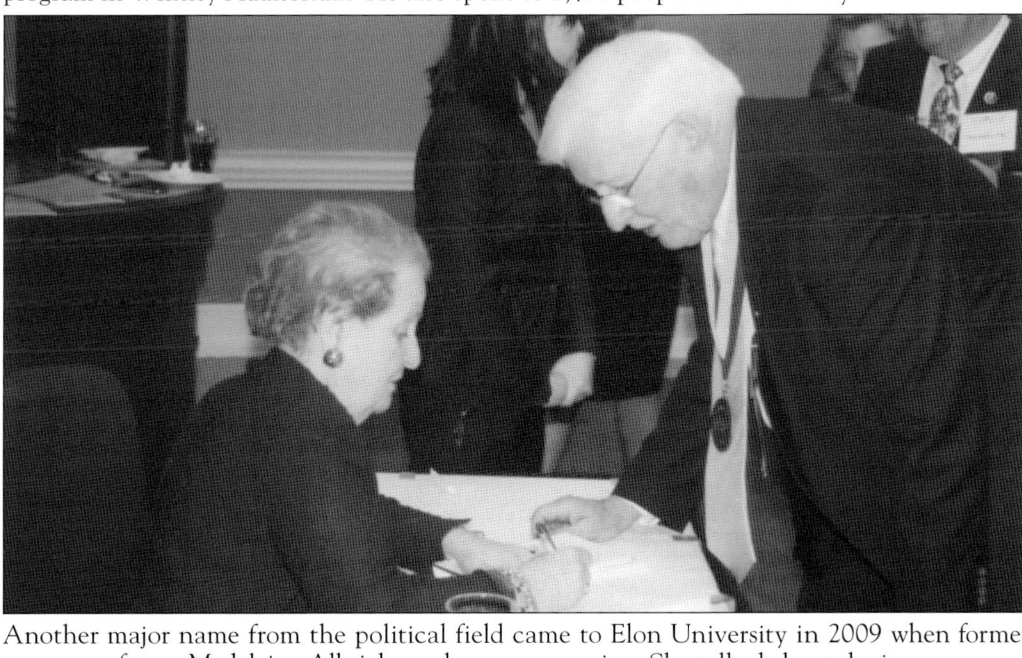

Another major name from the political field came to Elon University in 2009 when former secretary of state Madeleine Albright spoke at convocation. She talked about the importance of education in a changing world and encouraged learning about other cultures and other countries and their places in the world. Albright signs a book here for Dusty Rhodes. Rhodes Stadium is named for Dusty and his wife, Peggy.

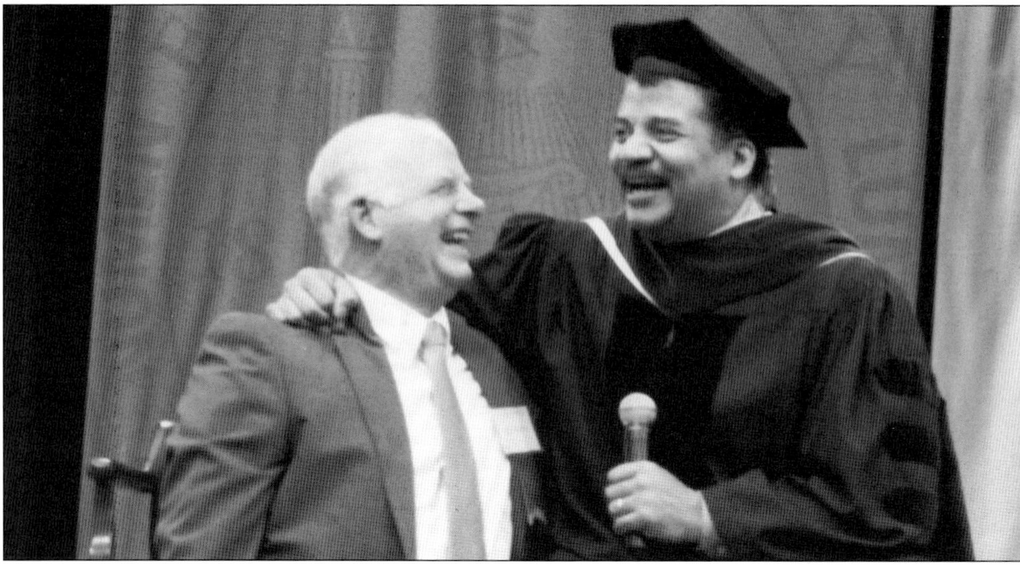

In April 2015, Neil deGrasse Tyson, director of the Hayden Planetarium in New York City, entertained the convocation audience with some laughs and audience participation. He is seen here with Wes Elingburg, member of the board of trustees. Tyson had a serious message, however, stressing the importance of science and literacy, urging students to be lifelong learners. (Elon University.)

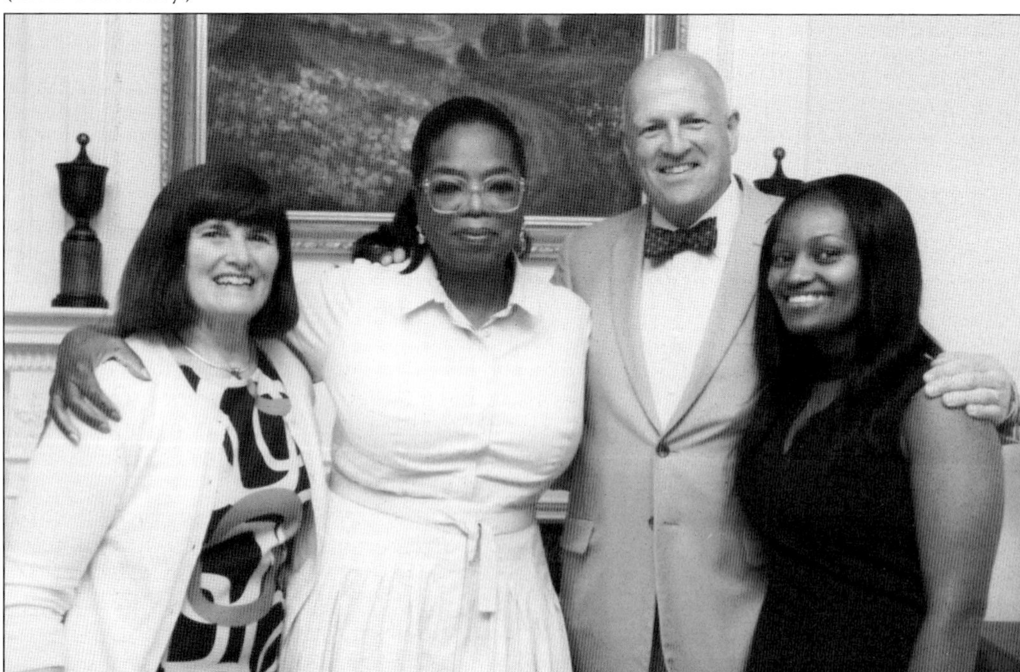

Oprah Winfrey surprised those at the baccalaureate service prior to Elon University's May 2017 graduation. She was there to see Nosipho Shangase the day prior to Shangase's graduation. Shangase was a graduate of the Oprah Winfrey Leadership Academy for Girls in South Africa. University president Leo Lambert and his wife, Laurie, are with Winfrey and Shangase prior to the service. (Elon University.)

Six

Elon's Neighbors

The town of Elon is one of a cluster of municipalities that stretch across the middle of Alamance County, several of them with common borders.

Beginning at the Guilford County line in western Alamance there is Gibsonville, a town divided between those two counties. Gibsonville abuts the town of Elon, which in turn shares a common border with Burlington, the largest of the municipalities. Burlington abuts Graham, the county seat that sits almost in the direct center of the county. And Graham and Burlington both link to the town of Haw River. That is a lot of local governments in a small area.

There is also the town of Ossipee just north of Elon, and the town of Green Level is just to the north of Haw River. The village of Alamance is south of Burlington, and the town of Swepsonville is south of Graham. The one most removed from this conglomeration of towns is Mebane on the eastern border of the county. It is a town also divided between counties, as part of it is in Orange County.

Gibsonville, Ossipee, Graham, Swepsonville, and Haw River were home to textile operations in the 19th and 20th centuries. Burlington was also a major hosiery and textile center, the location in which Burlington Industries was founded in 1923. At one time, this was the largest textile operation in the world. Burlington is now home to the headquarters of LabCorp, the world's leading health-care diagnostics company.

Green Level is a rural community, and Alamance is a former mill village. Mebane was a furniture center for many decades and is now home to a number of major industries located in two industrial parks. Mebane is also home to many who work in the Research Triangle Park and at the University of North Carolina at Chapel Hill and Duke University, all within a short driving distance. It has been one of the fastest-growing communities in the state in recent years.

North and south of this line, there are a number of other communities—Altamahaw, Glencoe, Bellemont, Union Ridge, Saxapahaw, Snow Camp, Eli Whitney, and Pleasant Grove—that make up Greater Alamance County.

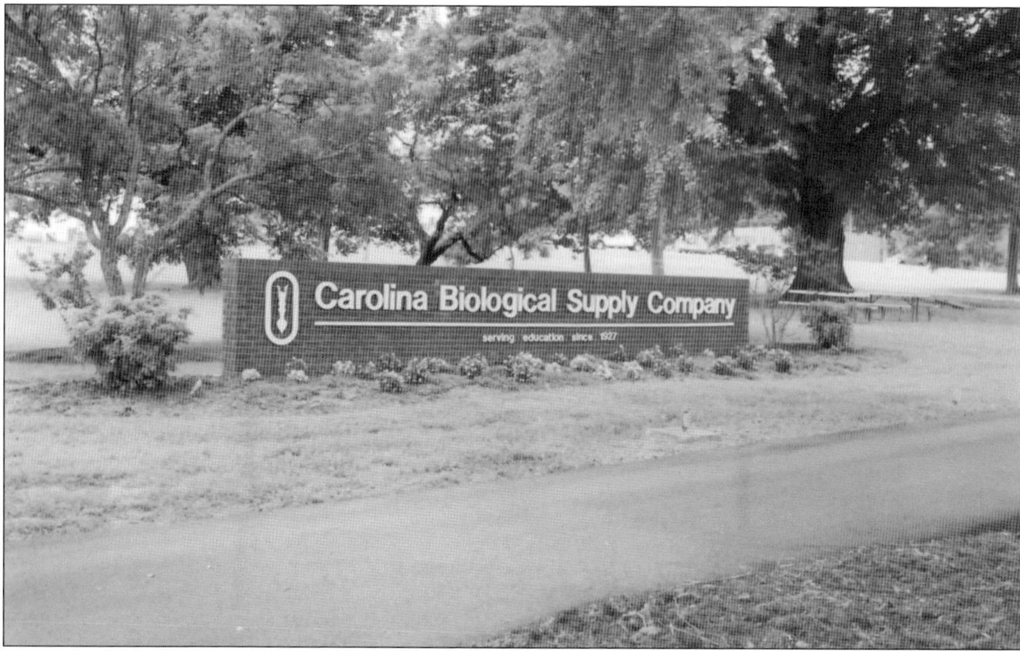

One of Elon's closest neighbors is a business located just over the town limits on East Haggard Avenue. Carolina Biological Supply Co. was organized by Dr. Thomas E. Powell Jr., an Elon College graduate who later taught biology and geology there. Powell started the company in 1927 to get the necessary scientific supplies he needed, and it was soon a national leader in its field.

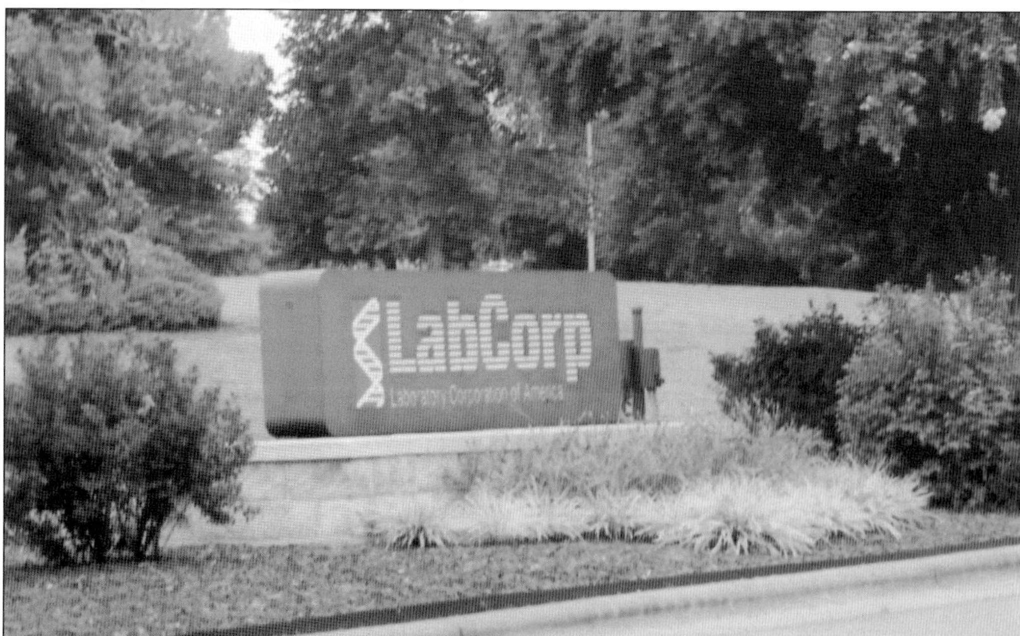

Next door to Carolina Biological Supply Co. is the major laboratory for LabCorp, the leading health-care diagnostics company in the world. LabCorp was begun in Burlington by Dr. James B. Powell Jr., a son of Dr. Thomas E. Powell Jr. The company began a small operation in the basement of an old hospital and now employs more than 50,000 people.

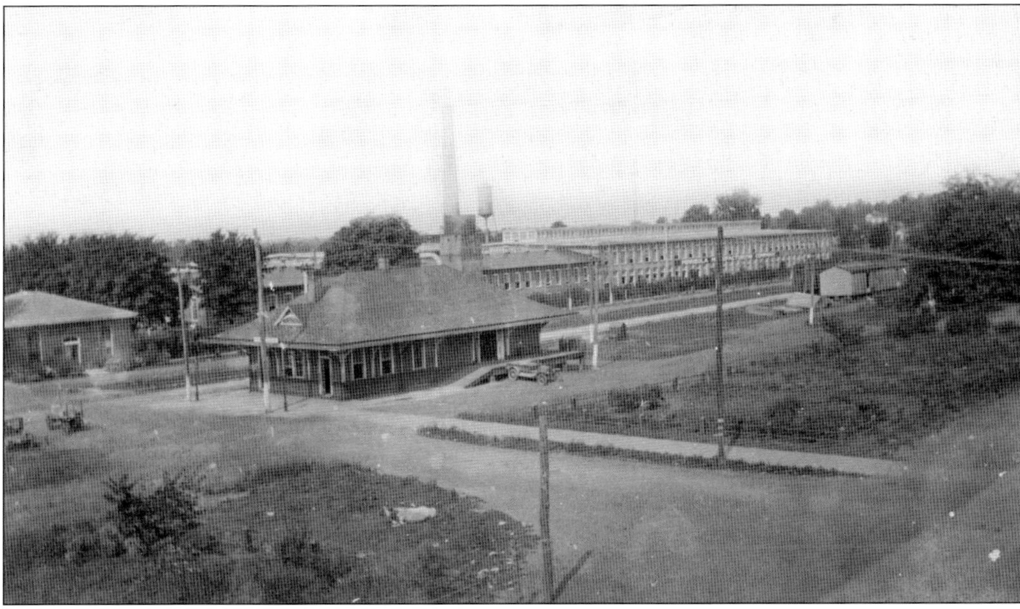

Elon's municipal neighbor to the west is the town of Gibsonville. Gibsonville, like Elon, started as a railroad depot established soon after the railroad came in the 1850s. The town was incorporated in 1871. There was gold mining there in the early years, but a textile mill was opened in 1886, and this an operation that would continue many decades as Minneola Mill.

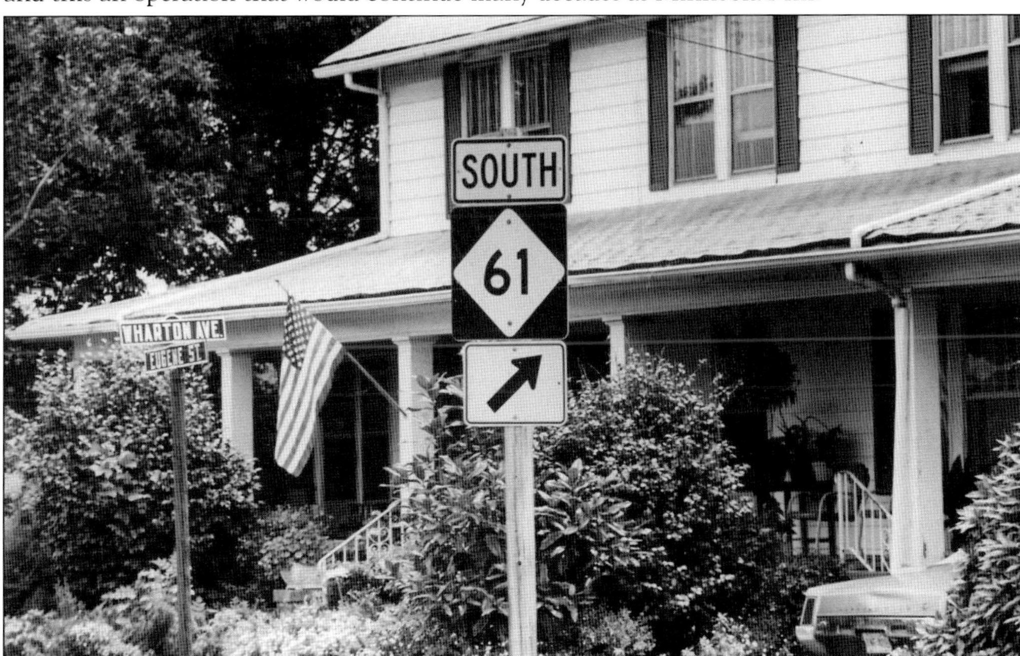

Gibsonville, like Elon, still has several old homes like this built around the turn of the 20th century. Most are private homes, but one, Burke Manor, is a popular bed-and-breakfast and restaurant. Gibsonville was on the major east-west highway across North Carolina in the early 1900s but was long ago bypassed by the new Highway 70 and the interstate. Highway 61 does still run north-south through the town.

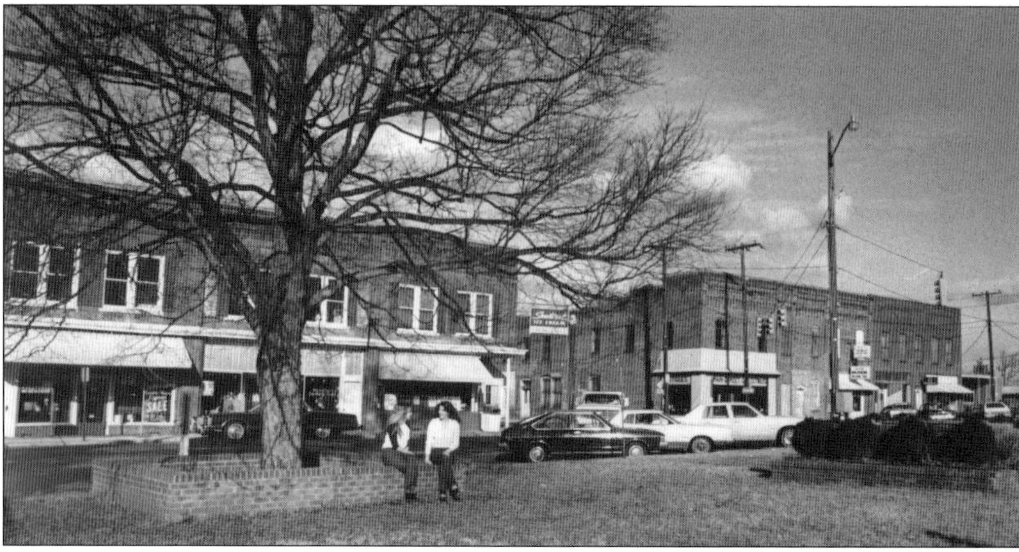

The textile mill closed down many years ago, but Gibsonsville remains an active town divided by the Alamance County–Guilford County line. The business area remains much like it has been for several decades, with a busy Main Street that features a unique display of miniature trains in a park near the middle of town.

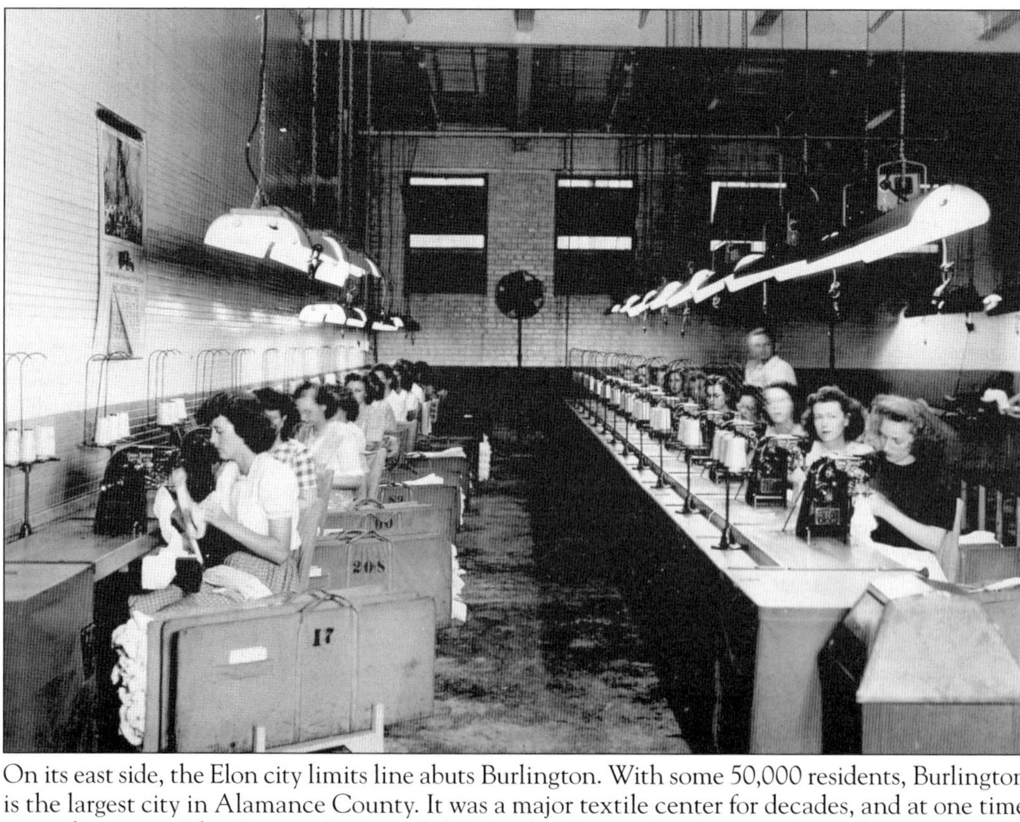

On its east side, the Elon city limits line abuts Burlington. With some 50,000 residents, Burlington is the largest city in Alamance County. It was a major textile center for decades, and at one time it was known as "the Hosiery Center of the South." This is the interior of the old May Hosiery plant on South Main Street in Burlington.

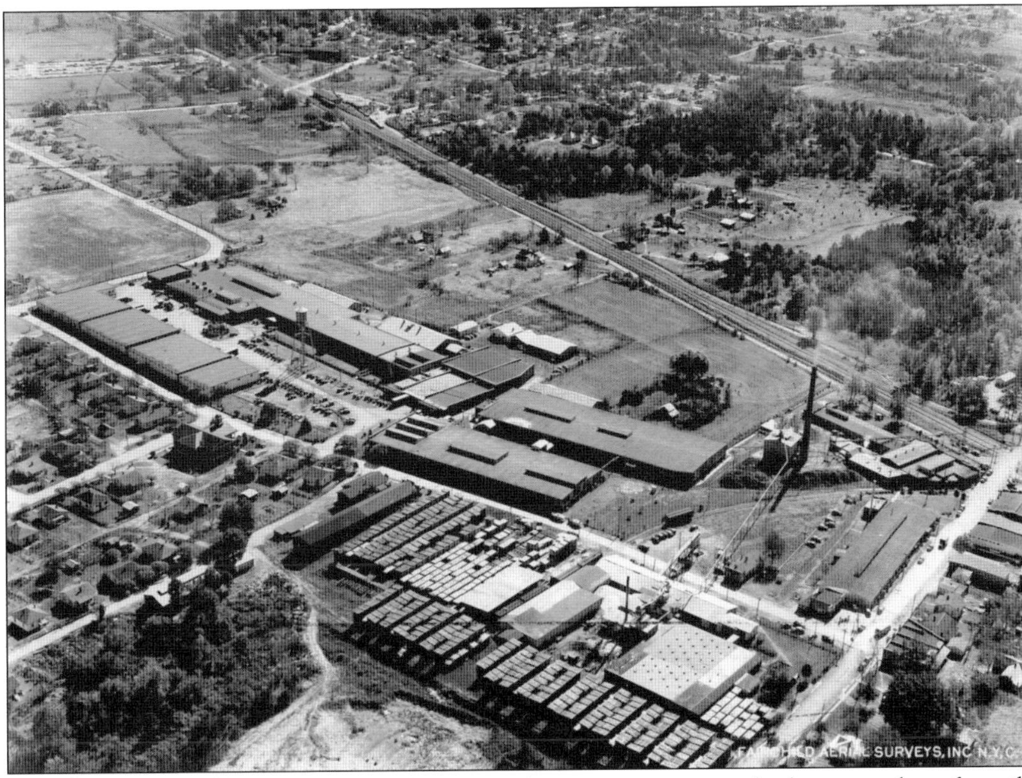

Burlington was the birthplace of Burlington Industries, at one time the largest maker of textile products in the world. It was started in 1923 as Burlington Mills, and this photograph shows the site of the original plant between Burlington and Graham in the 1960s. It became Burlington Industries in 1955 and had plants all across the nation and in several foreign countries.

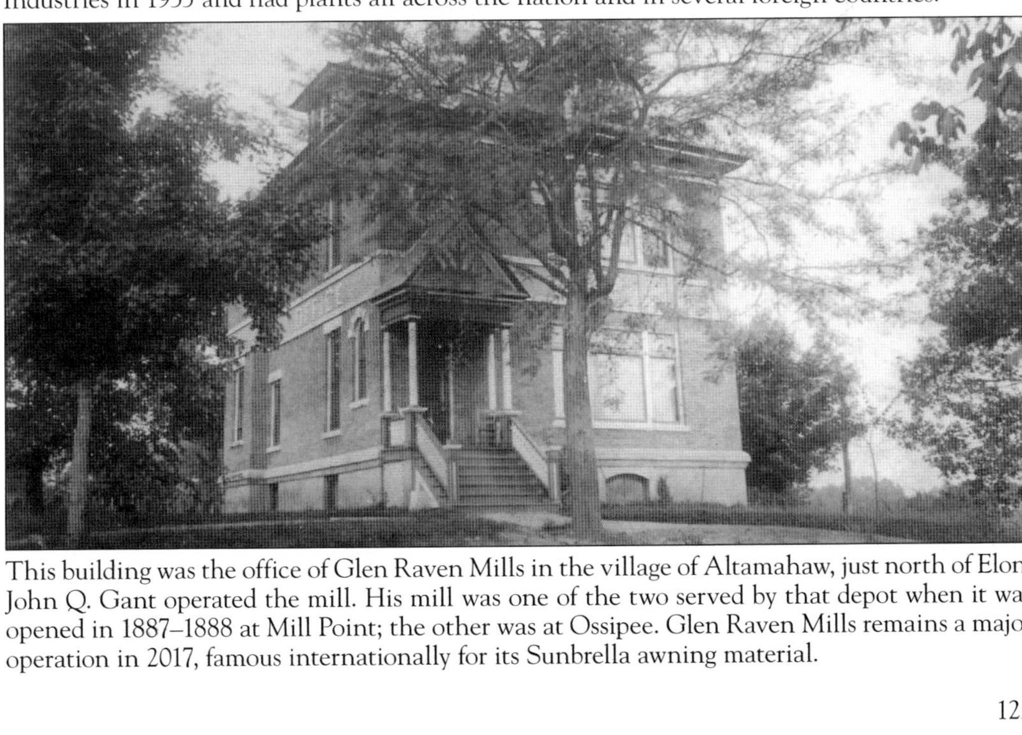

This building was the office of Glen Raven Mills in the village of Altamahaw, just north of Elon. John Q. Gant operated the mill. His mill was one of the two served by that depot when it was opened in 1887–1888 at Mill Point; the other was at Ossipee. Glen Raven Mills remains a major operation in 2017, famous internationally for its Sunbrella awning material.

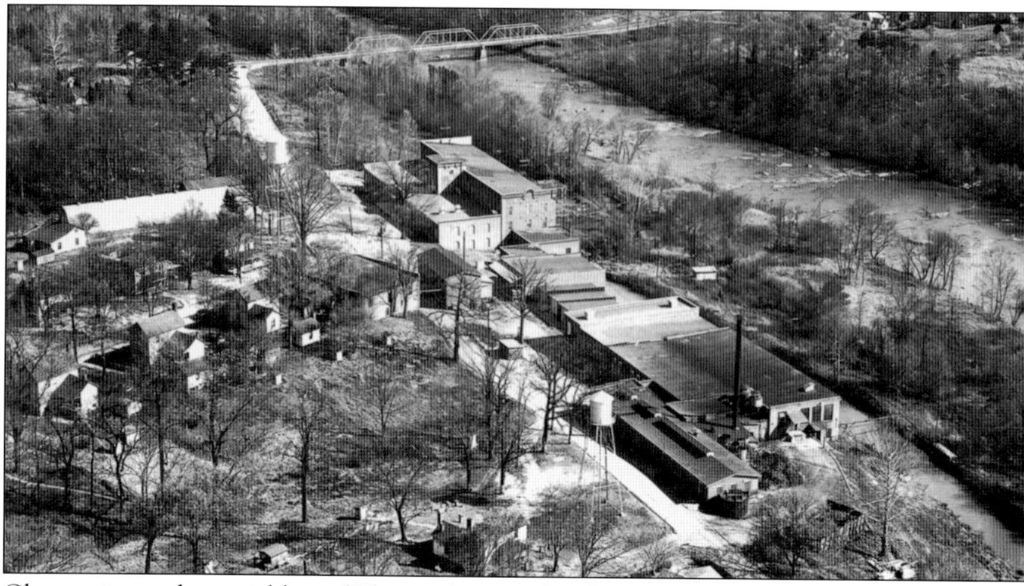

Glencoe is another neighbor of Elon and is a mill village like Altamahaw and Ossipee. This Glencoe photograph shows how a typical mill village looked. The water from Haw River was channeled into the mill to supply power to the looms as well as to the mill village homes at left, where the employees lived. In the early years, young children worked right along with their parents in the mill.

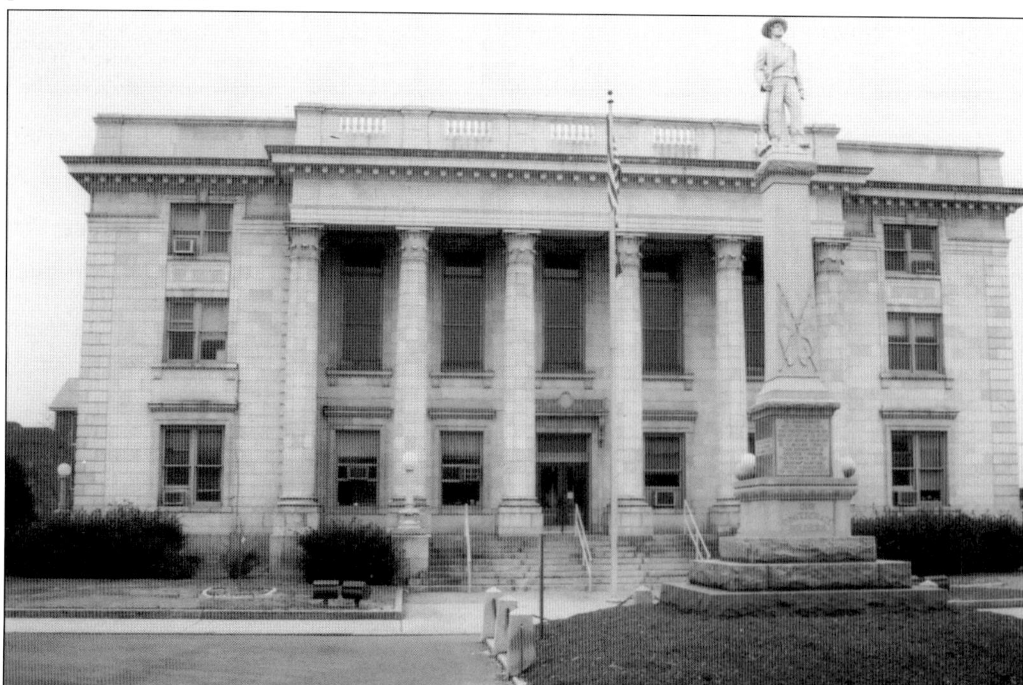

The city of Graham adjoins Burlington's eastern and southern city limits. When Alamance County was formed in 1849, Graham was created as the seat of county government. It too was home to textile and hosiery mills in the past. This courthouse was built in 1924, replacing the one built in the 1850s. It is on a square in the middle of town and is an official historic site.

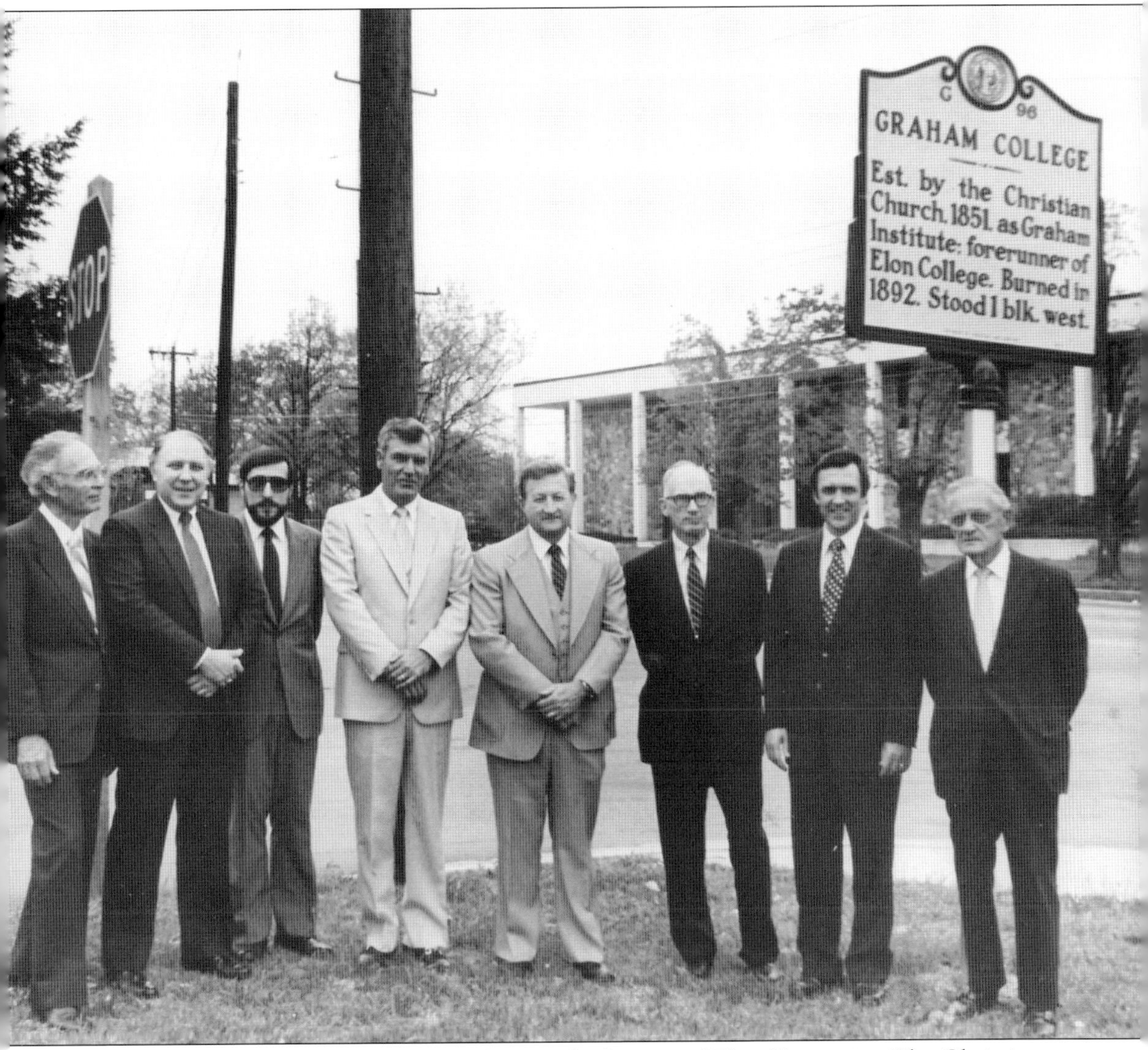

The city of Graham has an important place in the history of Elon University. The Christian Church founded the Graham Institute there on July 15, 1851, according to this historical marker on South Main Street in Graham. Part of the plan was to provide education for any young man preparing to enter the ministry, no matter the denomination. That school would eventually evolve into Graham College and then Elon College. This marker was unveiled on April 12, 1981, on South Main Street near the site of Graham College. Graham, state, and university officials participated. From left to right are Dr. Clyde Fields of the United Church of Christ; Dr. Robert McQueen; Joe A. Mobley of the North Carolina Department of Archives and History; M.L. Copeland of the Graham Historic Commission; the Rev. Donald Nance; William I. Ward Jr.; Dr. Fred Young, president of Elon University; and Myron Rhyne, mayor of Graham. (Elon University.)